ON THE COUNT OF ONE

The Art, Craft, and Science of Teaching Modern Dance

4th Edition

Elizabeth Sherbon

a cappella books

Library of Congress Cataloging-in-Publication Data

Sherbon, Elizabeth
     On the count of one : the art, craft, and science of teaching modern dance / Elizabeth
Sherbon. — 4th ed.
        p.   cm.
     Includes bibliographical references (p. 211).
     ISBN 1-55652-090-5 : $19.95
     1. Dancing—Study and teaching.   2. Dance notation.   3. Modern dance.   I. Title.
II. Title: On the count of 1.
GV1753.5.S48 1990
792.8—dc20   90-37649
                                                                                              CIP

Copyright © 1968, 1975, 1982, 1990 by Elizabeth Sherbon
Fourth edition

a cappella books
an imprint of Chicago Review Press

Editorial Offices:
PO Box 380
Pennington, NJ 08534

Business Offices:
814 N. Franklin Street
Chicago, Illinois 60610

Cover photo: Muriel Cohan and Patrick Suzeau, University of Kansas, Lawrence.
              Photo by John Daby
Cover design: Fran Lee
Interior design: Richard Carlin
Labanotation by Toni Intravaia
Checked by Muriel Topaz

This seal signifies that the notation contained in this work has been approved and meets the
qualifications for a Labanotation score as set forth by the Dance Notation Bureau.

Printed in the United States of America

Acknowledgments

The technical background for writing this book was provided by numerous teachers. In acknowledging them, I recall that old—yet ever young—teacher, musician, writer, director, martinet, chastiser, nemesis of the trifler and the lazy, profound inspirer of the serious student: the incomparable Louis Horst. Of equal importance is Martha Graham, the revealer and progenitor who completely changed the course of my life.

There are many others who pointed new ways. They include dance artists Hanya Holm, Doris Humphrey, Charles Weidman, Jean Erdman, José Limón, Martha Hill Davies, Ruth St. Denis, Dorothy Perkins, Lucas Hoving, Bessie Schoenberg, Margaret H'Doubler, Klarna Pinska, Gertrude Shurr, Robert Joffrey, and Lillian Moore. Artists in other fields include Toni Intravaia, Bernard Fraizer, Mary Jane Teall, Mary Jabara, Joshua Missal, Peggy McLuen, Miriam Gray, Miriam Green, and Robert Green. And there are other very special personalities, too: Dolo Brooking, Joseph Campbell, Saralyn Hardy, William Kuhlke, Marcia Grund. Each opened a uniquely different and important window of comprehension, perception, or art lore. In this sphere, perhaps my own students—those patient, distressing, delightful, irritating, rewarding, avid bundles of receptive energy—have been the most revealing teachers.

I am indebted to many for assistance and encouragement in the writing of this book. Without the original suggestion and delicate prodding of Dr. Gladys Taggart, the book would never have been started. With her usual perceptive tact, Dr. Joie Stapleton continued the prodding and encouragement at critical times. Dr. E. E. Bayles offered assistance at a moment of particular discouragement. I offer a special thanks to Judy Johanning, who was able to decipher my writing and notations when typing the manuscript, and to Janet Nakaji who transformed my stick figures into the illustrations in the book. Most of all, the book would never have been completed without the constant encouragement and the critical reading and many rereadings of Alice Bauman. Contact with the particular wisdom and stature of each of these individuals has been infinitely rewarding in countless ways.

For this edition, I am especially indebted to Arvella Frazier, Albert Weaver, and Richard Carlin. To Arvella who not only labored long hours at the computer and copier, but offered tactful advice and sensitive encouragement when most needed, all this when her own schedule was very demanding. To Albert for his most gracious and generous assistance in the area of computers. To Richard for suggesting that we prepare a new edition, and for his editorial care and guidance.

To ALICE BAUMAN,
whose comprehension and discernment
permeate all sections of this book

Contents

Preface

Many students and teachers have used *On the Count of One* since the publication of the first edition in 1968 and the subsequent revisions in 1975 and 1982. By the publication of the third edition, the book had grown greatly in size and scope from its original intent. In this new, revised edition, I decided to focus again on my original emphasis: the art, craft, and science of dance training. The heart of this book, according to those who have used it, comprises the chapters on dance technique that illustrate how progressive learning can occur. The explosion of dance publishing in recent years means that many topics that were briefly covered in the third edition can now be explored more satisfactorily by student or teacher by consulting these other, more comprehensive books (see the bibliography for a suggested reading list). For this reason, I was able to eliminate some of the ancillary material and return the book's focus to modern dance training.

Although the emphasis here is on the technical training, teachers should still introduce their students to the important background aspects of dance such as the history of dance and some brief information about the other styles of dance. Because there is never enough time in the usual technique class to cover all that is necessary, this will probably need to be in the form of handout sheets that include a short list of books available for those wishing more information.

Organization of the Text

This book focuses on the early technical training of the dance student whether the student aspires to be a teacher or a performing artist. It is very important that the student acquire an extensive vocabulary in the movement language of dance; this is the topic of Part I. The major portion of this text, Part II, is devoted to the art, craft, and science of dance technique. Understanding dance comes only through practice, through spending countless hours in the studio acquiring the physical feeling of movement along with the theory. Chapters 3 through 13 provide dozens of exercises buttressed by discussion of their technical and aesthetic characteristics and with suggested progression from the easy to more difficult exercises.

Part III is devoted to the teaching of dance. The author feels that this is important because too many schools do not stress the logical development in planning a full course of dance, of how beginning exercises are a preparation for more difficult techniques to be introduced later in a course. New dance teachers have a tendency to start with exercises they know best which are apt to be the last ones learned, often the more difficult exercises. This can be discouraging—and even injurious—to beginners. It is hoped that this tendency can be corrected with emphasis on understanding the relationship of earlier technical studies as preparation for the more difficult ones to be included later in the course.

Most of the exercises in this book are based on the techniques stemming from the creative genius of Martha Graham, Doris Humphrey, Hanya Holm, Jean Erdman, José Limón, and Robert Joffrey. Many of these exercises are now part of the standard training repertoire of many universities and schools, especially those offering a major in dance. The author's contribution is the organization for progressive development; the articulation of the three elements in dance movement—art, craft, and science—that must be coordinated; the suggestions for creative explorations; and the suggestions for the future teacher.

This author feels that dance teachers and students should learn dance notation and is certain that the time will come when dance teachers will not be able to get a teaching position unless they are able to read dance notation any more than music teachers could obtain a teaching position if unable to read music notation. In this book you will see Labanotation symbols by the dance technique illustrations.* These are for the benefit of students who have studied the notation system or are currently enrolled in such a class. In addition, Appendix A provides some basic information about Labanotation.

Although some lesson plans are included in the book, I must stress that these are not to be considered to be a formula but only a general guide for beginning teachers. As in all arts, there is no one way of progression, no one system of technique, but many.

---

* The author expresses deep appreciation to Toni Intravaia for preparing the Labanotation illustrations throughout the book as well as the information in Appendix A.

To the Reader

To those using this book, whether beginning teacher or beginning student, it should be considered a springboard or a temporary point of departure until you you are strong enough to work alone and make changes to fit your own technical growth or to suit the requirements of your students. Whether a teacher or a performer, you should remember that all classes and dancers are unique, requiring individual approaches in technical development. All need to make frequent re-evaluations, re-explorations, in a sense, a re-discovery of your philosophy, your approach to techniques and way of working. This should start while still a student. Teachers should find ways to help students think for themselves.

Whether you aspire to be a teacher or a professional performer, you need to know something of the periodic changes in style and philosophy in the arts. These changes have appeared throughout history. These new directions usually emerge as explosions of creative energy, instigated by the genius of one or many artists. The energy produced by these explosions gradually dissipates until another such eruption appears. If you do not know or understand this process, you may misunderstand new developments in the arts. Many people resist the new. Before you ridicule or dismiss new ideas in technique or composition, take time to examine the new as it appears. See if there may be something of value that could enrich or expand current techniques or horizons.

Whether a teacher or dancer you should understand this background in relation to the emergence of our current "modern dance" style which is already changing. You should discover the roles played in the development of "modern dance" by François Delsart, Isadora Duncan, Ruth St. Denis, Ted Shawn, Mary Wigman, Martha Graham, Hany Holm, Doris Humphrey, Charles Weidman, and Lester Horton. All of these individuals were searching for similar goals although they worked in different ways: to find a true foundation of movement within the instrument itself—the human body—instead of in the philosophy of some other century or culture. Knowing something of all these concepts can deepen your understanding of movement as you work in technique and composition classes. You should know of Louis Horst's role in forcing dancers to understand compositional form and his role in the growth and maturation of modern dance. A suggestion to teachers: You might suggest to your students that they use some of the above to gain further knowledge about dance for topics of themes in other classes or for research projects.

A brief note to the student dreaming of a career as a professional performer. First of all, be a realist. As preparation, consider investigating some of the local dance companies in your area. Currently there are many that are very good. Find out about auditions and what is required to become a member. I advise against taking off for New York or Hollywood immediately after graduation from college. You may be a star in your college dance group or in private studio recitals, but in a professional setting you will be a rank beginner, no matter how many years you may have studied. Wherever you go to study, a few may have new students audition to place them in a class; many just automatically put all new students in the beginning class. Dance classes, rent, and food are very expensive in major cities. You should know how you will handle such items. However, and probably most important, you must have that effervescence, that inner glow, and absolute belief in yourself that leaps from the stage to the audience. You must be mature enough to attend audition after audition where an atmosphere of cutthroat competition prevails and still hold onto your aspirations and artistic standards. If you are absolutely certain that you want a career in dance performance more than anything else and are prepared to handle all of the above: Good luck!

The wisdom of Louis Horst has a way of emerging when needed—sayings, comments, bits and scraps from conversations or from classes, seemingly forgotten—"You started it all wrong," he once said to me, "Why drift in on an upbeat? Jump in solidly on the count of one." Now it is time for you, the dance student and the beginning teacher, to jump in solidly on the count of one into mastering the art of learning and teaching dance.

Part I

THE LANGUAGE OF DANCE

Individuals should have the opportunity to develop themselves as unified wholes (emotionally, intellectually, and physically); to experience the challenge of molding and creating instruments of themselves; and to use those instruments for communication. This opportunity provides the wonder, excitement, and appeal of dance.

Ideally, dance training should start in the elementary schools as does training for art and music (or even before if it is well taught with material suitable for the preschool level of development). Starting training early is the only way dance can gain its rightful place in the nation's cultural life. Currently, too many students enter high school or college dance classes on a kindergarten achievement level of dance movement. To change the pattern, to expand dance in the schools, we need well-trained teachers. State certification, which has begun but is moving much too slowly, would ensure the availability of well-trained dance teachers.

The purpose of studying dance varies with each individual. Some students wish only for personal development, others wish to teach. Some will enter the fields of dance notation or dance therapy. A very few may become professional performers or join amateur or semiprofessional regional dance groups. Whatever the eventual goal, background and early training should include creative exploration; introduction to a variety of dance styles (folk, modern, ballet, jazz); a sound basis for technical development; and progressive technical development in the style selected for specialization. Whatever the eventual goal, thorough training should include courses in the history and philosophy of dance, in notation, and as much music as possible.

The craft of dance is the essential foundation of dance. It includes the practice of separate exercises for specific controls that increase the dancer's degree, range, and efficiency of movement. The craft gives the dancer a movement vocabulary, creating an awareness of rhythm, pulse, and phrasing. In addition, it helps students gain facility in combining movements.

Dance is found in the transition between position or planned sequences, that is, in the inner quality motivating the movements. The art transcends counts or meter; it is the intangible coming together of many elements. However, dance is not really experienced until the art aspects are understood and intermixed with the craft. Art aspects such as expressivity and motivation must become so much a part of the instrument that they are an automatic part of all movement. And finally, these movements must be structured into a composition and performed for an audience, which may be no more than other members of the class.

Dance is movement and cannot be satisfactorily captured in words. You must discover the essence of dance within your own instrument. To learn the use of yourself as a unified whole and to communicate to others with the instrument you have created are activities that enhance the experience of dance.

It is up to the teachers and young artists of this youthful art form to continue exploring expressive movement, to contribute their own creative energy for ongoing, vigorous growth. They must be willing to recognize and accept or discard new developments: to carefully evaluate the new in order to identify what is valid as an important contribution and what is a temporary exploration. The person who is unable or unwilling to re-explore and re-evaluate continuously, or who chooses to ride on the past (whether dancer or teacher) will simply contribute to the demise of modern dance.

Chapter 1 introduces the basic movement terminology used throughout the book. Additionally, it offers beginning movement exercises to prepare for the in-depth work later on. Chapter 2 discusses the relationship between music and dance. It gives the most basic rudiments of music and defines terminology that will be useful to the dancer.

The Vocabulary of Movement

Vocabulary (Movement)

The movement vocabulary of dance is based on certain fundamental concepts and basic motions that should be part of all dancers' early training. With understanding and practice, these concepts and motions become so rooted in the instrument that the qualities are automatic. The various elements are inseparable in actual use, but for clarity in the learning process they must be listed as distinct elements. These include the use of energy as well as the use of time, space, basic locomotion, axial movement, and other factors. This movement vocabulary can be introduced to beginners quickly, allowing students to acquire an easy use of the vocabulary in combinations as well as in separate elements.

Qualities of Movement

Traditionally, the use of energy in dance has been classified as *qualities of movement*. These qualities are categorized as primary and secondary. *Primary qualities* include swinging, percussive, and sustained movements. *Secondary qualities* include collapsing, vibratory, and suspended movements. While this classification is still valid, the whole area has been expanding, and within these categories there are infinite variations of dimension, proportion, dynamics, shapes, and combinations. The study of the use of energy through qualities of movement can be extended to include sequential movement, which involves an awareness of the flow of movement from one part of the body to another—that is, an awareness of sequential action and the way in which movements are connected.

Primary qualities of movement

Swinging movement in its simplest form is a pendulum-like motion of the arms, legs, or torso: back and forth, side to side, up and down. In swinging movement, there is usually a beginning accent, or definite starting impulse, with a feeling of freedom in the resulting action. The dimension of the resulting action depends on the amount of energy in the initiating impulse. Simple swinging movement can be carried into a circular action or a figure eight by exerting additional energy, or impulse, within the swing.

Percussive movement has a sharp, forceful initiation of energy combined with a very definite stopping or checking of the action. The action stops definitely, as though meeting an immovable object. This type of movement is suggestive of striking, hitting, or kicking.

Sustained movement is smooth, continuous, and seemingly unaccented. There is a starting impulse, but it is so much a part of the continuing action that is usually not apparent.

Secondary qualities of movement

Collapsing movement is a variation of swinging movement and emphasizes the beginning of the swing (the downward action). The recovery, or follow-through, is necessary but minimized in this type of movement.

Vibratory movement is a variation of percussive movement in which the initial force, stop, and recovery are so rapid that the resulting action becomes a shaking, trembling oscillation, or vibration.

Suspended movement is a variation of sustained movement in which there is a momentary sense of hanging in space, a denial of gravity. In suspended movement, there is often a more marked initiating accent or impulse than in a simple sustained movement.

Dynamics

Dynamics refers to the amount of, and the way in which, energy is used either in separate movements or within a movement theme. There may be a great deal or very little energy used. Energy may be exerted in an explosive burst, in an expanding or diminishing surge, with staccato accents, or as various combinations of these. Variation in the use of dynamics is an important element in making movement expressive and meaningful.

Time

In too many instances, dancers either do not know musical notation and time signatures or they do not discipline themselves to maintain a set tempo. Instead they count their own steps in a measure or phrase. When the steps are slow they count slowly; when the steps are fast, they count as fast as necessary. Dance students should acquire the discipline of counting correctly. See Chapter 2 for more details on basic rudiments of music for dancers.

Space

The awareness and use of space is an important part of the dancer's movement vocabulary and one of the most significant contributions of American dance to the movement vocabulary. Early training should include exploration and practice in this area.

Directions

The beginning dancer will have no difficulty understanding directions but will need some practice experiencing them with a feeling of moving in space. The directions are: forward; backward; sideways (left and right); diagonal (diagonally forward [left and right], and diagonally backward [right and left]). Some teachers include around (or circular) as part of direction, and some give this a separate category. Directions can be practiced in relation to a place called "the front of the room" or in relation to the dancer's own front, back, or whatever. When using Labanotation, direction is always in relation to the dancer's own front and back.

Circular movement has many variations. A circular movement can be performed while standing in place with only a lean of the torso in the various directions. A circular path (of varying size) can be followed while facing one direction, or it can be followed while facing the line of direction in the circle. Similarly, the dancer may back around the circle, go sideways while facing toward the center of the circle or facing out, or even while zigzagging the path of the circle. Another element may be added by moving in such a way that there is a feeling of centripetal force pulling toward the center of the circle or the reverse, a centrifugal force pulling away from the center of the circle. Then too, the element of tempo can be added. But talking about these concepts is not enough; the beginning dancer needs to experience all of them through movement explorations.

Level

The ability to change level adds an important dimension to the dancer's vocabulary. At first, the dancer should explore simple changes in level while remaining in one place; then the dancer should do so while moving in space; and later while leaping, jumping, and falling.

Dimension

Dimension is the actual size of movements or steps. Dimension is a somewhat subtle aspect of the use of space, and it affects all of the foregoing movements. Movements may be large and expansive, or they may be diminutive. Dimension must be explored and understood as an important element in expressive movement.

The various uses of space should first be explored as separate elements, then combined with each other, and finally combined with the various qualities of movement, various steps, and the added discipline of time.

Basic Locomotion

There are five basic dance steps: walk (*pas*), run (*couru*), leap (*jeté*), hop (*sauté*), and jump (*elevé*)*; all other dance steps are combinations of these. However, certain combinations of these basic steps are used so universally that they are often included under basic locomotion. These basic locomotor steps are organized according to their rhythmic base, either even or uneven. Nine of the steps have an even rhythmic structure.

Even rhythm

The primary steps of even rhythm (walk, run, leap, hop, jump) should not need detailed descriptions. Beginners, however, may need clarification regarding the differences among leaping, hopping, and jumping. In a leap, the weight is transferred from one foot to the other. In a hop, the weight stays on the same foot. In a jump, the landing is on both feet at the same time, although the takeoff may be from one or both feet.

---

* The French ballet terms are used here, and throughout the book, as an aid to students with ballet training. Modern dance movement, however, is different than the movement styles of classical ballet.

The secondary steps of even rhythm are: schottische, waltz, mazurka, and pas de Basque. These are combinations of the basic steps, but they are so fundamental to dance that many prefer to include them as basic steps.

The *schottische* is performed on four even counts. It consists of three steps and a hop. Generally, it is performed by progressing forward with the free foot swinging across the front of the other foot on the hop. Actually, the steps may be taken in any direction and the free foot may swing or lift in any direction: forward, sideways, or backward. A word cue for the schottische is, ''Step, step, step, hop.''

Experiment with the differences in feeling and in coordination when performing the following variations of the schottische:

1. Move forward with the basic schottische step, and swing the free foot diagonally across in front of the supporting leg on the hop. Repeat this, but move backward, then sideways, and finally around instead of forward.
2. Move forward with the basic schottische step, but lift the free foot backward on the hop. Repeat this while moving backward, sideways, and around.
3. Move sideways with the basic schottische step, but lift the free foot sideways on the hop. Repeat this while moving forward, backward, and around.

For beginners, this is not as easy as it may sound.

The *waltz* is performed on three even counts, and is usually a step forward, a step to the side, and a closing of the free foot to the standing foot with a shift of weight on the closing foot. Beginners often have difficulty remembering to take the weight on the closing foot. The variation of this most often used in modern dance is the *waltz run*, sometimes called a *triplet*. This is performed with three steps or runs forward, the first step of each three being accented with a small *plié*. The steps or runs should be even in both time and distance covered by the steps. The second and third steps are usually taken on half-toe. Most teachers cue the students by saying, ''Down, up, up; down, up, up.''

The *mazurka* uses a basic beat of three. It is probably the most difficult step for beginners to master and should not be taught early in the course. Here are brief instructions: Starting with the feet close together, slide the right foot diagonally forward, taking the weight on it. With a very small leap, cut the left foot under the right foot, changing the weight to the left foot. Hop on the left foot while bringing the right foot in close to the ankle of the left foot. Instead of a count, a work cue is usually most helpful to the beginning dancer. ''Slide, cut, hop; slide, cut, hop'' is an easy description of the step. These instructions must be kept even, with each word receiving the same amount of time. Be sure to repeat the sequence starting with the left foot.

The *pas de Basque* step, which may be either even or uneven in rhythm, received its name when it was incorporated into the vocabulary of ballet. It was taken from Basque folk dances. Although the name connects the step with this small geographical area, it is a basic step in many folk dances around the world (but with different names). There are probably more variations of the pas de Basque than any other basic steps.

Basically, the pas de Basque is a step (or a leap) to the side, a step forward (or backward), and a closing of the free foot to the other foot with a definite change of weight. When danced on an even rhythm, the steps are smooth, with each step taking the same amount of time. The basic beat is three.

The pas de Basque may be performed smoothly, with the steps definite and moderately slow or with the steps so small that it is hard to see the change of weight. The first step to the side may be taken as a small or very large leap with the knees lifted high. The tempo may vary from very slow to extremely fast. In style, it may be danced as though wearing wooden shoes (as in many of the Basque dances), boots, or with the sense of caressing the earth with bare feet, which is the manner of many dances of the Orient. Or, the style can be balletic in character, emphasizing an elegant use of the feet as though the dancers are presenting a jeweled heel to the audience. When the pas de Basque became a part of the ballet vocabulary, nobility wore shoes with jeweled heels, and in ballet the step should have this elegance.

Uneven rhythm

The primary steps of uneven rhythm are the slide, gallop, and skip. These should not need detailed description. However, to aid the complete beginner: The *slide* is a sideways movement; the *gallop* is a forward or backward movement keeping one foot in front while the other comes up to it. Both are basically a step from which the dancer rises quickly into the air. Then the other foot is brought close and takes the weight on landing, technically a small leap. Both the slide and gallop are usually performed quickly and lightly. A *skip* (a step and a hop on first one foot, then the other) is most often danced forward, though it can be taken in any direction, including turning. The slide and gallop can serve as a base for learning a ballet *chassé*.

The secondary steps of uneven rhythm are the polka and the pas de Basque.

The *polka* is usually danced forward, though it may be danced sideways, backward, or turning. The basic beat is two, but it starts on an upbeat. The usual description is hop, step forward, close the free foot and change weight, and step forward. The count is "one and two; a one and two." The feet alternate when the polka is repeated. Many beginners have difficulty learning the polka from this type of analysis. An easier approach is to start by dancing four gallops with the right foot in front, and without stopping dance four gallops with the left foot in front. Practice this until the change can be made smoothly. A small hop facilitates the change from one foot to the other. Repeat this, but gallop twice on each foot instead of four times. This is a polka step.

The *pas de Basque* was described under even rhythm. When it is danced on an uneven rhythm, the basic beat is two instead of three, and it is counted "one, a two; one, a two" or "one and two; one and two." This is almost always danced with a leap to the side instead of a step. It usually has a robust quality with many variations.

Basic Axial Movements:
Flexion, Extension, Rotation

Basic axial movements can be done with or without locomotion. The three principal categories are flexion, extension, and rotation. These movements are done in relation to joint areas in the torso and extremities. The movements are vital to dance, and all dancers should become thoroughly familiar with their own instruments; they should know how each part moves separately in isolation and in relation to all other parts. Each dancer should explore the movement of separate parts and discover the difference in feeling and bending (*flexion*), stretching (*extension*), and turning on one's own axis (*rotation*). Be sure to include all areas: fingers, toes, wrists, ankles, elbows, knees, shoulders, hips, torso or spine, and neck. Localize movement in various areas of the spine (neck, chest, midsection, and hip areas). After practicing the three types of movement within these limited joint areas, combine two, three, or more areas and use the three types of action. The variations are infinite.

The basic axial movements may be combined with the explorations in use of energy and qualities of movement.

One type of exploration, which can be called the *cat exercise*, is a useful warmup exercise. With this exercise, the students flex, extend, and rotate in all joint areas with an awareness of sequential movement from one part of the body to the other. Further awareness can be attained by doing these movements while lying on the face; lying on the back; sitting; kneeling; standing; and by combining them with simple locomotion. The concept of efficiency of movement can also be explained by pointing out that a cat's movement flows smoothly from one part to another with no extraneous movement; cats never tighten muscles to the point of cramping.

Vocabulary (Nonmovement Positions)

There are several elements of dance aside from actual movement that should be a part of the dancer's vocabulary. Nonmovement vocabulary includes the standard dance positions. Traditionally, ballet uses five standard positions. Many teachers of modern dance now use these ballet positions, and some teachers have added other positions and established a different numbering system.

Since movement (specifically in this case, dance movement) is a language, the various movements, positions, steps, qualities, and movement combinations serve as a vocabulary to be used for communication in much the same way as words are used for oral or written communication. The larger the vocabulary, the greater the possibilities for meaningful communication.

Art Aspects of Dance Positions

Each of the following dance positions (as well as the hundreds of other possible positions) should impart a different feeling of personal orientation. For instance, when you stand in first position you should feel differently than you do when you stand in second position or in any of the other positions. There should be a feeling of consistency in the position and shape between the arms and legs, and both should have a relationship to the center of the torso.

Feel that the arms are attached from the center of the back and that the impulse to move comes from there. Feel that the wrists and hands are extensions of the arm—but they must be flexible extensions. When using the arms and hands, feel as though the energy is progressing from the center of the body out through the end of the middle finger. When raising the arms over the head, hold the shoulders down; it is very easy to lift the shoulders when the arms are raised. Some beginners find it difficult, if not impossible, to hold their shoulders down, but they should work toward this goal. Beginners need frequent reminders to keep their shoulders down without tightening their neck, arms, or upper torso. (Work to make students aware of their shoulders so they can recognize when this is happening and correct themselves.) When the arms are curved, be aware of the relationship of the little finger and the palm of the hand in completing the curve. Sense a perpendicular line going through the center of the torso. As a general rule when working in the standard ballet positions the fingers should not cross this center line when the arms are in front of the body, overhead, or moving between these positions. Similarly, be conscious of the side seam of the leotard or trousers. When the arms are at the sides, the middle finger should be in line with this seam. Do not misunderstand: These stipulations are for standard positions, beginning technical training, and learning awareness and relationships. They are not for composition, exploring expressive movement, or improvisation.

Be very aware of the relationship of the legs to the hip area and to the torso. There should be a feeling of pulling up out of all the joints, with the arches lifted and with a particular awareness of an elongation at the front of the hip-joint area. This elongation should be localized and not produce a stiffening in any area. For leg movements, work for a feeling of complete freedom in the hip joint itself.

Safety Aspects of Dance Positions

For all the positions listed, weight must be distributed equally on both feet. Guard against stiffening the knees or forcing them back. Such movement can injure the knee, ruin the shape of the leg, and interfere with the alignment needed for balance and turns. Also, it is particularly easy to shift the weight to one foot in positions in which one foot is in front of the other. Feel that the shaft of the torso is halfway between the center of both longitudinal arches.

Turnout of the feet must be an individual matter. This cannot be too strongly emphasized. It is imperative that the turnout come from the hip joint and not from either the foot or the knees. An increased amount of turnout must come gradually and not be forced. One of the best ways to increase turnout is to maintain and consistently use the amount of turnout already acquired. It is very easy, especially when standing on one leg as for brushes, to let the supporting foot gradually creep around to a parallel position.

All students, advanced as well as beginners, and all teachers need to check constantly on knee placement or alignment; the knees must point directly over the center of the toes. In addition, the hips should be kept parallel to the front and not rotated toward the back or to one side. It is very easy to rotate the hips toward the back foot when standing with one foot in front of the other.

As a general rule, when the arms are raised either in front or to the side, they should be held just below shoulder level. If the arms are at shoulder level or above, there is a tendency to lift the shoulders, causing tension in the shoulders, neck, and upper torso.

Standard Dance Positions (Posés)

At the time ballet technique was systemized, five positions of the feet and arms were established, and have since been known by the numbers one to five. For ballet, these positions were supposed to be universal regardless of country or school. However, this standardization did not occur. Although the foot positions seem to be used uniformly in ballet schools, there is a divergence in arm positions.

Most modern dance schools now use the standard ballet numbering for these five positions, though a few schools have established their own numbering system. All the modern schools and some ballet schools also use a parallel foot position, and many use diagonal positions. In addition, there are a number of individual variations and combinations of these positions, including some with a turned-in rotation that should not be given to beginning students.

Parallel position

In the parallel position, stand with the feet parallel but not quite touching, the arms hanging in a long curve at the sides, and the middle finger in line with the side seam of the leotard or trousers. The arms, legs, and spine should be elongated but not stiff. There must be no undue tension in the shoulders, neck, knees, or wrists.

Parallel position

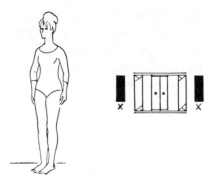

First position (première)

In the first position, stand tall, with the legs turned out from the hip joints and the heels touching each other. Various arm (*bras*) positions are used in both ballet and modern versions of this position. Some schools use the arm position described for the parallel position: arms hanging in a long curve at the sides. Some schools advise holding the arms in a long curve in front of the torso with the fingers not quite touching. Other schools have the arms raised in front just below shoulder level, again with the fingers not quite touching. There are also variations in the position of the fingers, including the thumb touching the first finger; the thumb touching the middle finger; and the fingers somewhat elongated with the middle finger dropped slightly below the others.

First position

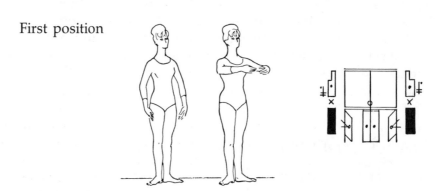

Second position (seconde)

There is less disagreement about the second position than any of the others. The main discrepancy is in the distance between the feet. Stand with the legs turned out (from the hips), the feet approximately 12 to 14 inches apart, and the arms extended sideways just below shoulder level. When deciding the distance to use, some consideration should be given to the length of the individual's legs. Those with longer legs can use a wider stance. A safe guideline is to have the heels approximately under the hip joint.

The arms should be in a long curve; the palms of the hands should be down; and the elbows should be carried to the back. This control seems to be difficult for beginners. If the arms tire in the shoulder area, they are being held incorrectly; but, if they tire at about the center of the upper arm, the arms are probably being held correctly.

Second position

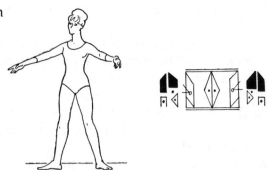

Third position (troisième)

The third position is often considered an in-between position or a semififth position, and many teachers omit it. Others use it for beginners but call it the fifth until students can control enough turnout for a true fifth position. The legs are turned out from the hips with one foot in front of the other. The front heel is at the instep of the back foot, with equal turnout maintained in both legs.

Third position

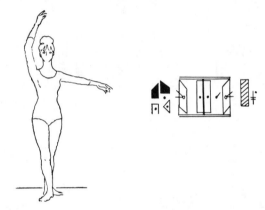

Most schools have the arm on the side of the back foot raised sideways as practiced in second position. The other arm is curved over the head. When an arm is raised over the head, the hand should not be carried too far back, and the fingers should not cross the center line of the torso. Again, the shoulders must be held down when the arms are raised over the head. One school, however, is consistent with the idea that this is an in-between position. In this school, one arm is held in a long curve at the side, raised halfway between lowered and shoulder level, with the other arm half-raised in a long curve in front. The front arm is on the side of the forward foot.

Third position, variation

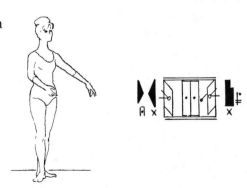

Fourth position (quatrième)

In the fourth position, stand with the legs turned out and one foot about 12 inches in front of the other foot. There are two basic opinions on the exact placement of the feet. The position most often used has the forward heel straight ahead of the big-toe joint of the back foot. Some schools, however, teach a foot relationship similar to that of the first position, but with the feet placed with one about 12 inches in front of the other. This position is easier for beginners with limited flexibility. Still other schools use both positions, calling one a closed (*fermeé*) fourth position and the other an open (*ouverte*) fourth position.

There are two arm positions in common use with the fourth position. One is the same as the version of the third position in which one arm is held overhead and the other is extended sideways. The other arm position has one arm overhead and the other raised in a long curve in front, with the hand on a level with the center of the chest.

Fourth position

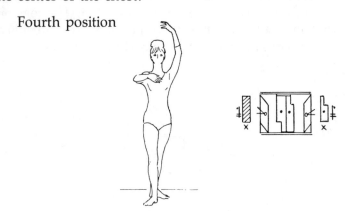

Fifth position (cinquième)

The foot location for the fifth position varies only in the degree of cross over. The legs are equally turned out from the hips, with one foot in front of the other. In the early days of ballet, the front heel was on a line with the end of the toes of the back foot. However, because most dancers cannot safely control this degree of turnout, many schools now place the heel at the big-toe joint of the back foot. This shift may seem too subtle to be important, but it does make a difference in the safe use of the knees. In either case, the hips must be kept parallel to the front.

Again, there are two arm positions in use with the fifth position. The arms may be raised in a long curve overhead (*en haut*) or they may be carried in front in a long downward curve (*en bas*), with the fingers not quite touching. Many schools use only the overhead position. Other schools use both positions, calling them fifth high (*en haut*) and fifth low (*en bas*).

Fifth position

Fifth position

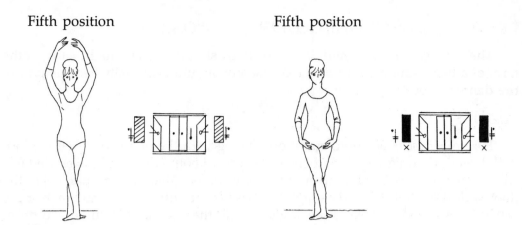

Arms high

Arms low

Diagonally closed position

To assume the diagonally closed position, stand with the back foot turned out and the front foot at right angles to the back foot. The back foot is more turned out than the front foot. Keep hips parallel to the front. It is easy to let the hips rotate toward the back foot.

The arms are almost straight and are aligned with the direction of the feet. The arms are not touching the body; the palms of the hands are turned toward each other, not down.

Diagonally closed position

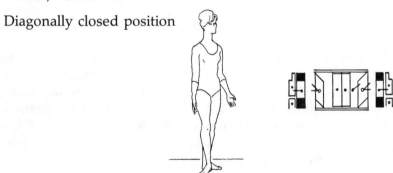

Diagonally opened position

To assume the diagonally opened position, stand with the back foot turned out, with the front foot at right angles to the back foot and 18 inches diagonally opened from the back foot. The arms are raised to just below the shoulder level on line with the direction of the foot.

Diagonally opened position

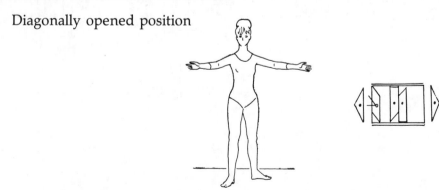

Advanced Dance Positions

The *arabesque*, *attitude*, and *relevé* positions should not be taught early in the term of a beginning modern dance course but should eventually become part of the dancer's vocabulary.

Arabesque

For an *arabesque* position, stand on one leg with the other leg lifted behind. Both knees are straight but not locked, and one or both arms can be extended forward. The torso can be held up straight, or it can be tilted forward parallel to the floor with the lifted leg held as high as possible. Be sure there is no break at the waist when raising the leg; a break will permit the head and shoulders to drop.

Arabesque

Attitude

For an attitude position, stand on one leg with the supporting knee straight. The other leg is lifted either in front (*en avant*) or behind (*en derrière*), with the knee bent and well turned out so that the foot crosses the torso. Generally, the arm on the side of the lifted leg is raised over the head as for third or fourth positions, and the other arm is extended to the side just slightly below shoulder level. Sometimes the arms are reversed. At times, the torso may be slightly rotated so the arm extended sideways is slightly toward the front.

Attitude   *Attitude*

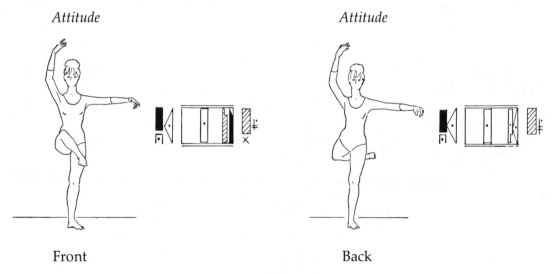

Front   Back

Relevé

Relevé is a rising to half-toe, usually on both feet, although some teachers use the term when rising to half-toe on one foot. The rise may be a slow press with knees straight or a quick springing action with or without a preparatory *plié*. Either way, it is important to hold the turnout from the hips and the ankle alignment. A feeling of pressing the heels very slightly forward will help with the balance.

Movement as a Unified Whole

All movement combines some aspect of each of the elements of energy, time, space, and axial movements, and all can be combined with locomotion. A keen awareness of pulse (underlying beat) or rhythm and phrasing is essential for a feeling of dance movement. There must also be a perception of the differences in feeling among movement qualities, differences that give shading and nuance to dance as communication. Additionally, the dancer must perform basic locomotor and axial movements with ease. At first, all of these elements of dance vocabulary must be consciously stressed. As facility develops through practice, the elements will become so much a part of the instrument that they will blend with all movement. Verbal knowledge of dance vocabulary is of little importance until it is combined with the technical controls of the craft and experienced through dance performance.

Chapter 2

The Dancer and the Music

From the beginning of life, time is manifest as a pulse, a measured beat or rhythm. Pulse and rhythm, either physical or visual, are found in all nature and art. This is particularly true in all aspects of dance. Dance students need at least an elementary knowledge of music basics from the start of their dance training.

In too many instances, dancers either do not know musical terminology, including music notation and time signatures, or they do not understand this terminology fully or use it accurately.* In many cases, dancers count their own steps in a measure or phrase. When the steps are slow they count slowly; when the steps are fast, they count as fast as necessary. Dance students, from the outset, should get in the habit of knowing the meter and acquire the discipline to count correctly.

As a dancer, you should have some ear for music and be able to hum a melody. Better still, you should study music. Take piano, voice, or basic music theory lessons. Learn to dance to your own singing; it will be to your advantage.

Remember that music is a partner, not a servant. Tempos should not be changed at the last minute in order to insert new dance movements or to permit difficult variations that were not planned in the original score. Also, music must never be forced to fit a dance idea that is different in character or meaning. Any cuts that are contemplated should always be planned with the composer, and if cuts are needed in music of the past, ask a trained musician to help you make them. Understand, and thereby use, the phrasing, melody, dynamics, and rhythm of music to dance intuitively. Learn to recognize musical motifs (see page X), and keep in mind that dance movements should realize transitions, cadenzas, introductions, codas, and other musical elements. Finally, remember that the rehearsal piano is just that: for rehearsal. The final score may use an ensemble of brass instruments, strings, etc.

Most important, however, recognize what is within the music and let it become part of you as dance.

---

* A glossary of musical terms is given in Appendix B.

Basic Terminology

Meter and measure

In music, the pulses or beats are partitioned into units called measures. The first beat of each measure is accented (emphasized). The number of beats per measure is the *meter* of that measure: 4 beats equals a meter of 4, 3 beats equals a meter of 3, and so on. A meter of 6, with a strong accent on 1 and a weaker accent on 4, divides into two groups of 3. A meter of 5 can divide into 2 + 3 or 3 + 2, with strong accents on 1, and weaker accents on 3 or 4. Meter in music is a recurring pattern of stress with an established arrangement of strong and weak pulsations or beats.

Note values

The shape of a note marks its duration. The whole note, written as an open circle, is used as a unit of measurement; it usually has 4 beats or counts. A half note is an open circle with a stem; two half notes equal one whole note. A quarter note is a filled circle with a stem; four of these equal one whole note. An eighth note is a filled circle with a stem plus a flag; eight of these equal one whole note. Two or more eighth notes are joined by a beam across the ends of the stems, instead of individual flags. A sixteenth note is a filled circle with a stem plus a double flag; sixteen of these equal one whole note. Two or more sixteenth notes are joined at the ends of their stems by a double beam. The whole system is simple arithmetic.

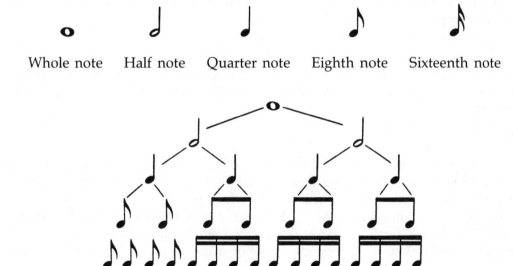

Whole note   Half note   Quarter note   Eighth note   Sixteenth note

When a time value has been subdivided into three equal parts instead of two, the group of three notes is called a triplet and marked with a "3":

Time signatures

To indicate the meter in music, the basic beat or count per measure, a time signature is used. The time signature is written like a fraction without the slash. The lower number indicates the kind of note that is given one count; the upper figure gives the number of beats in each measure. Thus, in ¾ there are recurring groups of three quarter notes (or any division thereof) equaling 3 beats, the first with a strong stress. In ¼ there are 4 beats, with a quarter note equaling the beat. Here there are two primary accents: the strongest on 1, the lesser on 3, with 2 and 4 having none.

Tempo

Tempo refers to the speed of music: fast, slow, moderate, etc. Any meter or rhythm can be performed at any tempo.

Rhythm

Rhythm is the organization of music with respect to time. Rhythmic patterns are created through repetitions of accents.

Phrase

A phrase in music serves the same purpose as a sentence in literature. It may be as long as necessary to complete a musical thought. It may consist of as few as two or three notes or be as long as 20 measures. The musical phrase always ends with a cadence, a device creating a pause or resting place, thus completing the thought.

Motif

The briefest intelligible unit of musical thought, a motif can consist of as few as two notes or as many as several measures. It is characterized by a distinctive rhythm and melody.

Accent

A strong accent indicates the beginning of each measure. An accent stresses a note by leaning on it, emphasizing it, making it louder than the rest. Accents may occur not only as the first beat but elsewhere in the measure (see the discussion of meter and measure above). However, any note may be accented for the sake of the music. Such an accent is indicated by the sign placed over or under the note or by the letters *sf* (*sforzando*, forced or strongly accented) placed similarly.

Syncopation

Syncopation occurs when the accent is placed either on an unusual beat, such as on 2 and 4 in ¼ meter, or on the second division (or second or third in triplet division) of a beat:

Tying a weak beat over a measure line to a strong beat creates an accent on that weak beat and eliminates the strong beat:

Rests

Rests are resting places, indicating silence for the duration of the rest symbol. In musical notations rests are written as follows:

whole rest   half rest   quarter rest   eighth rest   sixteenth rest

Downbeats and upbeats

Downbeat refers to the accent on the first note of a measure. The name is derived from the motion of the conductor in marking time for the orchestra or choral group. Similarly, an *upbeat* is one that occurs on the last note of a measure and is conducted with an upward motion preceding the downbeat. Some phrases may begin on an upbeat.

Dotted notes

A musical note may be given a longer time value by adding a dot after it in musical notation. The dot adds one-half the value of the note.

Counting Rhythmic Patterns

For a straight basic beat with a ¼ signature, dancers keep count of both the number of measures and the number of beats. For example, in ¼ time you would count: One, 2, 3, 4; Two, 2, 3, 4; Three, 2, 3, 4; Four, 2, 3, 4. Here's an example in ¾ time in notation:

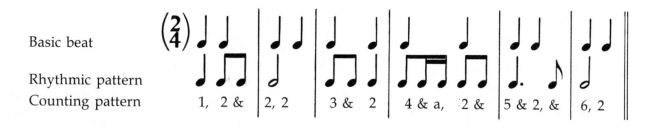

Basic beat							
Rhythmic pattern							
Counting pattern	1, 2 &	2, 2	3 & 2	4 & a,	2 &	5 & 2, &	6, 2

Part II

THE ART, CRAFT, AND SCIENCE
OF DANCE TECHNIQUE

Chapter 3

Relaxation

Relaxation means an efficient release of tension in localized areas. It is important to learn to relax areas not needed for a specific movement. Learning to do this means understanding the use of antagonistic muscles and how not to work against oneself. In other words, relaxation indicates complete efficiency of movement.

One of the causes of poor alignment is the extreme tension in our daily lives. For many individuals, this tension becomes localized in the back, shoulders, or neck. Soreness or stiff neck is practically a national malady. This uncontrolled tension can be the basis for poor posture and many of our so-called awkward movements. It is important to learn to relax when possible.

It is rare that members of a dance class will be so tense that several of the relaxation exercises will need to be performed before other types of movement can be attempted. It is suggested that the first relaxation exercise (3.A.1) be introduced to the class followed by beginning dance movements. In subsequent classes, introduce more of the relaxation exercises as needed by the class. All classes will differ.

3.A. Relaxation: Lying

3.A.1. Basic relaxation

Art. The stillness and inactivity will be disturbing to some individuals. There is such a constant blare of noise in our lives—television, radio, traffic—that becoming aware of silence and stillness can be both unsettling and revealing.

Craft. Lie on the back, the knees bent, with the soles of the feet on the floor, the arms comfortably at the sides on the floor, the neck straight with the spine, the face straight up, and the eyes closed. Keep only enough tension in the legs to keep the knees from flopping out. When teaching this relaxation exercise, speak slowly with a soothing voice just loud enough to be heard easily. Do not rush the movement. Talk the students into relaxing.

Here is a suggested order of instruction:

Close the eyes and try to shut out awareness of anyone else in the room. Feel
that there is a straight line from the base of the neck and head to the hips. Let the back of the head feel heavy on the floor. Feel the tension going out of the neck. Let this relaxation continue down the spine. Feel as though the weight of the shoulders is pressing into the floor. Let the floor support the entire back. Let the small of the back relax into the floor. (Those with swayback will not be able to do this.) Think of the backbone as a hollow tube containing a column of air. When inhaling, feel as though the air is going down the spine to the tail. As the air is exhaled, feel the air going to the top of the head. Keep the breathing even and slow.

Other helpful instructions include telling the class to relax the eyeballs and the tongue. However, some classes or individuals find this so funny that they laugh and destroy all that has gone before. If you intend to use this, you might discuss it very briefly before starting the exercise.

Each class needs a different time allotment for this relaxation. Finish the exercise very quietly by having the students open their eyes, and then with their knees still bent roll over to one side and slowly sit up.

Sometimes as many as half the class members will make spasmodic movements of the hands, feet, and head. Many will keep opening their eyes and turning their heads to see what others are doing. It may be necessary to tell the class that there is nothing to see. It may help to have students start by tightening the muscles of the body then collapsing or letting go suddenly. Some may need to do this several times before achieving complete relaxation.

Relaxation

Science.   Never jump up quickly to a standing position following any of these relaxation exercises. Do not follow this relaxation with strenuous activity without a slow, careful warmup.

3.A.2. Long relaxation session

If time permits, or if there is an unusually tense group of students, a whole lesson on relaxation may be taught. This exercise can be used for such a lesson or used by students outside of class during stressful times.

If possible, turn out the lights and post signs on the doors directing no one to enter. There must be no interruption.

Art.   See Exercise 3.A.1.

Craft.   Lie on the floor on the back. Close the eyes. Try to block out all extraneous sounds; concentrate on the feel of the muscles. Use a soothing tone of voice when teaching this exercise; speak slightly slower than normal and only loud enough to be heard.

Tense all muscles as tightly as possible. Let go, feeling as though everything is sinking into the floor: the back of the head, the neck, the shoulders, the elbows and hands, the lower back, the hips, the thighs and calves, the feet. Be aware of the contrast in feeling between the tightness and the relaxation. No one must make any effort to keep up with anyone else. Find the tempo that is right for you; any faster or slower will cause some feeling of tension. Find your own tempo as we progress.

Using only enough energy to perform the movement, slide one arm along the floor until the arm is about even with the shoulder. When you feel this position has been reached, slowly slide the arm on the floor back to the starting position. (The teacher should pace the instructions to the slowest member of the class. Those arriving in position earlier should wait.)

Repeat this movement with the other arm. Be sure to slide the arm slowly on the floor with no lifting.

Check to be sure everything is still sinking into the floor. Slide one foot along the floor until the sole of the foot is on the floor and the knee is pointing toward the ceiling. When you feel this position has been reached, slowly slide the foot back to the starting position. Repeat with the other foot.

Repeat the arm slide with both arms at the same time but with the backs of the hands on the floor. Be efficient; use only muscles needed to move the arms with no change in the back.

When the arms are back at the sides, use the least amount of energy possible to roll slowly to one side; curling easily into a fetal position, let the underneath arm find the most comfortable position. Feel that everything is still sinking into the floor. Slowly lift the top arm toward the ceiling, making no effort to stretch; use only an easy lift as though floating toward the ceiling, then return the arm to the side.

As easily as possible, roll onto the back and continue the roll to the other side. Assuming an easy fetal position, let everything sink into the floor. Easily let the top arm rise toward the ceiling and return to the side.

(At this stage, if you are giving yourself instructions while in bed trying to sleep, stop here and assume the usual sleeping position. In the usual class situation, however, it is necessary to rise gradually to a standing position since you or your students will be going to other classes.)

Come to a sitting position as effortlessly as possible. Find whatever position is comfortable for you. Let the head drop forward toward the chest as dead weight. Let the head just hang, and as the muscles in the neck and back gradually relax and elongate, the head will drop further forward (but do not bend the torso forward). Do not hold this position too long; think of it as a pause. Gradually roll the head to one side with the ear approaching the shoulder. Do not run or twist the head. Pause long enough to feel the muscles on the opposite side of the neck elongate. Do not raise either shoulder. The arms and shoulders should just hang.

Slowly roll the head to the back, to the opposite side, and again hang the head forward. Repeat the sequence rolling in the opposite direction.

(This head-rolling sequence may be used alone by a person who is sitting at a desk to relieve tense muscles in the neck, back, and shoulders.)

As easily as possible come to a standing position. From the sitting position roll to both knees and use the hands on the floor to help in standing. Forget about grace or dance movements; try to find the easiest way possible to stand. Keep the eyes closed and walk in a small circle around yourself. When you feel that you have returned to the starting position, walk in the opposite direction.

Easily raise the arms overhead toward the ceiling and let them return to the sides. Make this an easy lowering, not a drop. Open the eyes and let the head turn easily and slowly from side to side, and walk calmly to your next class.

Science. Any section of the exercise may be repeated more than once if needed. Each class is different and the teacher must adjust to the needs of each class. This usually takes from 30 to 40 minutes, and there should be no strenuous activity following this exercise.

3.B. Relaxation: Sitting

3.B.1. Semi-yoga position

Art. Become sensitive to the movement possibilities of the neck and spine. Become aware of the sequential action of movement down and up the spine. Let the movement come naturally. Do not force it, but move as easily as possible. As always, be efficient; use only the parts needed.

Craft. This exercise is performed slowly. Sit with the knees bent, the toes of one foot in the bend of the knee of the other leg, the torso erect but not stiff, the head balanced easily on the top of the spine, and the arms hanging down with the hands just resting on the knees. The feet should not be under the legs. Here-after, this will be referred to as the semi-yoga position.

Lower the head to the left so the ear goes toward the shoulder. There should be no rotation. Let the head hang until the muscles of the right side of the neck begin to relax. It will feel as though the muscles on that side of the neck are getting slightly longer. Do not exert a muscular pull; let the weight of the head do all the pulling. Slowly lift the head upright and repeat to the right. Slowly lift the head again and lower it toward the back. Slowly lift the head upright and hang it forward. As the muscles in the back of the neck relax, let the relaxation continue down the spine so the head gradually pulls the whole torso forward. As the muscles in the back relax, the torso will bend forward over the legs. Let the hands slide along the floor. There will be a great deal of individual variation in the degree of bend. Then, starting at the base of the spine with movement progressing segment by segment up the spine, return to the beginning upright sitting position.

Basic relaxation: Sitting

 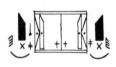

Science. When relaxing these muscles, it is very important to let the weight of the head do all the pulling. The movement should progress slowly, smoothly, and sequentially. Do not bounce. Ease and localized relaxation are the keynotes of this entire movement sequence.

3.B.2. Relaxation with the soles of the feet together

Art. Although there is only a small change in position in the following exercises, each will feel different from the others. Students should be encouraged to be aware of the change in feeling in these and in all exercises.

Craft. Sit with the soles of the feet together, the back erect but not stiff, and the arms hanging so that the hands are just outside the knees. Using a sequential relaxation movement starting with the head, let the head pull the whole torso into a forward bend. Let the head go as close to the floor as individual flexibility permits, but do not force the bend. The arms should slide forward along the floor as the bend increases. Starting from the base of the spine, return to the sitting position, with the movement flowing from the base of the spine to the top of the head. The head should be the last part to come to place.

Relaxation with the soles of the feet together

Science.   See Exercise 3.B.2.

3.B.3. Relaxation with the legs extended to sides

Art.   See exercises 3.B.1 and 3.B.2.

Craft.   Sit with the legs extended and spread as far apart as possible. There will be a great deal of individual variation in the degree of spread. The knees should be straight but not locked, and the arms should be raised sideways just below the shoulder level. Repeat the sequential relaxation movement into a forward bend with the head leading. The arms should lower toward the legs and slide out along the legs or along the floor as the bend increases. Return to the upright position, with the movement starting at the base of the spine and flowing to the top of the head.

Relaxation with the legs extended to sides

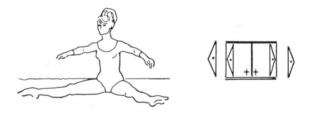

Science.   The height of the arms is important in these exercises. If the arms are at shoulder level or above, the shoulders will lift, which they should not do. It is easier to keep the shoulders down if the arms are held just below shoulder level.

Watch the alignment of the back. There will be a tendency for some to round the back and collapse the midsection. Also watch the ankle alignment. There should be a straight line down the front of each leg through the top of the arch. The legs must not rotate inward when they are extended straight forward or to the side.

3.B.4. Relaxation with the legs extended forward

Art.   See Exercise 3.B.2.

Craft.   Sit with the legs extended straight forward and the knees straight but not stiff. The arms may be extended forward just outside the legs and just below the shoulder level, or they may be raised sideways. Repeat the sequential relaxation, with the head pulling the torso into a forward bend. As relaxation reaches the rib-cage area, permit the arms to join the relaxation movement by letting them slide along the floor as the bend increases. Return to the upright position, with movement progressing sequentially from the base of the spine to the top of the head.

Science. See Exercise 3.B.3.

3.C. Additional Exercises to Release Tension

3.C.1. Lifting head back

This is particularly good to release tension in the upper back after sitting bent over a desk or typewriter.

Art. See Exercise 3.B.1.

Craft. Stand easily with good alignment through torso. Lift arms with elbows bent, so that the upper arms are straight out from the shoulders and the lower arms back as far as possible so there is a pull in the upper back.

Science. Be sure the head is lifted back and not collapsed so the head drops or hangs toward the back. Be sure the lower arms stay on line with or slightly in front of the ears, not behind the ears. Be sure the upper arms stay on line with or slightly below the shoulders but not above shoulder level.

3.C.2. Head tip

This is good for stiff neck or soreness in neck, upper back, or shoulders.

Art. See Exercise 3.B.1.

Craft. Sit easily on a chair or on the floor with the back erect but not stiff. Let the head hang forward until the muscles in the back of the neck relax or feel as though elongating. Slowly lift the head upright, then let the head hang straight to one side so the ear goes toward the shoulder without dropping either forward or backward. Again let the head just hang. Slowly lift the head to an upright position, then let the head hang to the back. Slowly lift the head to an upright position, then let the head hang to the opposite side with the ear going toward the shoulder. Repeat exercise two or three times.

If the neck is very tense or sore, this may be somewhat painful at first. In this case, it may help to apply heat before starting the exercise.

Science. Be sure the weight of the head does all the pulling without exerting any other muscular pull and that the ear goes toward the shoulder without letting the head rotate forward or backward.

3.C.3. Head roll

Art. See Exercise 3.B.1.

Craft. Sit easily in a chair or on the floor with back erect but not stiff. Let the head drop forward, then slowly roll the head to one side, continue on to the back, to the other side, and again forward. Do three or four rolls in one direction, then reverse going in the opposite direction.

Science. Be sure this is slow and easy, with the weight of the head doing all the pulling and with no resistance to the pull of the head.

3.C.4. Relaxed roll

This exercise is excellent for reducing tension in the shoulders and neck when suffering from a stiff neck or a tension headache.

Art. See Exercise 3.B.1.

Craft. Lie on the back completely relaxed with the arms on the floor over the head. It may be necessary to stretch completely and then collapse a few times to arrive at a point of complete relaxation. Using a very localized movement, let the right knee bend and reach the right leg across the left leg. Pull with the leg until the whole body flops over. Staying relaxed, reach the left elbow across the head to the right and pull with the elbow until the whole body flops over the back. Some students will lift the arm straight up toward the ceiling instead of just pulling the elbow close to the head. Permit the knees to bend as the pull twists the torso.

Relaxed roll

Science. Avoid pushing with the elbow or knee to start the roll. This usually indicates that the student is tensing in the torso and resisting the pull of the arm or leg.

3.C.5. Breathing exercise

There are many other relaxation exercises. Deep, sustained breaths followed by slow exhalation may help. Do not take deep breaths to the point of hyperventilation.

3.C.6. Localized stretch

Another way of working to relax specific muscle groups is to assume a position that stretches a localized area or muscle group and to hold the position until the muscles relax. Particularly tense individuals may find this painful at first, but if the position is held the pain will subside and they will feel the muscles elongating and releasing the tension. Care must be taken to be sure the position is not actually straining a muscle and that there is no danger of tearing muscles.

Chapter 4

Control of Center, Alignment, and Balance

In this chapter, we discuss three areas involving control: control of center, alignment, and balance. Control in each area results in a feeling of freedom that is essential for later exercises.

Control of Center

Awareness and conscious use of the center (*midsection* and *center of gravity* are two of many synonyms in current use) are essential for genuine control of movement. Also necessary is a sense of energy going out from the center and returning to the center. Dancers need much help in exploring this phase of movement. Control of the center provides a freedom in the use of arms and legs and in control of posture; it is the focus for balance and turns, and it is the base for authority in movement. Precise control of the big muscles that carry the weight and supply the power should be acquired in the first years of dance training; this control leaves the groups of smaller muscles free for style, quality, speed, and line.

For this book, the basic dance techniques conceived by Martha Graham and the terms "contract" and "release" will be used as the foundation for this control of the center. However, teachers should feel free to select other terminology.

4.A. Lying on the Floor

4.A.1. Preliminary exercise: Hip thrust

Art. Sense where movement originates and be particularly aware of how movement flows from one part of the body to another.

Craft. Lie on the back with the knees bent and the soles of the feet on the floor, arms extended out to the sides and on the floor, palms of the hands down. Lift the hips as high as possible, keeping the shoulders on the floor. Return to the starting position by pulling the small of the back down. Try to touch the small of the back to the floor *before* the hips touch the floor. There should be a sequential action moving down the spine as one part after another touches the floor. As the hips touch, keep the entire back pressed to the floor for about three counts. Repeat two or three times. For beginners, the feeling of pressing against the floor provides a tangible point of reference not possible in a sitting or standing position.

Hip thrust

Science. It is important to have a feeling of pulling into the movements. Avoid a percussive jerk or "crunch" into a contraction or release. Also, it is important to breathe normally whenever practicing these exercises.

4.A.2. Contractions lying down: Basic contraction and release

Art. An awareness of the workings of the spine will be the most important aspect of this exercise and the following ones. With this awareness, develop an understanding of the relationship of the spine's flexion and extension to the workings of the arms and hands as well as to the legs and feet.

Craft. Lie on the back with the legs out straight and the arms at the sides. Contract (tighten) the abdominal muscles, pressing the small of the back into the floor. This is similar to the hip-thrust exercise (4.A.1.), but it will be more difficult because of the leg position. Localize the movement so the neck, shoulders, and legs do not tighten. The movement should be deep enough that the knees bend slightly; the shoulders, arms, and head should be slightly off the floor, but the head should be hanging down with the neck relaxed. Now release (straighten out) along the floor to the original position. This should be a definite elongation and not just a collapse.

Basic contraction

Science. The flexion of the knees and the lift of the shoulders and arms from the floor must come as a result of the contraction in the center and not as separate movements. Especially important is the fact that the knees, head, and shoulders must not initiate the movement but must follow or be a result of the contraction in the center of the torso. Guard against arching the back or pushing the abdomen up or out on the release.

After this is mastered, the contraction may be deepened to come higher off the floor.

4.A.3. Contractions lying down: Side contraction

Art. See Exercise 4.A.2.

Craft. To the basic contraction exercise, add a rotation in the upper torso so that one shoulder and elbow are raised higher than the other. Lift the elbow on the high arm and the face will turn as a result of the lifting. This may be taken to a half-sitting position. Do not attempt this until complete control has been achieved when lying on the back in the basic contraction.

Side contraction

Science. See Exercise 4.A.2.

4.A.4. *Contraction lying face down*

Art. See Exercise 4.A.2.

Craft. Lie face down, with the arms extended at the sides at about shoulder level. Contract and release as in Exercise 4.A.2. In this position, the small of the back will round toward the ceiling. There will be a feeling of pressure of the thighs and hands against the floor.

Contraction lying face down

Science. The hip bones and rib cage must maintain contact with the floor. Be sure the hips do not lift. Guard against starting the movement in the thighs and hands or hips. There is a difference between feeling pressure there as a result of the contraction and as a result of starting out by pressing with the thighs and hands before the contraction.

4.B. Sitting

4.B.1. *Contractions: Semi-yoga position*

Art. Although a sitting contraction is essentially the same as one executed while lying on the floor, it feels quite different. Become sensitive to the differences in total organization as positions change. Maintain a sense of the totality and completeness of movement as each exercise is repeated.

Craft. Start in a semi-yoga position with the spine erect but not stiff and with the arms hanging down at the sides, outside the legs. At first, perform an extremely small contraction and release in the lower torso. Keep the tempo slow and even. Think of this as a pulse. Gradually increase the range of movement until the chest, shoulders, and head become a part of the movement.

Science. Be sure the starting movement is a true contraction involving the back and not just a tightening in front with a counterresistance in the back. Also be sure the movement is a true contraction and not a collapse; many beginners perform the latter. The contraction should produce a lift, not a slump. Be sure it is not a percussive crunch.

In the semi-yoga position, be sure the foot is not placed under the leg. Also be sure the release is a straightening up—a lifting through the top of the head—with a feeling of elongation of the spine, not just a pushing forward of the abdomen causing a swayback. Through *all* the sitting contractions, guard against tightening the neck and the throat area on the release so the head stays back. The elongation of the spine must continue all the way up through the neck to the top of the head but with no extra tension. Be efficient.

4.B.2. *Sitting contraction with the soles of the feet together*

Art. See Exercise 4.B.1.

Craft. Sit with the soles of the feet together, the torso erect, and the hands resting on the ankles. Perform a deep contraction, lifting the head back with the face parallel to the ceiling. Hold the contraction as the torso bends forward as far as possible. (There will be a great deal of variation in individual flexibility in this movement.) Permit the head to go forward toward the floor to complete the bend. While bent forward, release, carrying the movement from the base of the spine though the top of the head. Hold the release as the torso lifts to the original sitting position.

Sitting contraction with the soles together

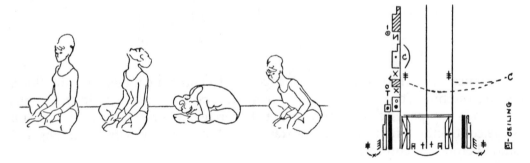

Science. See Exercise 4.B.1.

4.B.3. *Sitting contraction with the legs extended to sides*

Art. See Exercise 4.B.1.

Craft. Sit with the legs stretched out sideways, the knees straight and pointing toward the ceiling, back erect, and the arms extended in a long curve sideways just below shoulder level. The contraction and release are performed as in Exercise 4.B.2. However, the arms and legs will move as a result of the action. On the contraction, the ankles will flex and the elbows will straighten, forcing energy out through the heel of the hand and causing the wrist to flex. On release, the ankles will extend, causing the toes to point, and the arms and wrists will again round as at the beginning.

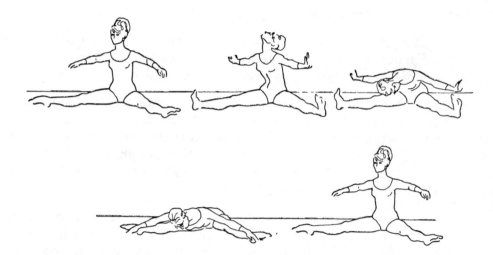

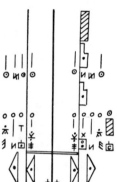

Science. See Exercise 4.B.1.

4.B.4. *Sitting contraction with the arms overhead*

Art. See Exercise 4.B.1.

Craft. Sit as in Exercise 4.B.3. but with the arms raised overhead in a long curve and the fingers not quite touching. On the contraction the ankles will flex, and the elbows will bend, bringing the upper arms in front of the head; the lower arms will be parallel to each other and to the ceiling. The face will lift toward the ceiling. Hold this position as the torso bends forward bringing the upper arms parallel to the floor. On the release, as the back straightens, the ankles will extend and the arms will round into their beginning position. This position is held as the torso lifts to its starting position. The arms move in and out, not up and down (except as the torso bends and lifts). The movement of the arms and legs must come as a result of the contraction and release, not as separate movements.

Sitting contraction: Arms overhead

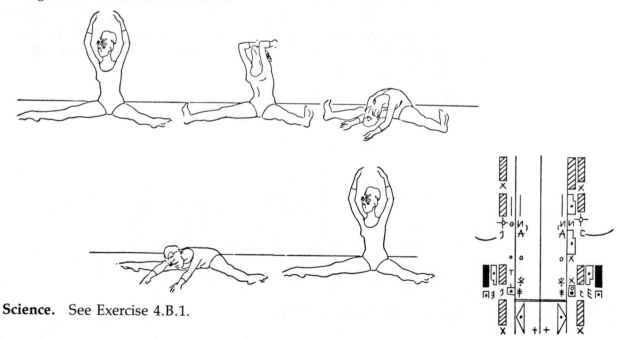

Science. See Exercise 4.B.1.

4.C. Contractions: Standing

4.C.1. Basic Exercise

Art. The problem of balance will add somewhat to the difficulty of this exercise, although this will be counterbalanced by the pleasure of greater mobility. There should be an awareness of a new organization of the entire person.

Craft. Stand with good alignment, the knees straight but not locked, and the arms extended to the sides just below shoulder level. Start with very small movements of contraction and release. Try to recognize the very first inside tightening that starts the contraction before it becomes deep enough to be visible as movement. This first inside tightening is the basic control for balance. Gradually increase the range to involve a slight shoulder action.

Science. Guard against locking the knees or forcing the knees backward. On the contraction, be sure the spine rounds slightly. Beginning students often resist this by locking the spine so that it cannot move; the locking is often accompanied by tightening the throat, holding the breath, and locking the knees. Guard against this or warn the students about it. They seldom are aware of this until told. In their first attempts, beginners may need to place a hand at the small of the back and have something tangible to push against.

If students have real difficulty with this, you are probably progressing too rapidly; they are not ready for this degree of difficulty. It may be necessary to return, briefly, to Exercise 4.A.1., hip thrust. Having the floor to push against provides a point of reference.

4.C.2. Standing contraction: Inner beat

Art. See Exercise 4.C.1.

Craft. This is related to the contraction but is much smaller. Find the inside muscles that start the contraction, but do not go to the point where the back rounds. It is felt, but no actual movement is visible. The tightening should result in a feeling of a very slight pulling up in the lower abdominal muscles balanced by a similar upward lift in the lower back. Guard against going too far; this should not become an actual contraction. Acquiring this control and awareness is an important factor in balance. Use this exercise when introducing balance on half-toe and when introducing turns on one foot.

Standing contraction: Inner beat

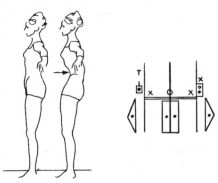

Science. See Exercise 4.C.1.

4.C.3. Standing contraction: Back wave

Art. See Exercise 4.C.1.

Craft. Stand with the legs close together but not touching, the knees slightly bent, the torso bent forward at the hips (not the waist) so it is parallel to the floor, and the hands resting (not pressing) on the knees. Perform a deep contraction, rounding the back toward the ceiling. Release to the original position. On the release, feel as though the top of the head (not the chin) is pushing toward one wall and the hips are pushing toward the opposite wall. This is movement in opposite directions. The movement should ripple or wave sequentially along the back. Finding the feeling of a truly straight back in this position may be difficult for some.

Standing contraction: Back wave

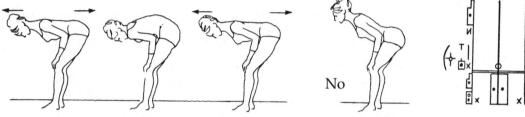

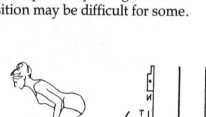

Science. Be sure the back is straight in the starting position. Many students will hunch or round the shoulders. Be sure the neck is used as an extension of the spine and not as a separate appendage. There will be a tendency to lift the chin instead of keeping the face parallel to the floor. On the release, the elongation should be so complete that the abdomen flattens. There is a tendency for beginners to push the abdomen toward the floor, which causes a swayback.

Alignment

Dancers need to be constantly reminded of the importance of alignment. With proper alignment, dancers gain control of the center of the torso and of the chest area without experiencing tensing in the shoulders and neck. Alignment is also necessary for precise balance.

4.D. Basic Control

Art. When all parts of the body are properly aligned, there should be a feeling of freedom. With practice in this control, there will come a marvelous sense of easy movement in the arms and legs and a feeling of effortlessness in the carriage of the head with no tension in the neck and shoulders. Try for a feeling of complete lightness, of weightlessness. Be aware of the relationship of one part of the body to another.

Craft. The following movements are localized; use only the parts of the body mentioned; do not involve any other part. Work as easily as possible and avoid overtensing. After completing one movement, sustain it as the next is added. Most movements will be so small they will be felt rather than seen. The teacher will see the result of the movement rather than the actual movement.

Stand with feet parallel and almost touching. Perform the following sequence:

1. Lift the arches slightly, but not enough to shift weight to the outside of the feet. Keep weight evenly distributed on three parts of each foot: behind the big toe, behind the little toe, and on the heel.
2. Lift each thigh slightly to feel a slight tightening in the knee area and up into the front of the hip-joint area. Do not push back or lock the knee or hip joint.
3. Stretch up in the waist area, localizing the stretch between the lowest rib and the hip bone. This tends to flatten the abdomen if done correctly. Do not hold your breath or lift the shoulders.
4. Lift the rib cage slightly. Feel as though the rib cage is being raised by a pull at the top of the sternum (breast bone). Do not throw the shoulders back or tighten the neck. (To help beginners control specific muscular movements, find different ways of directing these movements. Search for a variety of work descriptions in order to reach all the students in a class and to help them elongate the torso efficiently.)
5. Lengthen the neck slightly as though the head is being lifted by the top of the ears. Do not lift the chin or tilt the head.
6. Holding all these movements without undue tension, pull the scapulae (shoulder blades) slightly toward the spine or toward each other. Do not move the shoulders. They will move slightly owing to the scapulae movement, but they should not be thrown back or moved independently.
7. Tighten the buttocks slightly. Do not think of tucking under. Rather, feel that the backs of the thighs and the buttocks are pulling slightly toward each other.

The shoulder girdle should be resting on the upright, central shaft of the torso. If all this has been performed efficiently using enough tension but not too much, it should be possible to rise easily on half-toe with a feeling of floating toward the ceiling. It should be possible to swing the arms easily without disturbing the balance and to move the head easily. Each individual will need to experiment with this to find the least amount of tension possible to accomplish the alignment.

Science.   This procedure uses the skeleton for support. When the bones are properly aligned, it should take very little muscular effort to hold the upright lift in both the front and back of the thighs and in the torso and shoulders. Muscle control in the back of the thighs is often neglected.

Balance

Precise balance is important for dancers. It requires complete alignment control and an exquisite center awareness. Acquiring balance and versatility in the use of space should bring a feeling of elation.

4.E. Balance on Two Feet

Art.   Balance requires a serene center, both physically and psychologically. To set the stage, establish a quiet, unhurried atmosphere. This atmosphere is so closely related to that of the relaxation, alignment (4.D.), and inner beat (4.C.2.) exercises that it may be advisable to return, briefly, to these exercises or at least remind the students of them. Strive for a feeling of complete suspension and an ease in balance.

Craft. Stand in good alignment, feet parallel, arms down at the sides but with a feeling of air between the arms and torso. There should be a sense of the heels barely touching the floor, with the weight held more over the balls of the feet. Do two inner beats in moderate tempo and with a sustained quality. Start a third inner beat, and let this inside center tightening be the energy source for rising to half-toe. Do not depend on the small ankle muscle to do all the work. Be sure to hold the alignment in the back, knees, and ankles. Feel energy going straight through the top of the head and a counterforce pushing out through the balls of the feet. Think of the rise as a floating movement rather than as a sudden perch. Lower the heels to the floor without changing the alignment.

Science. Guard against giving slightly at the small of the back by pushing the rib cage forward and up just before reaching the peak of the lift, at the starting point, or when returning the heels to the floor. These are vulnerable points for beginners. At times, this may be so small it will be difficult for the teacher to see. It is very important to establish the center as the source of control. If students depend solely on the ankles or tighten the shoulder area, they will not acquire sureness of balance or any appearance of suspension. Another area often forgotten as part of alignment is the lift in the back of the thighs into the buttocks. There must be an equal lift in both the front and the back of the thighs.

Most beginners need constant reminding about ankle alignment. Do not permit the ankles to swing out. The straight line through the ankle from the top of the arch and up the front of the leg is necessary for true balance. This alignment is also an important safety factor in elevation. Carelessness in acquiring control of ankle alignment is the cause of most ankle sprains.

4.F. Balance on One Foot (*Relevé*)

Art. In exploring balance on one foot, the sense of center must be even stronger than for balance on both feet. Maintain alignment with a strong pull up in the center of the torso (with no tension in neck or shoulders) and a strong pull up on both the front and back of the thighs. The balance becomes a little more complicated as other elements come into play. Here is a small detail that may help. Visualize a suspension bridge between two towers. Then, when balancing on one foot, try to discover two points that can aid in suspending the position or movement. Feel that there is a taut string between these two points. (Try to maintain control of the center during this exploration.) One point usually will be in the middle of the thigh of the lifted leg and the other point will be in the area of the rib cage. The exact placement of the two will vary slightly with the standing position and the direction of the lifted leg (front, side, or back). This visualization is more an awareness of a concept than an actual physical control.

Craft. Some degree of ankle strength and control on both feet should be acquired before trying balance on one foot. To begin the exercise, stand on both feet, either in parallel or first position. Lift one foot forward just off the floor. Holding torso alignment and lifting from the center as described above, rise smoothly to half-toe. Rise as though being lifted by a string attached to the top of both ears. Be completely efficient in the movement, using the least amount of energy needed. There must be no unnecessary movement in any part of the body or in the extremities. When balancing on one foot, the base of support shifts from a point between both legs to a point over the supporting leg.

Science. Watch for tension in the neck and wrists. This is an indication that center control has been lost. Guard against having the lifted leg pull the hips out of alignment. This displacement is a very common error. Sometimes the displacement is so small that it is hard to see or for the dancer to feel. Dancers should learn to feel any displacement for self-correction.

All the practice on rising to half-toe (whether with one or both feet) should be mixed with small *pliés*, with the heels pressed to the floor to counteract the extreme contraction in the calf of the leg. Neglecting this stretch in the back of the lower leg is an important cause of overdevelopment of the calf muscle and of the subsequent shortening of the Achilles tendon; this latter can affect jumping and leaping efficiency and in extreme cases may result in muscle tear.

4.G. Shift of Balance

Art. The coming down from a balance should occur because the dancer chooses to return to earth, not because he or she has to.

Craft. With feet in first position, rise to half-toe on both feet and without coming down shift the balance to one foot. Then, still without coming down, return to balance on both feet then shift the balance to the other foot and control the coming down to rest on the full foot. Try this in various positions, and vary the direction of the lifted leg.

Science. See Exercise 4.F.

4.H. Balance Variations

Art. See exercises 4.E., 4.F., and 4.G.

Craft. The following are variations of balance exercises.

1. Vary the tempo. After acquiring some sureness in the slow rise to half-toe, try a fast step directly onto half-toe and hold.
2. Modify the level of the lifting leg to include low, medium, or high.
3. Change the level of the heel of the lifting leg after rising to half-toe and while maintaining balance.
4. Change the direction of the step into balance.
5. Combine balances (one foot or both feet) with *pliés* and brushes, torso movements, and the movement explorations described in Chapter 3.
6. Use balances employed for a coda or finish with various technical combinations.
7. Vary the dimension and direction. In other words, vary the degree of rise on the toe of the standing foot and the size and direction of the step into balance position.
8. Vary the torso position.

The possible combinations are infinite.

Science. See exercises 4.E., 4.F., and 4.G.

Chapter 5

Flexibility

Flexibility is important in fine tuning a dancer's instrument. In this chapter, we examine exercises that will increase flexibility, from sitting and standing stretches to the flexion, extension, and rotation of the torso.

Flexibility with Control

Sitting and standing stretches both begin with relaxation exercises. These exercises are important to prevent muscle tensing when we want to do the opposite—to stretch the muscles. Basic controlled stretches help increase dancers' flexibility.

5.A. Sitting Stretches

5.A.1. Basic stretches

Sitting stretches are commonly called "bounces." Because they should not be uncontrolled bounces, it is better to call them "stretches." Sitting bounces or sitting stretches have been part of standard warmups almost from the beginning of modern dance. Recently, however, they have become controversial, as some people have pointed out their potential harm. And when performed incorrectly these exercises are definitely injurious. However, many teachers feel that, when correctly executed, the exercises may be beneficial for stretching, warmup, and discovering how to hold the torso in relation to leg and torso movements. These sitting stretches should not be given to beginners early in a course. It is impossible to execute the exercises correctly until the students are able to sit upright without rolling back in the small of the back or tilting the pelvis. The bend must come from the hip joint with the torso well lifted and with a forward pull, not from the waist with a downward pressure.

Art.   Dance occurs through movement between poses, or positions. Encourage an awareness of transitional movement, of how one moves between or connects movements. The following stretch exercises are simple, but they can and must be performed with a dance quality. Communicate through voice quality, choice of metaphor, and personal enthusiasm the excitement of moving completely.

In all the stretches, feel that the neck is an extension of the spine. Precede the bend by feeling a lifting up and over in the midsection. Have a sense of trying to touch the rib cage to the thighs rather than trying to touch the head to the knees or floor.

Craft. Start the sitting stretches with sitting relaxation exercises as described in section 3.B. of Chapter 3. After reaching the maximum forward bend, start an easy, small stretch by pulling forward. Gradually increase the energy used to a strong forward pull. The emphasis should be on the forward pull and not on a downward bounce. End in an upright, lifted sitting position. After a series of four to eight stretches in any of the following positions, come to a centered, erect position before repeating or changing sides or position.

Science. None of the following sitting stretches should be given until students are able to sit up with the back straight without tilting the pelvis or allowing the lower back to roll backward. Until they reach this capability, students will not be able to bend from the hip joint. When the bend is taken from the waist, the exercise may injure the back or stretch and loosen the muscles that should tighten to hold the back. Keep both buttocks on the floor, even if this curtails the degree of the bend. The ankle alignment must be maintained. Be sure that the foot is not permitted to roll in.

Students should be encouraged to experiment with doing these exercises incorrectly to understand and experience their purpose. This can also stimulate self-correction. Doing this just once will not be injurious. Have the students place their hands on each side of the lower back and try bending from the waist, then pull up and bend from the hip joint. They should feel the back muscles loosen and spread on the first move and tighten on the second. Also, try a side bend permitting one buttock to lift off the floor and then keeping both on the floor. This should help the students feel where the stretch should be.

5.A.2. Sitting stretches in semi-yoga position

Art. See Exercise 5.A.1.

Craft. Use the semi-yoga position with arms hanging and the hands over the knees. Proceed as described in Exercise 5.A.1.

Sitting stretches in semi-yoga position

Science. See Exercise 5.A.1.

5.A.3. Sitting stretches with the soles of the feet together

Art. See Exercise 5.A.1.

Craft. Each of the following positions will provide a stronger stretch in a slightly different place. Beginners should start with the arms down and the hands resting on the knees (not grasping the knees). With more experience, the arms may be raised to just below shoulder level. Later, the student may grasp the ankles and exert a stronger pull. Be sure that the pull is forward and not a downward bounce.

Sitting stretches with the soles of the feet together.

Science. See Exercise 5.A.1.

5.A.4. *Sitting stretches with the legs extended to sides*

Art. See Exercise 5.A.1.

Craft. For this position, the legs should be spread as wide as possible while keeping the knees straight and the back erect. Be sure the knees are straight but not stiff. There will be a great deal of variation in the degree of spread. It is possible to develop a wider spread, but this must be very gradual; it must never be forced. Each student should find the greatest degree of spread that still permits keeping the back straight. The ankles may be either flexed or extended, but they should not be loose and forgotten.

Sitting stretches with the legs extended to sides

Science. See Exercise 5.A.1.

5.A.5. *Sitting stretches with the legs extended forward*

Art. See Exercise 5.A.1.

Craft. The legs are extended straight forward with the knees straight but not locked. Maintain a straight line down the front of each leg, through the ankle, and the top of the arch. The arms may be extended sideways or forward along the legs. Later, the ankles may be grasped with the hands to aid in a forward pull for greater flexibility. Be sure the ankles are part of the action whether they are flexed or extended.

Sitting stretches with the legs forward

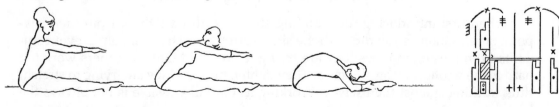

Science. See Exercise 5.A.1.

5.A.6. Sitting stretches with side bend

Art.   See Exercise 5.A.1.

Craft.   Sit with the legs extended sideways. Bend sideways over one leg, the lower arm inside the leg with the elbow reaching toward the floor, and the higher arm well extended overhead. Do not drop the higher arm over the face. Keep both buttocks on the floor. When first trying this exercise, students may benefit by feeling the difference in the stretch when both buttocks are down and when one is permitted to lift off the floor. The stretch in the torso will come in a different part of the torso.

Sitting stretches with side bend

Science.   See Exercise 5.A.1.

5.A.7. Sitting stretches with torso rotation

Art.   See Exercise 5.A.1.

Craft.   Bend over one leg as in Exercise 5.A.6. but rotate the torso to face the leg. The arms should extend over the leg. Later, the students may try to reach the hands beyond the toes or grasp the ankle for a stronger pull. Again, be sure both buttocks stay on the floor.

Sitting stretches with torso rotation

Science.   See Exercise 5.A.1.

5.A.8. Sitting stretches with forward pull

Art.   See Exercise 5.A.1.

Craft.   Start as in Exercise 5.A.7., but instead of keeping the stretch over one leg, move the torso forward between the outstretched legs using four pulls forward in the process of moving from one leg to the other.

Science.   See Exercise 5.A.1.

5.B. Basic Standing Stretches

When first introducing the standing stretches, discuss them from the viewpoint of relaxation as you did with the sitting stretches. This will help prevent students from tensing muscles they are trying to stretch. Many beginners work too hard in the wrong way on stretches. They tighten muscles they are trying to stretch, thus working against themselves. Working as hard as possible is not always the best way.

5.B.1. Forward bend

Art.   See Exercise 5.A.1.

Craft.   Start with relaxing the torso and arms in a forward bend. Go as far as possible, just hanging from the hip joint; then start an easy bounce or pull to bend further and gradually increase the amount of energy used, thereby increasing the degree of the stretch. Feel a stretch from the heels to the top of the head with the arms participating.

Basic standing stretches

No

Science.   The knees should be straight but not locked. Do not force back behind the knees. Dancers need frequent reminders about this. It may help to try to keep the weight over the toes. Be sure the legs are perpendicular to the floor with the hips over the heels and not at an angle diagonally behind the heels.

In forward and sideways stretches, be sure there is a long curve from the heels to the top of the head on the high side and not a crunching down on the low side. In the sideways stretch, the arm on the high side should be extended over the head, not dropped in front of the face, with the other arm diagonally down at the side.

In a backward stretch or bend, be sure to get a high lift in the upper chest area with a *very slight* pushing forward of the hips. Be sure not to drop in the small of the back or push the abdomen forward. Feel that the back is very long. For forward stretches with a flat back, the position of the arms and head are important. The face should be parallel to the floor, with the neck an extension of the spine. The arms must be straight out from the sides. If they are carried back toward the hips, the back will round. If the arms are lifted above shoulder height, hyperextension of the back will occur and it will be harder to keep from lifting the head.

5.B.2. *Standing stretches: Variations*

Art.   See Exercise 5.A.1.

Craft.   Try these variations:

1. Change the tempo and range of the stretches.
2. Vary the position of the feet. Beginners should use a semi-second position: feet apart with a comfortable turnout. Intermediate students may keep the feet parallel (together or slightly separated). Advanced students may use a fifth or fourth position.
3. Change direction and stretch forward, sideways, backward, and diagonally forward.
4. Alternate stretches in the various directions with *pliés* on one or both legs.
5. Modify the use of the back, holding it either rounded or straight.
6. Combine these variations into definite patterns.

Science.   See Exercise 5.B.1.

Torso Flexion and Extension

The upper torso is usually the least flexible part of the body. The following flexing and extending exercises will help correct that condition. Exercises include chest arches in various positions and shoulderstands.

5.C. On Floor

5.C.1. *Chest arch on back*

Art.   The spine is a miraculous instrument with endless movement possibilities. Explore these possibilities. Do not work too hard at first; rather, try to discover how easily the movements can be performed and in how many directions. Discover the feeling of sequential movement up and down the spine.

Craft.   Lie on the back, arms extended from the sides at about shoulder level, with the palms down. Raise the rib cage until the top of the head (not the back of the head) is on the floor. Press the palms against the floor and keep the elbows straight. Get as high an arch in the upper back as possible. To return to the floor, lift the head and round the back, rolling down to the starting position with the head returning last. After getting the feel of this movement, let the arch lift the torso to a sitting position; keep leading with the chest, the head hanging back. Continue the movement forward with the chest leading toward the knees. At the maximum bend forward, let the head carry on forward and, if possible, touch the knees. Hold this rounded position returning backward to the floor, sliding hands out on the floor. The head should be the last part to touch the floor.

Alternating this exercise with the basic contraction and release on the floor is an excellent warmup for the back at the beginning of class.

Science. Be sure the top of the head is on the floor in the starting arch. This places the arch in the upper back. If the back of the head is on the floor, the arch can shift to the small of the back. Some beginners may try to lift the hips instead of leaving them on the floor.

This exercise is a sequential movement and should be smooth and flowing. There should be no bump on the roll back to the floor. A critical point occurs just before reaching the sitting position. Many beginners permit the chest to cave in at this point.

5.C.2. Chest arch on side

Art. See Exercise 5.C.1.

Craft. Lie on one side, with the torso, the neck, and the head in a straight line and with the knee flexed on the underneath leg. Extend the lower arm underneath the head so that the ear rests on it. The other arm may be bent toward the front, with the palm of the hand on the floor to stabilize the position. Keeping the movement localized, raise the rib cage, getting a high arch between the lower side and the floor. Keep the head on the arm. After getting some control and easy flexibility in the action, let the arch lead to a side sitting position. Both knees will bend for the sit. This should be a sequential movement, with the head the last to come up. Then the head should move to the other side and be the last to return to the floor. For both the lifting and the return to the floor, movement should start on the side of the rib cage. Roll over and repeat on the other side.

Chest arch on side

Science See Exercise 5.C.1.

5.D. On Hands and Knees

5.D.1. Chest arch and round

Art. See Exercise 5.C.1.

Craft. On hands and knees, with the knees directly under the hips and hands under the shoulders with fingers pointing toward each other, pull down with the rib cage and let the elbows bend outward and the chin lift. Return by lifting the middle of the back, letting the top of the head go toward the floor. This is a continuous flowing action. The exercise is sometimes known as the "cat back."

Chest arch on hands and knees

Science. Guard against starting the downward movement by pushing into a swayback position rather than pulling down the rib cage.

5.D.2. Chest arch on hands and knees: Variations

Art. See Exercise 5.C.1.

Craft. The following are variations of Exercise 5.D.1.:

1. Descend with a chest lead, but return with a contraction in the lower back.
2. Perform circular motion with a chest lead. Still on hands and knees, lead down with the chest, as in the first variation, but not far enough to bend the elbows. Then, lead with the chest to the right as far as possible without moving off base. Then lead up, rounding the upper back as high as possible, and finally lead to the left as far as possible. Continue this circular action, increasing the tempo as control is achieved. Try to keep an even beat. Reverse the direction. As control increases, let this become a fast but small, continuous circular movement instead of a four-directional sequence.
3. A similar exercise may be performed by localizing movement in the hips.

Science. This is a very localized movement. The movement should be as easy as possible while moving as completely as the localization permits. Be sure not to resist the movements by inefficient tension.

5.E. Shoulderstand

5.E.1. Basic shoulderstand

Art.   See Exercise 5.C.1.

Craft.   Lie on the back, the arms down at the sides with the palms of the hands on the floor. Roll up on the shoulders, lift the feet toward the ceiling, and brace the hips with the hands keeping the elbows on the floor. Try to get as straight a line as possible from the shoulders to the pointed toes. Next, keeping the knees straight and extending the arms on the floor for balance, touch the toes to the floor overhead. Again, lift the feet toward the ceiling and stretch back up as straight as possible. Begin the return to the starting position by rounding the upper back. Slowly roll down to the floor, segment by segment. At the same time, bring the feet overhead, and with the hands pull the legs toward the chest (knees still straight). When the buttocks touch the floor, release the hands from the legs and bend the knees to permit the feet to return to the floor. This produces a different kind of stretch in the spine than any of the other exercises. Then slide the feet along the floor until the legs are again stretched out. Do not lower the legs with the knees straight, as this can cause strain in the lower back.

Shoulderstand

No

Science.   See Exercise 5.C.2.

5.E.2. Shoulderstand: Variations

Art.   See Exercise 5.C.1.

Craft. Here is a more difficult variation of the shoulderstand for advanced students. Proceed as in the shoulderstand to the point where the toes touch the floor overhead. Instead of lifting the feet, however, bend the knees, bringing them to the floor on each side of the head. This should not be forced. From here, either roll down to the starting position or return to the upright position, with the feet stretched toward the ceiling for the following variations: (1) Keeping the knees straight, perform a scissors action with the legs going forward and backward; and (2) open the legs sideways and then close them.

Shoulderstand variation

Science. See Exercise 5.D.2.

5.F. Flexion and Extension on Knees with Hands Grasping Heels

Art. See Exercise 5.C.1.

Craft. Start on the knees with the torso forward, the back straight and perfectly level, and the hands grasping the heels. Take a deep contraction, rounding the back toward the ceiling. Holding the contraction, lift the torso up and back so there is a straight diagonal slant from the knees to the shoulders. Arch the back by pushing the hips forward, still holding the heels. Return to the diagonal slant by taking a strong contraction. Arch the upper back and sit on the heels, and then sweep forward to assume the beginning position. The numbers under the illustrations indicate the timing and counts for performing this exercise.

Chest arch on knees with hands grasping heels

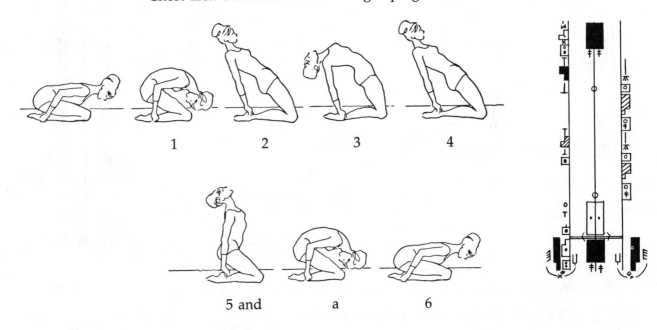

1   2   3   4

5 and   a   6

Science. See Exercise 5.D.2.

5.G. Standing Arch

5.G.1. Basic standing chest arch

Art.   See Exercise 5.C.1.

Craft.   Performing the chest arch in a standing position is quite different than lying on your back or on hands and knees. You will need to adjust to the additional factors of balance, length, and mobility that pertain to standing up. At first, keep the movement small, sustained, and sequential. Later, experiment with changing quality, dynamics, tempo, and dimension. Stand with the feet parallel and the knees easy, arms down at the sides. Start with a small torso sway, the chest leading; alternate forward and backward directions. Gradually increase the range and energy until the whole torso, arms, and head are pulled into the action.

Science.   See Exercise 5.D.2.

5.G.2. Standing chest arch: Variations

Art.   See Exercise 5.C.1.

Craft.   The following are variations of Exercise 5.G.1.:

1. Change the foot positions both in width and dimension.
2. Increase the dimension so the feet are lifted then lowered to the floor. The knees should be easy, taking part in the movement as needed.
3. Use the side chest lead, or use the above variations with side movement.
4. Let the lead carry on into locomotion. Again, vary the dynamics and dimension.
5. Use a circular chest lead.
6. Let the circular chest lead carry on into locomotion, including turning.
7. Repeat all of these variations, using a contraction as the motivating force.
8. Combine or alternate leads from the center and from the chest area.
9. Stand with good alignment, the feet parallel, and the arms raised overhead. Using a chest lead, swing the torso forward and down into a contraction and permit the knees to bend. Still holding the contraction, swing the arms behind, then forward and up to the starting position, straightening the knees at the same time. Bend the knees again as the arms swing down and through, and again straighten the knees as the arms swing forward and up, the body returning to the starting position.

Science.   See Exercise 5.D.2.

Torso Rotation

In this section, we continue with exercises designed to increase torso flexibility. These exercises involve torso rotation: turning the body around a vertical axis.

5.H. Previously Listed Rotation Exercises

5.H.1. Sitting stretches with torso rotation

The sitting stretches in Exercise 5.A.7., in which the torso faces the leg, employ a torso rotation; these exercises may be cited or introduced here if not previously introduced.

5.H.2. *Side contraction*

Exercise 4.A.3. uses a small rotation in the torso.

5.I. Additional Rotation Exercises

5.I.1. *Sitting torso rotation: Upright*

Art. The rotation of the torso—the turning of the body around a vertical axis— should be performed with an awareness of space, a sense of viewing the far horizons of the universe. The axis should be a serene center. However, the calmness of this center should be like the eye of a hurricane. The outward turning may be wild or gentle, but there must be a central control and a patterned direction of energy release.

Craft. Sit with both knees bent, one leg in front and the other behind. The arms should be just below shoulder level, with one arm curved over the forward leg and the other extended to the side. Lift the hip on the side of the back leg, turning the torso toward the forward leg. The degree of turn will vary by individual. After the maximum hip movement has been reached, the torso will continue to rotate and the head will continue still further. The arms stay parallel to the floor and follow the torso action.

Be sure there is no compression in the center of the torso caused by bending or collapsing in the waist area as the hip lifts. The torso must remain erect and the arms must move with the torso. On the return, as the hip pushes toward the floor, lift the area between the hip bone and the lowest rib, but take care not to lift the shoulders or arms. The return should be to an exact center, with no turning toward the back leg or dropping in the middle; these latter movements would permit the pelvis to tip and the body to roll back onto the tail.

For some beginners, it may be necessary to start with the arms down, one hand on the moving hip and the other with the fingers resting on the floor and sliding along as the torso turns. The hand on the hip can help the student find the hip action. With the fingers on the floor, the student can see the circular path followed during the rotation.

Sitting torso rotation: Upright

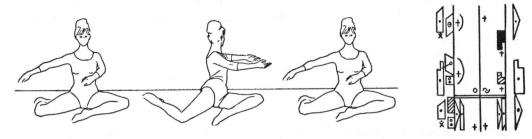

Science. When sitting with knees bent, one leg in front and the other in back (called the "swastika position" by some), it is important to allow for individual variations in this positioning of the legs. This position is difficult for students with limited flexibility in the hip joints (especially for men). Permit students to try different leg placements so they do not strain their knees. Never force students to put both buttocks on the floor; this degree of flexibility must come very gradually for those who do not have it naturally. Some never acquire the kind of flexibility that permits sitting on both buttocks in this position.

In sitting torso rotations, it is important that the movement start in the hip
for both the turn and return. For additional control, use the principle of energy
moving equally in opposite directions, particularly on the return. As the hip presses
to the floor, the torso must lift up from the center. Acquiring an understanding
of the relationship between the torso and the hip at this point can be helpful in
all the standing exercises to follow.

5.1.2. Sitting torso rotation: Going to the floor

Art. See Exercise 5.1.1.

Craft. Start as in Exercise 5.1.1., but, as the torso rotates, lift the forward arm
in a long curve overhead. Have a feeling of turning into the arm. The other arm
stays parallel to the floor, extended sideways. After reaching maximum rotation
in the torso and head, reach for the floor with the raised arm and with the back
of the hand going to the floor lean back, placing the elbow on the floor. Feel as
though you are trying to touch the elbow to the back foot. This is not possible,
but it gives a tangible point of reference. Move the other arm into a long curve
overhead as the elbow goes to the floor (the elbow should not drop in front of
the face). Next, rotate the torso to face the floor and swing the whole torso, with
the arms parallel to the floor, to the front, keeping close to the floor. Complete
the movement by lifting up to the original position with the hip pressing to the
floor but the torso lifting. Be sure to come to a true center; do not continue movement on toward the back leg.

There are many variations of this exercise. The arms may be used differently
and a contraction may be used to start the swing back to the front.

Sitting torso rotation: Going to the floor

Science. See Exercise 5.1.1.

5.1.3. Sitting torso rotation: Back leg extension

Art. See Exercise 5.1.1.

Craft. Start as in the previous exercise with the leading arm lifting overhead
and the other arm extended sideways, but rotate only enough to face the side of

the room. Extend the torso over the leg, place the hands on the floor, and bring the shoulders near and parallel to the floor. Extend the top leg until the knee is straight. Keep the knee straight and, localizing the movement in the hip joint, raise and lower the leg four times. On the fourth time, do not lower the leg. Instead, with the leg still elevated, raise the torso as high as individual control permits, rotate the torso to face the front, and sit on both buttocks. Meanwhile, rotate the hip joint of the raised leg so it remains at the side with the top of the arch up toward the ceiling. Do not permit the leg to swing to the front.

This exercise may also be used in connection with leg extensions.

Sitting torso rotation: Back leg extension

Science. See Exercise 5.I.1.

5.I.4. Sitting torso rotation: Front leg extension

Art. See Exercise 5.I.1.

Craft. Proceed as in the torso rotation going to the floor (Exercise 5.I.2.), but instead of swinging along the floor to return to place, contract and bring both buttocks to the floor as the torso returns to face front. At the same time, raise the front leg as high as possible with the knee straight and the toe pointed. Finish with a release, bringing the arms over the head in a long curve, bending the knee to place the foot on the floor.

Science.   See Exercise 5.I.1.

5.I.5. Torso rotation: Hip lead

Art.   See Exercise 5.I.1.

Craft.   All movement in this rotation is sequential, starting with the hip lead. The movement progresses through the torso to the head, which completes the action.

Start by lying face down with the elbows bent and the hands on the floor near the shoulders. Lift the left hip, moving it over the right hip, and come to a sitting position; the whole body follows the hip. Finish with the head bent forward. At the same time, bend the left knee and then place the sole of the left foot on the floor close to the left hip. Place the right hand on the floor close to the right hip, but keep the arm straight under the shoulder. At the same time, bend the left elbow and place the left arm in front of the torso.

Torso rotation: Hip lead

In the next part of this exercise, the left hip pushes as high as possible toward the ceiling with weight supported on the right hand and both feet (the side of the right foot and the toes of the left foot, with the knee bent and the right knee straight). The left arm reaches straight up. The head acts last, with the face looking toward the ceiling.

In the third part of the exercise, the left hip is pulled down to a sitting position, as before. The head is held back until the last minute, and then it is brought forward. Finally, in a return to the starting position, the left hip is pulled across, rotating the body. The head faces over the shoulder as long as possible and it is the last to come to place.

Perform the entire exercise slowly with four counts for each of the four main sections (roll to sit, rise, return to sit, roll to face) until sequential control of the action is achieved. Then speed up the action with three counts for each movement, then two counts, and finally one count. The one-count sequence should be a whiplike action.

Science. See Exercise 5.I.1.

Chapter 6

Hands, Arms, Feet, Ankles, and Hips

In this chapter, we work on exercises designed to increase the flexibility of the hands and arms, the feet and legs, and the hips.

Hands (*Mains*) and Arms (*Bras*)

The hands and arms are extremely flexible parts of the body. The exercises in this section will help you increase their flexibility. When performing the exercises, work for smooth, fluid movements.

6.A. Hands

6.A.1. Progressive localized movement

Art. The human hand is a phenomenal mechanism. Examine with wonder the details that allow for its movement. Then explore the limited directional movement of the elbow, and compare it with the greater mobility of the shoulder joint. Become aware of the increased movement possibilities when the three work together. Discover the possible variations in tempo and dynamics when flexing, extending, and rotating both in localized movement and in combinations of movements.

Craft. Without involving the wrists or other areas, move the fingers quickly and easily, flexing and extending all the finger joints. Move each finger separately with no relationship to the movement of the other fingers. Keep the fingers going in this chance movement and add a separate wrist action. Then keep both of these areas moving, adding a separate and free elbow movement. Continuing all of these movements, add a separate and free shoulder action. This progression will feel strange to many, but it can also be very intriguing.

Science. Avoid inefficient use of tension in hand and arm movements. Use just enough tension to permit movement to flow from one part to another.

6.A.2. *Finger fan*

Art. See Exercise 6.A.1.

Craft. Use one hand at a time when first trying the finger fan. Later, move both hands at the same time. Hold one hand in front of you with the palm up, just above the waist level. Have the elbow comfortably bent. Bend the little finger into the palm and allow the other fingers to follow in succession. The succeeding fingers should resist slightly so that it feels as though the little finger is pulling the others into the palm. Reverse the action, with the first finger leading the others into a complete extension. Stretch the finger joints. Do this a few times to get a flowing, continuous motion.

Now add a wrist rotation to the action. Starting with the palm up, have the little finger lead into flexion, closing the fingers. Rotate the wrist so that the palm is down and have the little finger lead into an opening of the fingers. Then have the first finger lead into a closing of the fingers; rotate the wrist so that the palm is up again, and have the first finger lead into a finger extension. Start the whole pattern again, with the little finger leading into a closing. The exercise should be a smooth, sequential action. After acquiring reasonable facility, increase the tempo of the fan. Work for a smooth, flowing, continuous action.

This is particularly good for dancers whose hands tend to be stiff. It benefits all dancers to have hands that are more flexible and expressive and that can be involved in the total movement.

Science. See Exercise 6.A.1.

6.A.3. *Hand ripple*

Art. See Exercise 6.A.1.

Craft. Again, start with one hand and later use both hands at the same time. Hold one hand in front with the palm down, just above the waist level. Have the elbow comfortably bent. Movement should be smooth and flowing though small and slow at first. Lift the knuckles without closing the fingers in too far. At the same time, drop the wrist slightly. Reverse the action, raising the wrist to its former level, dropping the knuckles, and forcing energy through the fingers; extend the fingers to the utmost. All action should start in the knuckles or wrist with the fingers moving as a result. The action must not start in the fingers. After acquiring some facility in this small area, add the rest of the arm as described in Exercise 6.B.1.

Science See Exercise 6.A.1.

6.B. Arms

6.B.1. *Arm ripple*

Art. The emphasis should be on the outward movement with the inward motion minimized. This inward motion is necessary only in order to go out again; the bending of the joints is small. Work for a feeling of fluid, smooth, sequential action. It may help to visualize the way movement progresses in a squirrel: along the back and through the tail.

Craft. Extend the arms sideways just below shoulder level but with no extra tension in the arms. Keep the hand and wrist action as in Exercise 6.A.3. As the wrist lifts, bend the elbow slightly. Straighten the elbow and permit the action to flow sequentially through the wrist, then to the area of the knuckles, and finally out through the end of the middle finger. Reverse the action, being careful not to flex the joint areas too far. After acquiring smooth-flowing control in this exercise, change to the spiral arm ripple (Exercise 6.B.2.).

Science.   See Exercise 6.A.1.

6.B.2. Arm ripple with spiral action

Art.   See Exercise 6.B.1.

Craft.   Instead of an up-and-down or in-and-out feeling in the flexion and extension of the arm, try for a spiral feeling, as though energy is coiling down the arm from the shoulder to the end of the middle finger. To produce this feeling, add a very slight rotation in the shoulder, elbow, and wrist. Be sure that the palm of the hand faces down throughout the movement and the shoulders do not lift. Instead of bending the elbow down, bend it toward the back and then down slightly when leading into the extension. Many will find this requires particularly good coordination. Do not hyperextend the elbow, but do stretch through the knuckles into as deep a curve as possible on the back of the hand so the fingers go up slightly.

Science.   See Exercise 6.A.1.

6.B.3. Arm swings and circles

Art.   Be aware of the arm moving as a whole unit, freely and without any extra tension. At the same time, feel that the arm is a long appendage.

Craft.   Have each arm move as one piece from the shoulder with a free, easy swing. Swing the arms one at a time then both together. Swing forward and backward, then across the front and to the side. Let the swing become a complete circle in both of these directions. Change dynamics during the swings or the circles. For instance, start with a strong impulse from the center of the torso and lead into an arm circle, slow to a feeling of suspension at the top of the swing, and end with a loss of energy so that the arm drops.

Science.   See Exercise 6.A.1.

6.B.4. Arm swings and circles: Variations

Art.   See exercises 6.B.1. and 6.B.3.

Craft.   The following are variations to arm swings and circles:

1. Let both arms move in parallel lines.
2. Let the arms move in opposite directions.
3. Let one arm swing while the other arm circles.
4. Increase the range by permitting swinging or circling action to lead into locomotion.
5. Extend the reach on the arm swing so that the opposite (or same) leg extends into the air.

There are countless variations.

Science.   See Exercise 6.A.1.

6.B.5. Arm movement with changes in quality

Art. See Exercises 6.B.1. and 6.B.3.

Craft. Repeat the previous types and directions of arm movements, but vary the quality. Use a percussive, sustained, or a vibrating quality. For example, using some of the actions described in Exercise 6.B.4., take a movement to a point of suspension and then add a collapsing quality.

Science. See Exercise 6.A.1.

6.B.6. Push and pull

Art. See exercises 6.B.1. and 6.B.3.

Craft. Explore movement possibilities, alternating a pushing and a pulling action. Discover how these movements start from the center of the torso. Try these movements first with total arm involvement, and then repeat as completely localized action in the fingers, wrists, legs (with no arms), head, and so on. Try combinations of movement, alternating the push and pull. Vary dynamics in the total combination. Or, when combining the push and pull, have the push strong and the pull weak, reverse, and so on. Let the push and pull lead into locomotion in various directions.

Science. See Exercise 6.A.1.

6.B.7. Peripheral arm movement

Art. See Exercise 6.A.1.

Craft. Discover differences in feeling by contrasting Exercise 6.B.6. with strictly peripheral arm movements (movements completely localized in the arms with no torso involvement). In order to contrast with the preceding exercises, these movements should have no central involvement. This type of movement should feel completely different from movement involving the torso.

Science. This will require more concentration if it is to use energy with complete efficiency.

6.C. Hands and Arms: Variations

Art. See exercises 6.A.1., 6.B.1., and 6.B.3.

Craft. The following are variations of movements for hands and arms:

1. Use a figure-eight type of movement for total arm involvement in small, localized areas.
2. Pass the lead from one part to another.
3. Try the various types of movement mentioned in the previous exercises, but use limp wrists, fingers, or elbows. This should give a very different feeling.
4. Repeat these movements with the joints very stiff.
5. Try some exercises with the fingers spread wide or pressed tightly together.

The possible combinations of arm and hand movements are infinite.

Science. See exercises 6.A.1. and 6.B.7.

Feet (*Pieds*) and Ankles (*Cou-de-pieds*)

The feet and ankles, the very foundation of the instrument, are probably abused more than any other part of the body. The abuse is found in the shape and size of shoes and hose and in poor movement habits. This abuse, which results in painful, misshapen feet and ankles with limited use, is unfortunate and unnecessary. It can also be a factor in the poor alignment of torso and shoulders. The common abuse of the feet and ankles can be largely overcome through continued dance training, especially when students correct themselves outside of dance class as well. Another important cause of foot abuse is walking on cement, not only on the street but now in most buildings. To help cushion against this impact, we should all wear shoes with thick rubber soles.

6.D. Basic Exercises

6.D.1. Basic ankle flexion and extension

Art.   Examine the feet and ankles with awe, for they are marvelous structures. With your hand, explore the parts that create the diversity of movement possibilities. Strive to make both the ankles and the feet as sensitive as the hands. Try to feel the grain of wood in the floor with the soles of the feet. Work for maximum flexibility, for control of each small segment in both localized and total movements.

Craft.   Sit with the back in good alignment and both legs extended straight ahead. The hands may be on the floor slightly behind the hips, but do not hunch the shoulders. Alternate flexing and extending the ankles. Pull the toes toward the shin as far as possible, then extend the ankles with a feeling of trying to touch the toes to the floor. Although this is not possible, it does give a tangible point of reference.

Science.   In both flexion and extension, be sure the ankles maintain a straight alignment with the leg and the top of the arch.

6.D.2. Foot ripple

Art.   See Exercise 6.D.1.

Craft.   The foot ripple is a variation of Exercise 6.D.1. Sit as before, with the legs extended in front. As the ankles bend, flex the feet at the metatarsal arch so that the top of the arch is pulling toward the torso but the toes are pointing in the opposite direction. As the ankle extends, push toward the floor with the ball of the foot and point the toes toward the torso. This exercise should be a sequential, smooth-flowing, continuous action with the toes the last to follow the movement sequence.

Science.   See Exercise 6.D.1.

6.D.3. Ankle rotation

Art.   See Exercise 6.D.1.

Craft.   Sitting in good alignment, the legs extended to the front, the arms either curved in front or with the hands on floor slightly behind the hips, rotate or circle the ankles. Start with flexion toward the torso, circle out, extend forward, circle in, and return to the starting flexion. Go as far as possible in all directions. Circle in the opposite direction. This may be performed with four to eight circles out, then the same number in. Or, the out and in circles may alternate.

Science. See Exercise 6.D.1.

6.D.4. Ankle flexion and extension with leg rotation

Art. See Exercise 6.D.1.

Craft. Sit up with the back in good alignment, the legs extended straight forward, and the arms held in a long curve forward over the legs or resting on the floor on each side of the hips. Flex the ankles as for a foot ripple. Hold this flexion and, with the knees straight, rotate the legs out from the hips. At the same time, tighten the buttocks. This should cause a slight bounce of the whole torso. Hold the tightening of the buttocks and the leg rotation while extending the ankle and arch (pointing the toes). Then hold the ankle extension while rotating the legs back to the original position.

Ankle flexion and extension with leg rotation

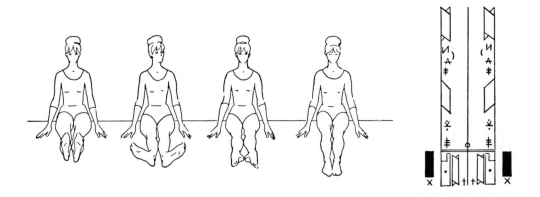

Science. Be sure the back is held up in good alignment during the exercise. It is easy to slump, rounding the back and tilting the pelvis. As mentioned, the tightening of the buttocks should cause a slight bounce of the whole torso. However, be sure this bounce does not result from a partial or total lift of the shoulders. When the legs rotate back to place, be sure the action does not carry into an inward rotation. Dancers must learn to check their own ankle alignment.

6.D.5. Push off with toes

Art. See Exercise 6.D.1.

Craft. Sit with the back straight, the knees bent in front, and the arms extended out at the sides. Without using any other part of the body, push hard enough with the feet and toes so that the torso rocks back and the toes lift slightly from the floor. Return to the starting position. The exercise can be done with the arms around the knees, but this may cause a temptation to use the arms to help in the rocking action.

 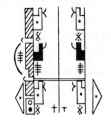

Science.   See Exercise 6.D.4.

6.D.6. Lift in longitudinal arch

Art.   See Exercise 6.D.1.

Craft.   Sit with knees bent and the soles of the feet on the floor. Hold the knees together with the hands so they cannot flop out. *Slightly* lift each longitudinal arch. Do not lift so high that the ankle curves out. Hold a straight alignment. The ball of each foot should remain on the floor. When the legs can be controlled, perform this without holding the knees with the hands. This exercise can also be performed standing. A straight alignment should be maintained in the standing exercise as well.

Lift in longitudinal arch

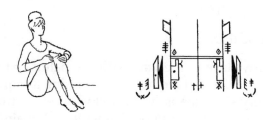

Science.   See Exercise 6.D.1.

6.D.7. Lift in metatarsal arch

Art.   See Exercise 6.D.1.

Craft.   This lift may be performed either standing or sitting. If sitting, bend both knees, with the soles of the feet on the floor. If standing, place the feet parallel. The lift is a very small movement, requiring close observation to be seen. Try to lift the metatarsal arch by a crosswise pull under the ball of the foot. Do not cause a lengthwise lift by curling the toes underneath. This exercise is difficult for most adults, probably because of years of foot abuse and poorly designed shoes.

Science   See Exercise 6.D.1.

6.D.8. Knee and ankle touch against wall

Art.   See Exercise 6.D.1.

Craft.   This exercise has two principal benefits: It promotes complete ankle extension; and it reveals a particular relationship among the lower leg, the upper leg, and the back. Stand a thigh's length from a wall, with the hips parallel to the wall. Lift one leg so that the thigh is at right angles to the hip. The relationship of the foot to the knee should be such that the top of the arch, the ankle, and the knee all touch the wall at the same time rather than one after the other. The touch should be controlled so the knee or arch does not bang against the wall. Perform the exercise a few times with one leg, then the other. Or, make the exercise more like a prance by alternating the legs. Keep the back and the standing leg in good alignment throughout.

Science. See Exercise 6.D.1.

6.D.9. Sequential foot action

Art. See Exercise 6.D.1.

Craft. Think of the foot as being as flexible and sensitive as the hand. Stand on one foot and move the other as though trying to feel the texture of the floor boards. Next, formalize this movement into a small, slow prancing action. Have just enough weight on the moving foot so that work is required to lift the foot, but keep the tip of the toe in contact with the floor. Lower the foot to place. Make this a sequential action, with the movement flowing through each small segment of the foot in both the lifting and returning to place. Perform this a few times with one foot, then the other. Next, alternate the feet.

Science. See Exercise 6.D.1.

6.D.10. Achilles stretch

Art. See Exercise 6.D.1.

Craft. Start fairly close to the wall with the palms of the hands on the wall just below shoulder level and the elbows bent. Using a sequential foot and ankle action and taking very small steps, walk backward away from the wall but keep the hands on the wall. Go as far as possible while still maintaining a straight line through the back and hips. Return to place and repeat. The heel must go completely to the floor on each step. There will be a great deal of individual variation in the distance covered.

Achilles stretch

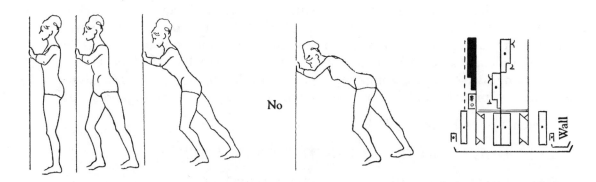

Science. Do not permit the hands to slide down the wall, thus allowing a bend at the hips. At the end of each step, as the heel goes to the floor, be sure the back knee does not bend with the front knee. Keep a straight line from the top of the head to the back heel.

6.D.11. Pedaling and prancing

Art. See Exercise 6.D.1.

Craft. Stand with good alignment, weight equally distributed on both feet. Use the action described in the sequential foot action exercise (Exercise 6.D.9.), but keep the motion continuous with one foot lifting as the other is lowered. At first, be sure each foot lifts enough so that only the tip of the big toe is touching the floor, not the bottom of all the toes. Start slowly, then gradually increase the tempo and range of movement until the knee is lifting as it was in the exercise at the wall (Exercise 6.D.10.). Be sure the knee lifts because of the foot action; many beginners use the thighs instead of the foot movement to lift the leg. For further variation, do three prances and then hold one count. The legs will alternate for the hold.

Pedaling and prancing

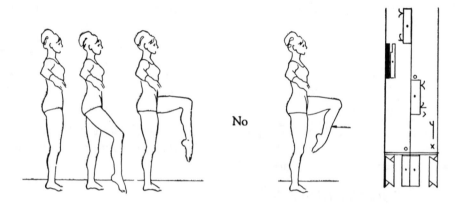

No

Science. See Exercise 6.D.4.

Hip Rotation

The rotation exercises in this section will help keep the hip joint free from tension and free to move without resistance.

6.E. Preparatory Exercises

6.E.1. Lying on the back

Art. At all times, there should be a feeling of freedom of movement in the hip joint.

Craft. Lie on the back with the legs straight and the arms extended sideways. Raise one leg as far overhead as possible, keeping the knee straight; carry the leg sideways, trying to touch the extended arm; swing the leg down to the other leg; raising the leg again, cross over and extend it to the other side, trying to touch the opposite arm. The moving hip will lift from the floor on the crossover, but both shoulders should remain in place. Keep the back on the floor when the leg extends to the same side.

Hip rotation

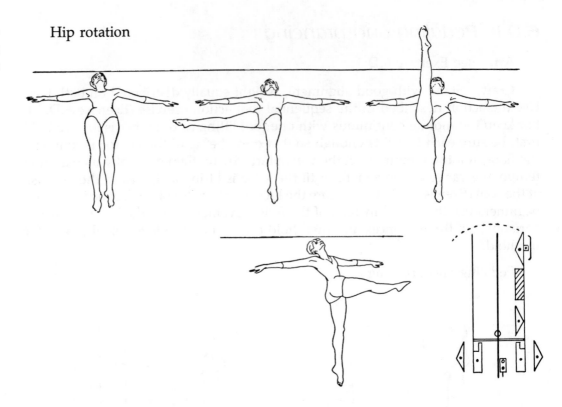

Science. It is important to keep the hip joint free to move without resistance. Inefficient tension in the hip that resists the circular movement may cause a catch or even a cramp during this movement.

6.E.2. Standing knee lift

Exercise 8.H. (in Chapter 8) may be used as preparation for hip rotation exercises.

6.F. Standing Leg Circles

6.F.1. Leg circle forward

Art. See exercises 6.E.1. and 8.H.

Craft. Stand in first position, brush the foot forward, with knee straight and holding turnout, until just the toes are lightly touching the floor. Lift the leg slightly so toes are just off the floor; carry the leg to the side, still holding turnout, again lightly touching toes to the floor; lift toes off the floor and carry leg to the back; repeat the toe touch and lift; return to the side position, repeat the toe touch, lift, return to the front, and so on. The emphasis should be on control in the thigh, a light touch with toes well pointed, and feeling the control of the turnout in the three directions.

Science. It is important to keep control in the thighs, with no tension in the hip joint itself, so the leg is free to move. The standing leg must support the body with no pressure on the floor with the moving foot.

6.F.2. Leg circles forward on the floor (ronds de jambe en dedans à terre)

Art. See exercises 6.E.1. and 8.H.

Craft. Stand in first position with arms extended sideways. Holding turnout in the legs, brush one leg forward until only the toes are on the floor; keeping the heel pressed forward, circle the leg out to the side, to the back, and then brush the foot in to return to first position with the heel on the floor. Repeat several times, making this a smooth continuous action. There should be a small *plié* before repeating on the other side.

Science. See Exercise 6.F.1.

6.F.3. Leg circles backward on the floor (ronds de jambe en dehors à terre)

Art. See exercises 6.E.1. and 8.H.

Craft. Reverse the action in Exercise 6.F.2., with the foot moving back, then to the side, then front. It is most difficult to hold the turnout when starting the changes of direction from back to side, and from side to front, and when closing to first position.

Science. See Exercise 6.F.1.

6.F.4. Leg circles off the floor (ronds de jambe en l'air)

Art. See exercises 6.E.1. and 8.H.

Craft. Proceed as in exercises 6.F.2. and 6.F.3., but instead of putting the toes on the floor, keep them off the floor, still with the knees straight and toes well pointed, holding the turnout during the action. Beginners should not try for a high leg lift. Height will come later, as control and strength develop. This movement may be performed two or three times forward (the number should be limited), then two or three times starting backward, or the front and back may alternate. In this latter case, instead of ending in first position carry the foot through first to a slight hold (front or back), to reverse direction. Be sure the heel touches the floor on the pass through first position. This should be performed moderately fast, almost with the feeling of a swinging movement.

Science. See Exercise 6.F.1.

Chapter 7

Pliés, Rises to Half-Toe, and Jumps

The movement from *plié* to rise to half-toe and to jump is a good illustration of sequential development. In this chapter, separate exercises are given for each of the three moves, but the last two cannot be performed without the first or second preceding. And the first movement, the *plié*, is one of the most vital in the dancer's vocabulary.

Pliés

Although a *plié* is defined as a knee bend, a great deal more is involved than this definition implies. Mastery of the *plié* is so vital and complicated that it must be taught early rather than from exploratory unfolding. When correctly performed, the *plié* aligns and strengthens the back, thighs, ankles, and feet. If incorrectly performed, it can be seriously injurious to these areas. Dance careers have ended suddenly and painfully because a dancer failed to habitually use correct knee action and back control. Teachers must accept responsibility for teaching the *plié* correctly. And students must accept responsibility for themselves—to constantly check their own performance.

7.A. *Plié* Preparatory Exercises

7.A.1. Flex and point

Art. In this exercise, discover the relationship between the bend of the knee, the hip, and the ankle. Be aware of how the thigh muscles straighten the knee. Be sensitive to the ankle extension (the pointing of the toe) and the existence of a straight line down the front of the leg through the ankle and center of the foot. This is also a preparation for performing the hop when standing.

Craft. Lie on the back, one leg extended straight on the floor, the other raised toward the ceiling. The knees are straight, the ankles extended, and the toes pointed. The hands should hold the raised leg at the back of the thigh, not the calf of the leg. The latter puts too great a strain at the back of the knee. Hold the thigh in place so it cannot move back and forth. Bend the knee in a small movement and flex the ankle. Next, straighten the knee and extend the ankle (point the toe). Complete this exercise four to eight times, then repeat with the other leg.

Flex and point

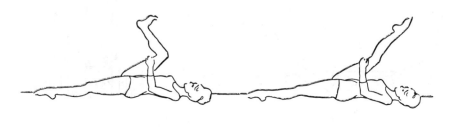

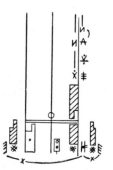

Science. Be sure the straightening of the knee is an extension and not a snap. When extending the ankle, be sure to keep it in a straight line, with no supination (sometimes called "sickle foot" or "clubbing"). If the beginner thinks of a toe point as an ankle extension, it will be easier to hold the correct alignment.

Keep the thigh in place as the knee straightens by using the front thigh muscles for the straightening. The lower leg aligns with the upper leg, not vice versa. It is very easy to let the upper leg move back and forth as the knee bends and straightens. While this is not injurious, an important element of the exercise is lost.

7.A.2. Flex and point: Variations

Art. See Exercise 7.A.1.

Craft. The following are variations of flex and point:

1. Repeat Exercise 7.A.1. without holding the leg with the hands, but do not permit the thigh to move.
2. Increase the tempo of the exercise, but keep the action very neat and exact. The quality should remain constant as the timing changes.
3. Still lying on the back, with both legs extended toward the ceiling, flex and extend both legs at the same time.
4. With both legs extended toward the ceiling, alternate the flex and extend, with one leg extending as the other flexes. On the first try, this is tricky even for the fairly advanced dancers.

Science. See Exercise 7.A.1.

7.A.3. Plié preparatory exercise: Sitting knee lift

Art. Explore the relationship of the coordinated flexion and extension of the hip, knee, and ankle. Become aware of a simultaneous lift in the lower torso and a complete attenuation of the left leg from the hip joint to the end of the pointed toe.

Craft. Sit with the legs opened wide to the sides, the knees straight, the ankles extended, the back and head well aligned, the arms curved in front just below shoulder level, the fingers not quite touching, and the shoulders down. Keeping the heels in place (not letting them slide along the floor), flex the ankles as the knees lift. Next, extend the knees and ankles. The torso should stay erect with no tensing in the wrists, shoulders, or neck.

Plié preparatory exercise: Sitting knee lift

Science. Be sure the straightening of the leg is an extended stretch and not a slap on the floor. The lift in the lower torso should not be accompanied by a lift in the shoulder or tension in the wrists or neck. An outward rotation of the leg from the hip should be encouraged if ankle alignment can be maintained. The leg rotation should never be inward. Be sure there is no forward or backward tilting of the pelvis. Maintain total back alignment.

7.A.4. Sitting knee lift: Variations

Art. See Exercises 7.A.3.

Craft. The following are two variations of the sitting knee lift: (1) Alternate legs, first lifting one knee and then the other; and (2) telescope the action so that one knee straightens as the other one lifts.

Science. See Exercise 7.A.3.

7.A.5. Plié *preparatory exercise: Sitting front extension*

Art. See Exercise 7.A.3.

Craft. Sit with good alignment, the legs forward, the knees bent, the ankles flexed, the toes on the floor, the heels off the floor and touching each other, and the arms rounded in front just below shoulder level. Keeping the back very lifted but with no tension in the shoulders and neck, push the heels forward (keeping the ankles flexed) until the knees are completely straight. At the moment the knees straighten, tighten the buttocks. Holding all this, extend the ankles to point the toes, maintaining turnout from the hips (keep the little toes as near the floor as possible). Next, flex the ankles and, at the same time, bend the knees to start back to the original position. When the knees start to bend, instantly lift the heels off the floor, but keep the ankles flexed and toes on the floor.

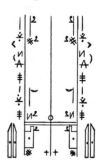

Science. This exercise (which is basically a *plié* in the first position, or a jump) is excellent for illustrating the relationship between the action of the hips, thighs, knees, ankles, and back, and the degree of hold necessary for correct use of a turned-out position. The exercise is difficult and cannot be used too early in a course.

It is very easy to let the pelvis tip and the back round when performing this exercise. If this happens, its value is lost; you are probably introducing it too early in the course or have not given enough preparatory exercises.

7.B. Standing *Pliés*

It is customary for many modern dance classes to start *pliés* in the parallel position. It is generally better, however, to start them in the first position, with a precaution that students use only the degree of turnout they can control safely. Beginning students can control the knee placement over the toes in this position more easily than they can in the parallel position. Also, it is easier for them to find the control for straightening the knees by trying to bring the inside of the upper thighs together. In a parallel position, beginners tend to brace the knees together rather than hold in the thighs when bending the knees. When straightening a parallel position, most students tend to snap the back of the knees, stopping the movement there instead of pulling up into the thighs.

A good order of positions when introducing *pliés* to beginners is: first; second; parallel; third (or fifth, depending on class development); and fourth. In the short six-week course, the first, second, parallel, and third positions are all that should be used. It takes more time than these short courses provide for students to gain enough control of backs, legs, hips, and knees for fourth and fifth positions. Other areas, such as movement explorations and locomotor skills, are more important in these short courses than mastering a complete vocabulary of *pliés*.

Pliés may be performed as small (*demi-*) *pliés* or deep (*grand*) *pliés* and in combination with other movements. They may be performed with or without a forced arch (never a forced arch on *pliés* for beginners) and in all positions.

7.B.1. Standing small pliés (demi-pliés)

Art. Performing the *pliés*, either small or deep, should feel like breathing. Although maintaining the alignments and controls does require effort, try for a feeling of ease in performing *pliés*.

Craft. In the small *pliés*, the heels stay on the floor as the knees bend. Bend the knees over the toes whether the position is parallel or turned out. For a turned-out position, straighten the knees by pulling the inside of the upper thighs together; do not concentrate on the knees only.

Performing small *pliés* with the heels pressed to the floor is vital to prevent overdevelopment of the calf muscle. This part of the leg is used so much (on half-toe, in elevations, and in walking) that its contraction should be counteracted by the stretch in the small *plié*. Many students—and not just beginners—get at least part of their control by gripping the floor with the toes without realizing it. Stretching the leg, then, is usually accompanied by a contraction of the calf, and the value of the stretch is lost. Because this contraction is almost impossible for the teacher to see, students must learn to check it for themselves. A simple check is to perform the small *plié* with the toes off the floor.

Standing small *plié*

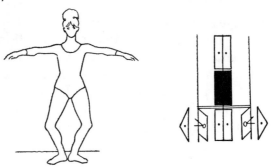

Science. The knees must always bend over the center of the feet or over the toes. The thighs should control the direction of bending. The bend at the ankle must be in alignment, without permitting the arches to roll in or out. Straightening is just as important as bending (and an area often neglected). While the knees straighten, the lift in the thighs must be continued in back as well as in front, with no forcing backward behind the knees.

The back must be held erect, and the shoulders must be directly over the hips. There must be no swayback and no tension in the shoulders or neck.

When performing *pliés*, be particularly conscious of energy going equally in opposite directions. As the knees bend, there must be a compensatory lift in the torso all the way through the top of the head. As the knees straighten, balance the upward rise by feeling energy going down through the heels into the floor.

In all *pliés*, deep as well as small, feel that the whole shaft of the torso is pushing to a point directly between both heels. Guard against shifting weight to one foot.

Remember that rising is just as important as descending. Guard against easing control so that the knees swing in when rising. Do not permit the pelvis to tilt at the moment the knees complete their straightening. This is a very common error and one often overlooked.

7.B.2. Standing small pliés with toes off floor

Art. See Exercise 7.B.1.

Craft. Perform the small *plié* as described in Exercise 7.B.1., but with the toes lifted slightly off the floor. Do not overdo the lift of the toes; just be sure they are off the floor. Keep the heels on the floor. The first time this toe lift is tried, it is apt to be quite a revelation. Dancers find that they have not really been holding in the thighs. The lifting of the toes off the floor should be performed occasionally in all the standard positions because the controls vary slightly with each of the positions. This should be used only as an occasional check, not as an everyday exercise.

Science. See Exercise 7.B.1.

7.B.3. *Standing deep* plies (grand plies)

Art. See Exercise 7.B.1.

Craft. Start the deep *pliés* as though performing small *pliés*. Press down until the heels have to leave the floor. Always go as low as control of the back and knees allows. Increasing depth must come gradually. When rising, press the heels to the floor as soon as possible. The heels must come to the floor before the knees straighten. The variation of rising to a forced arch and then lowering the heels should be used only with advanced students.

Standing deep *plié*

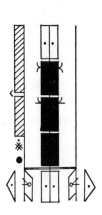

Science. Be sure to maintain outward pressure on the knees for both the descent and the rise, holding turnout. Never go low enough to sit on the heels, which causes loss of control in the thighs and strains the knees.

Do not introduce deep *pliés* to beginners until they have some control of back and knee placement. Increase in the degree of the bend (how low they go) should be gradual as the students gain control. It is worth emphasizing that increasing control must come gradually through use of the control already achieved.

7.B.4. *Standing* plies: *Variations*

Art. See Exercise 7.B.1.

Craft. The following are variations of standing *pliés*:

1. Stand in second position. *Plié* equally on both legs. Then straighten one knee without rising, causing the whole torso to move toward the other leg. Return to center and then straighten the other knee, pushing the torso toward the other leg. Throughout these movements, keep the hips on the same level, with no up-or-down movement. Use no arm movement. Move the whole torso from one side to center and to the other side, then back to center within one level.

2. Vary the tempo.
3. Make sequences combining small and deep *pliés*.
4. Work out sequences or combinations with other elements such as arm movements.
5. Finish a series of *pliés* with a rise to half-toe (*relevé*) and a balance on two feet or on one foot.
6. Combine *pliés* with brushes.
7. Combine *pliés* with simple turns.

Standing *pliés*: Variations

Science. See Exercise 7.B.3.

Rise To Half-Toe (*Relevés*)

Most teachers combine *pliés* with a rise to half-toe (called *relevé* in ballet).

7.C. Rise To Half-Toe

Art. See Exercise 7.B.1.

Craft. It is important to keep the knees straight and to maintain correct alignment of torso and ankles when rising to half-toe. The impulse for the rise should start in the middle of the torso with a sense of an equal lift in both the front and back of the torso. Have an equal lift in the front and back of the thighs. The feeling of lifting in the back of the thighs is often neglected. A common mistake is to expect the ankles to do all the work. The use of a slight inner beat as the impulse for starting the rise will add control.

Science. Any exercise on half-toe, especially an extended hold on half-toe, should be followed with a small *plié*, taking care to keep the heels on the floor. Work on half-toe requires a strong contraction in the calf of the leg, and, to prevent overenlargement of the calf, it is necessary to counteract this contraction with the stretch provided by the small *plié*. This *plié* also provides development of a more flexible and usable muscle. The hard, tight calf muscles that develop when small *pliés* are neglected are more apt to tear or break.

Jumps (*Elevés*)

The jump (called an *elevé* in ballet terminology) is an extension of the *plié*. It results in a moment of weightlessness when the dancer is elevated in space and experiences a lift of the spirits and a unique excitement.

7.D. Basic Exercises

7.D.1. Basic jump

Art. The thrill of the first experience of weightlessness during a jump should never be lost; in fact, it should increase as enough control is gained to prolong the moment of weightlessness. To attain the excitement that accompanies elevation, explore for a feeling of suspension and for variations in the use of energy.

Craft. To prepare for a jump, perform a small *plié* and let the straightening movement lift to half-toe. Next, use enough energy on the straightening to lift into the air. Cushion the landing with a small *plié*. The first jumps should be for ease and not height. All elevations should begin and end with a *plié*. Work for quiet landings. If there is no sound on landing, the mechanics are probably correct.

7.D.1. Basic jump

Science. The landing *plié* from an elevation should be so centered and controlled that the heels return to and stay on the floor. Do not permit them to pop off after the landing. Guard against collapsing in the midsection when landing. Such a collapse forces the air out of the lungs and is one of the factors in becoming winded. The collapse also throws a strain on the small of the back and completely stops movement, thus interfering with any transition to further movement. A helpful device for the beginner is to talk aloud while jumping. By talking aloud, the rib cage is held up and not dropped. Beginning students can manage to talk, but they often get tied up in knots if they are asked to think of specific control of the rib cage. Conscious control can come later.

7.D.2. Jumps: Variations

Art. See Exercise 7.D.1.

Craft. The following are variations of jumps:

1. Practice jumps in all standard dance positions.
2. Combine jumping and hopping.
3. Vary the rhythm, dimension, and tempo.
4. Use an ankle extension without a knee extension as the impulse to leave the floor. Do not straighten the knees. Stand in second position in *plié,* arms in second position. Use a strong ankle extension and push with the toes to leave the floor. Do not straighten the knees. Students should leave the floor but they should not try for height. Do not do more than eight at one time.
5. In a series of jumps, alternate the foot position from parallel to first position. This causes a leg rotation from the hip.
6. Jump, alternating a straight jump in parallel position with a jump in a turned-out position, while bending the knees and bringing the heels up under the center of the torso.
7. While in the air, keep the knees straight and bend at the hips, bringing the feet forward and up to the outstretched hands.
8. While in the air, raise the legs high in a wide second position, bringing the feet toward the hands.
9. Alternate jumps in first and second positions; combine jumps in various positions.
10. Turn while jumping.
11. Alternate a jump with the legs straight while in the air with a jump in which the knees are lifted high, one knee forward and one back. Alternate the legs in the forward position, as if running in place.
12. In third or fifth positions, change the relation of the legs while in the air; that is, the front foot goes to the back while the back foot comes to the front (called *changement de pieds* in ballet terminology).

Science. See Exercise 7.D.1.

Chapter 8

Brushes and Leg Extensions

The importance of flexibility and control is emphasized once again in this chapter. Exercises are given for brushes and leg extensions, two movements vital to a dancer's vocabulary. As usual, the exercises both progress in difficulty and illustrate the need for control with flexibility.

Brushes (*Battements**)

The brush is just as important as the *plié* for basic controls, and it needs drill in addition to exploratory exercises. As in the *plié*, many localized controls make up the total movement. It is vital to recognize the importance of control in the center, or midsection, of the body. Without this control there can be no freedom in leg or arm movements or in locomotion.

8.A. Preparation for Brushes (Lying on Floor)

8.A.1. Simple leg lift (lying on back)

Art. In spite of the work needed to acquire the necessary controls and alignments for brushes and leg lifts, it is important to give the impression of effortlessness. In time, with true efficiency in the movements, this effortlessness may approach a reality for the dancer.

Craft. Lie on the back on the floor, with the legs straight and the arms extended out at the sides. Keeping the leg straight and the toes pointed, raise one leg straight up toward the ceiling, then lower it to place. At first, try to raise the leg to a right angle to the torso with the toes pointing toward the ceiling. Later, bring the leg as far over the head as possible while still keeping both knees straight. Try for a feeling of the leg floating up toward the ceiling. The leg should feel long.

Science. Maintain control in the torso so the back does not pull into a swayback. The whole torso should feel extended along the floor. Guard against tight-

---

* *Battements*, literally "beats." There are many different kinds of battements performed on and off the floor. I am emphasizing here the brushing movement.

ening in the hip joint in an effort to keep the knee straight; many beginners make this mistake, thus working against themselves. It may help students to stand and experience a free swing of the leg from the hip to discover the feeling of the hip joint moving freely.

8.A.2. Simple leg lift: Sideways

Art.   See Exercise 8.A.1.

Craft.   Repeat Exercise 8.A.1., but with a sideways lift while lying on the side. Do this in both a parallel position with the side of the foot lifting toward the ceiling and in a turned-out position, with the toes pointing toward the ceiling. Note the difference in degree of lift and in the feeling of the relation of the leg to the torso.

Science.   See Exercise 8.A.1.

8.A.3. Simple leg lift: Backward

Art.   See Exercise 8.A.1.

Craft.   Repeat Exercise 8.A.1., but do so lying on the face with a backward lift.

Science.   See Exercise 8.A.1.

8.A.4. Simple leg lift: Variations

Art.   See Exercise 8.A.1.

Craft.   Try Exercise 8.A.1., but in both a parallel and a turned-out position.

Science.   See Exercise 8.A.1.

8.B. Small Brushes: Standing

8.B.1. Basic small brush (petit battement)

Art.   See Exercise 8.A.1.

Craft.   The term "brush" is descriptive. The sole of the foot brushes the floor as it moves away from the center, and brushes the floor as it returns. Stand with the feet in first position, with good alignment and the arms extended to the sides in second position. Brush one foot out to the side, gradually extending the ankle until the heel is off the floor, but the tips of the toes still touching the floor. Keep both knees very straight but not locked. Brush the foot back to place, still with both knees straight. This should be taken moderately slow at first.

Small brushes on floor: Standing

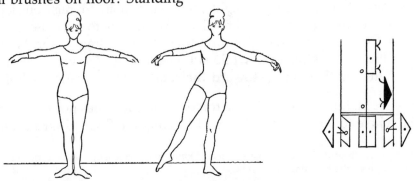

Science. The knees must be kept completely straight but not braced back and locked. At the same time, the ankle and hip joints must remain flexible and free. When brushing outward, have enough weight on the foot so the leg must work to get the foot out. The toe points at the end because of the ankle extension; keep proper alignment through the ankle. One device that may help beginners find the proper ankle alignment is to have the students press their fingers on the ankle at the spot where the ankle and the arch meet. They should press hard enough to hurt slightly. After the students stand up, the spot will tingle a little. The students may then extend that spot toward the side wall until the ankle is completely extended. To prevent clubbing the foot, beginners should think of the pointed toe as an ankle extension.

Check on the straightness of the knee of the moving leg at the beginning and end of the movement. Many beginners bend the knee slightly as the brush starts and again as the foot returns to place. For the return to place, students should concentrate on bringing the upper thighs together rather than the heels or the knees.

Guard against losing alignment of the hip area. It is very easy to push the standing hip out to the side or to sink down into it. Be adamant about keeping equal turnout in both legs. Of course, this turnout must come from the hips. Many students (and not just beginners), when performing a series of brushes with one leg, will let the standing leg gradually lose the turnout. One of the best ways to increase degree of turnout and control is to meticulously maintain the turnout already acquired.

8.B.2. Small brushes on the floor (à terre): Variations

Art. See Exercise 8.A.1.

Craft. The following are variations of the previous exercises:

1. Vary the tempo. After brushing out slowly, return the leg very quickly. This fast movement sometimes helps the beginner who has a tendency to bend the knee on the return to place.
2. Lift the arch slightly when brushing out and again when returning to place. This should be very slight; however, this lifted arch should be a constant factor in returning to place after students have gained some proficiency in performing brushes.
3. Concentrate on foot position. When the leg is extended to the side, maintain sufficient turnout (pressing the heel forward) to permit the tips of all the toes, not just the big toe (unless the big toe is unusually long in relation to the other toes), to touch the floor. When the leg is extended in front, press the heel forward and cup the arch so that the tip of the big toe is touching the floor. The point of touch should not be just the inside edge of the big toe or the outside edge of the little toe. On the return brush, maintain turnout with no pressure on the big toe. Keep control in the thigh so no weight is carried on the toes.
4. Vary dance positions. Practice small brushes from first position, parallel position, and fifth (or third) position.
5. Vary the direction. Practice small brushes forward, sideways, and backward.
6. Combine small brushes with *pliés*.

Science. See Exercise 8.B.1.

8.C. Brushes Off the Floor (*Grand Battements*)

8.C.1. *Small brush extension*

Art. See Exercise 8.A.1.

Craft. Start as for the small brush, but continue by lifting the foot off the floor. Be sure to use a lift, not a kick. The big toe should be the last to leave the floor and the first to touch the floor upon the return.

Brushes off floor

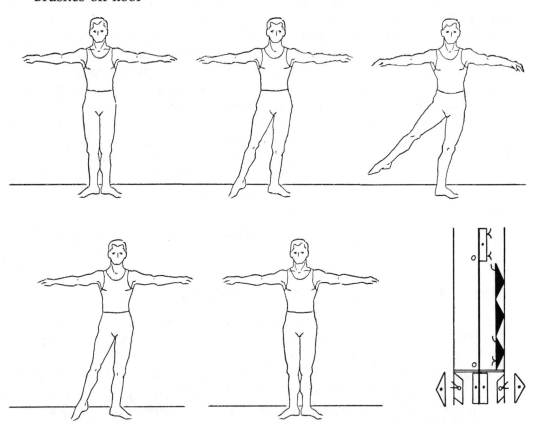

Science. Maintain equal turnout in both legs. It is very easy to let the standing foot creep around until turnout is lost. Another common error is to lose turnout when the leg is in the air but regain it as the leg returns to place. Also, work for complete ankle extension every time the leg goes out, and maintain upward lift in the midsection and the hip area of the standing leg.

Many beginners flex the ankle too soon and place the foot when returning to place, instead of brushing it back to place.

When performing brushes either forward or backward, guard against tilting the pelvis. The joint to use is in the hips, not the waist. Be sure the knee of the standing leg does not give slightly when the moving leg returns to place. This is often so slight a bend that it is easy for the teacher to miss.

8.C.2. *Brushes: Variations*

Art. See Exercise 8.A.1.

Craft. There are so many possible variations with brushes that one could write a book on these alone. This is fortunate because the movement needs so much drill that frequent changes of pattern and combinations help sustain interest. Here are a few possibilities:

1. Change level. Perform brushes on the floor, just off the floor, medium high, or as high as possible within the range of individual back and knee control. Beginners should limit the medium and high levels to first and parallel positions.
2. Vary the tempo and rhythm.
3. Combine brushes on and off the floor.
4. Combine the directions of forward (*en avant*), sideways (*à la seconde*), and backward (*derrière*). For example, using the fifth position, perform four brushes forward, four sideways (alternating the closing in front and back), and four brushes backward. The sideways direction can then be repeated, or you can change to the other side with some transitional movement. Or the entire pattern can be done on the other foot, if the side brush is not repeated after the backward brush (front, side, back, other foot, front, side, back).
5. Alternate directions, changing feet. Starting in fifth position, perform only one brush on each foot with each change of direction. For example, if the right foot is in front in fifth position, brush the right foot forward; brush the left foot backward; brush the right foot to the side and close back; brush the left foot to the side and close front; brush the right foot back; brush the left foot forward, and so on. This is also good for practice in changing weight quickly, particularly if there is a gradual increase in tempo.
6. Change directions quickly. Stand in fifth position with the left foot in front. (Do not get in the habit of starting all exercises on the right foot: Change around.) Brush forward, brush sideways and close back, brush back, then brush sideways and close front. Keep repeating this on the same foot, increasing tempo. Stop when you are no longer able to hold the turnout or perform each brush correctly and completely. *Plié* and repeat on the other foot. This is also good for practice in holding a turnout from the hips.
7. Change accent. Perform a brush with an accent on the outward motion. Repeat with an accent on the inward motion. These two accents can be combined if a half-count hold is added at the point of change.
8. Combine brushes with *pliés*. There are innumerable possibilities here. For example, perform a small *plié*, brushing out as the legs straighten, and go into a *plié* again as the foot brushes in. In this instance, both knees should start to bend as the foot comes in. Do not close and then *plié*. The combination of brushes and *pliés* may be tried in any of the positions except second position, either using one direction at a time or alternating directions as described in variation 5.

   The following, for instance, is a combination that requires versatility in coordination and is excellent for an intermediate level, though it is too difficult for beginners: *Plié* and brush twice, then close with both legs straight. Continue with a *plié* on one leg as the other leg brushes out, and straighten both legs on the close. Do this part two times. Try this front, back, side, and side. Add a transition to start on the other foot. Or, this may be done with the same foot front, side, and back and then with the other foot front, side, and back.
9. Perform brushes on half-toe. This combination is excellent for discovering the true use of the thighs and improving center control. A slight variation may be created by a change of accent: Have the accent on the outward motion when on full foot and on the inward motion when on half-toe.

10. Stand on one leg with the other foot at the ankle of the standing leg. Carry the foot out to the side so the toe lightly brushes the floor and ends just off the floor with the knee very straight. Bring the foot back to the ankle, again lightly brushing the floor with the toes and ending with the foot firmly against the ankle. Make this a sharp, staccato movement but do not permit the thigh to bob up and down. This variation can also be performed forward and back, though it is more difficult to control the turnout and the thigh movement.

11. Stand on one leg with the other foot at the ankle as described in variation 10. Without changing the position of the foot and without letting the thigh rotate forward and back, move the foot to the back of the ankle so the heel is against the back of the ankle with toes pointing slightly back. Bring the foot back to the front pressing it firmly against the ankle. The accent should occur when the foot is at the front: back, *front*; back, *front*; and so on.

12. Variation 11 may be performed with a triple beat, alternating the accent back and front: back, *front*, back; then front, *back*, front, and so on.

13. Stand in fifth position. Lift the front leg with the foot at the inside of the standing ankle so only the toes are touching the ankle and the knee is well turned out. Keeping the thigh still and moving the lower leg from the knee, perform small, fast, light beatings of the toes against the ankle.

14. An exercise that is excellent for developing clean and subtle foot movements begins in the fifth position. Lift the front foot to the standing ankle so the heel is in front of the ankle, with toes pointed slightly back and knee held out to the side. Lift the foot with the toes well-pointed and with the heel against the front of the leg so that the toes show on the outside of the leg. Lift the foot so that the toes just touch inside the standing knee. Carry the foot to the back of the standing leg so that the foot is halfway between the standing knee and the ankle, with the heel against the back of the leg but the toes showing on the outside of the standing leg. Lower the foot to the back of the ankle so the foot is in the same shape it was when it was placed at the front of the ankle, except that now the heel is touching the ankle with toes pointed slightly back. The instep should not be touching the ankle.

Close to fifth position back. Reverse the above: to back of the ankle, halfway up; to knee, halfway down in front; to ankle, in front; close in fifth position front. There are very subtle changes in ankle and leg position. Do this in six even counts, stressing exactness of the foot and leg positions. Gradually increase the tempo but stop when positions are no longer exact and cleanly placed. When this can be performed very quickly and cleanly, it is a base for development of versatile foot and leg movements.

Science. See exercises 8.B.1. and 8.C.1.

Leg Extensions

To perform extensions, dancers need a great flexibility within the hip joint and the surrounding area, but this flexibility must have a counterbalance of control in the center, back, and thighs. The word "flexibility" should always be coupled with the word "control." The dancer who possesses a long, lean figure often has a naturally high extension, but the shorter, less lean dancer usually has to work hard to achieve a high extension. However, there are exceptions.

8.D. Leg Extension Preparatory Exercises: Lying and Sitting

8.D.1. Back and front extension

Art. Extensions, like back bends, should come from a fullness, a bursting of energy that demands release in an excess of normal movement beyond the normal range. They should not be mere acrobatic stunts. The emphasis should be on lifting up. Even in the return, there should be no suggestion of giving in to the pull of gravity. The leg returns to earth because the dancer chooses to bring it down. The extension is a lift, not a kick. Beautiful and spectacular leg extensions can be an exciting aspect of dance. However, they must have an effortless quality to be effective.

Craft. Sit with both knees bent, one leg in front and the other behind. The hand on the side of the forward leg should be on the floor at the side of the hip; the other hand should rest lightly on the front ankle. Try to sit on both buttocks. (If a student cannot sit easily on both buttocks, do not force it.) Keep the back straight. Do not rest weight on the arm that is on the floor. Extend the back leg until the knee is straight and the side of the foot and heel are on the floor. Just before starting the extension, the knee should be lifted slightly from the floor. Next, bend the knee and return the leg to place. Then, extend the front leg with the little toe toward the floor. As the leg extends, raise the free arm overhead. Hold the front leg extension as the torso bends forward over the leg and then lifts back to place. Bend the front knee, returning the leg to the starting position. At the same time, lower the raised arm.

Many beginners need to take the back leg to the side in order to straighten the knee. Students need to experiment with the direction of the back leg extension to permit straightening the knee. This is an individual matter and must not be forced. Many beginners need to go almost straight to the side at first. A true back extension will develop gradually as flexibility increases. Several variations of this exercise can help increase flexibility. For instance, after extending the back leg, place the knee on the floor where it is. Maintain this position as the knee bends and the foot moves toward the torso; do not permit the thigh to slide forward. Similarly, when the front leg extends, slide forward slightly, increasing the spread between the legs. Maintain this spread as the front knee bends to return to place.

The flex and point (Exercise 8.A.1.) and the knee lift (Exercise 8.H.) exercises may be used as preparation or as warmup exercises for leg extensions.

Back and front extension

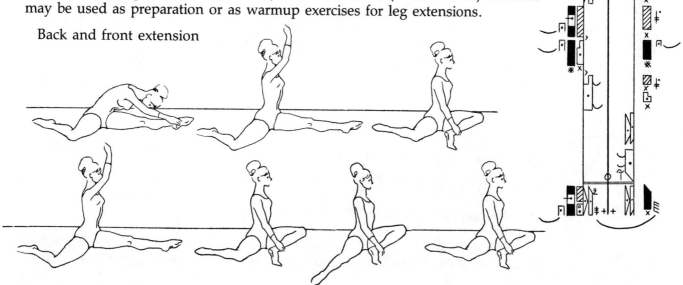

Science. Individuals should always do their own stretching. Never manually stretch another person either by pulling or pushing. Many dancers have been seriously injured as a result of this type of manipulation by teachers or fellow students.

8.D.2. Back leg lift

Art. See Exercise 8.D.1.

Craft. Sit with the back straight, both knees bent, one leg in front and the other behind, and with the arms raised to just below shoulder level—the arm on the side of the forward leg curved over the forward leg, and the other raised to the side. Rotate the torso to face over the hip on the side of the forward leg. Bend over the forward leg with the shoulders parallel to the floor and as close to the floor as possible, placing the hands on the floor with the elbows bent. Extend the back leg so that the knee is completely straight and the toe pointed. Maintaining a straight knee, and with movement localized in the hip and leg, raise the leg as high as possible, then lower it to touch the floor (do not drop the leg or rest the foot on the floor). Raise and lower the leg three or four times. The last time, raise the leg but do not lower it. While holding it up, lift the torso and arms as far as possible without strain in the small of the back, rotate the torso to face the starting position, and sit on both buttocks. At the same time, rotate the hip of the lifted leg so the leg remains at the side and does not swing forward.

Back leg lift

Science. See Exercise 8.D.1.

8.D.3. Toe touch

Art. See Exercise 8.D.1.

Craft. Sit with the back straight and the knees bent in front. Contract, rolling back just enough that the toes, not the whole foot, are touching the floor. Open the arms sideways as you contract. Keeping this angle at the hip joint and without letting the thighs move, lift the feet up by straightening the knees, return the toes to just touching the floor, then extend, and so on. Do not perform the exercise more than four or five times without straightening the back and resting the legs. The angle between the torso and thighs must be maintained throughout. It is easy to drop the thighs as the legs extend.

Toe touch

Science. See Exercise 8.D.1.

8.D.4. Side leg lift

Art. See Exercise 8.D.1.

Craft. Sit with the knees bent, one leg in front and the other in back. Place the hands lightly on the forward leg, one hand on the knee, and one on the ankle. The hands should just rest on the leg, not press down. Keeping the back straight, shift the weight slightly to the side away from the back leg but with no forward tip. Maintaining this position, use a completely localized movement of the leg to raise the back leg from the floor. The foot and the knee should leave and return to the floor at the same time. Do not permit the knee to lift higher than the foot. Guard against a tightening in the hip joint itself. The leg will not go very high. Do no more than four lifts on a side at one time.

Side leg lift

Science. If a cramp develops in the hip joint on any of these localized leg lifts, stop immediately and release the tension. This is caused by inefficient performance of the exercise: That is, the student is resisting the exercise by tightening antagonistic muscle groups that will interfere with or prevent lifting the leg. Common mistakes are: tipping the torso forward or rocking sideways and back as the leg lifts and lowers; and leaving the foot down or near the floor as the knee lifts. These incorrect movements use different muscle groups than the ones for which the exercise is intended. It may be valuable to have the students complete the exercise the wrong way once or twice to experience the difference.

8.D.5. *Side leg lift: Variations*

Art. See Exercise 8.D.1.

Craft. The following are variations of the side leg lift:

1. Sit as in the previous exercises. Begin in the same way by lifting the leg to the side, but after raising the leg, move it to the back and then forward to the starting position before lowering it. The range of movement will be small. Guard against lifting the knee higher than the foot. Do not let the torso tip forward or further sideways as the leg is carried to the back.

Side leg lift: Variation 1

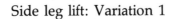

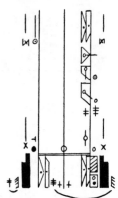

2. This exercise goes further than variation 1. After lifting the leg and moving it to the back, extend it by straightening the knee. Extend the leg as far to the back as possible. Keeping the extension, sweep the leg to the side, then bend the knee and lower the leg to place. Be careful not to tip the torso forward as the leg extends to the back.

Side leg lift: Variation 2

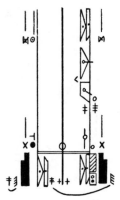

Science. See Exercise 8.D.4.

8.D.6. *Front extension along floor*

Art. See Exercise 8.D.1.

Craft. Sit with the knees bent, one leg in front and the other behind, and with the arms raised at the sides just below shoulder level. With the ankle extended (toe pointed), extend the front leg along the floor with the little toe as close to the floor as individual turnout permits. While the leg is extended, flex the ankle, then again extend it. Keeping the ankle extended, bend the knee back to the starting position.

Science. See Exercise 8.D.4.

8.D.7. Front extension off floor

Art. See Exercise 8.D.1.

Craft. This is a variation of Exercise 8.D.6. and is more difficult. It should not be used in short, beginning courses. It could be used toward the end of a full semester course, depending on how far the class has progressed.

Sit with one leg in front, the knee bent and the ankle extended, with the other leg extended to the side and the knee straight. Lift the front leg, trying to keep the foot as closely in line with the knee as possible. Grasp the heel of the lifted foot with the hand by placing the hand on top of the heel; use the same hand as foot. The other hand rests lightly on the other knee. While pulling the foot toward the face, extend the knee. Keeping the knee straight, flex the ankle, then extend the ankle and bend the knee to return to the starting position. Do this three to five times and then repeat with the other leg. Later, perform this exercise without holding the heel. In this version, the hand on the side of the moving leg rests lightly on the other elbow.

Front extension off floor

Science. There is usually someone in a beginning class who will insist that the arm is not long enough to permit the knee to straighten. Actually, the difficulty is in the lack of flexibility in the hip joint and lack of control in the thigh, or the student is depending on the arm instead of the leg to do all the work.

Work to maintain turnout when the ankle is flexed. The toes should point to the side wall and not over the shoulder. The back will be rounded but still lifted; however, do not roll backward onto the small of the back. The free hand should not be used on the front for support.

8.D.8. Front extension off floor: Variation

Art. See Exercise 8.D.1.

Craft. This is a more difficult exercise and should not be used for beginners. Start the same way as in Exercise 8.D.7. but without holding the heel. The hand on the side of the straight leg rests on that knee with the other hand resting on the elbow. After extending the leg and flexing the ankle, lower the leg almost to the floor, lift it, and carry the leg as far to the side as possible. Keeping the leg straight, again lower and raise the leg, keeping the side of the foot parallel to the floor. Bend the knee, bringing the foot back to the starting position. The accent should be on the lifting of the leg.

Front extension off floor: Variation

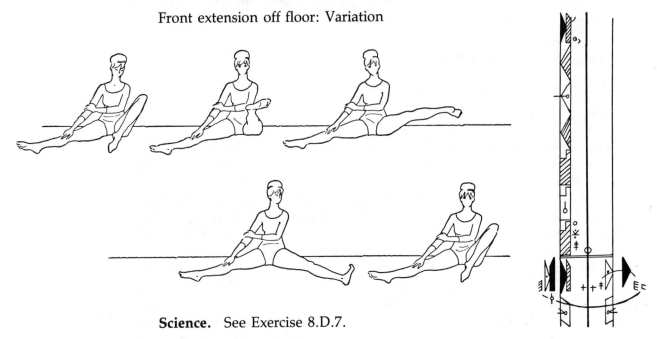

Science. See Exercise 8.D.7.

8.E. On One Knee

8.E.1. Extension from side sit

Art. See Exercise 8.D.1.

Craft. Sit on one hip. Both knees should be bent, with one leg front and the other behind. The hand on the side of the front leg should be on the floor; the arm on the other side should be extended out to the side. Starting with a contraction, bring the knee of the back leg and the corresponding arm in toward the chest. Next, swing the leg to a side extension while the arm swings high. (The force of the swing should lift the student to a hand-and-knee support.) Return to a sit on one hip while bringing the free hand and knee in toward the chest. Control the return to the sitting position. There should be no bump.

Extension from side sit

Science. See Exercise 8.D.4.

8.E.2. Back extension on hands and knees

Art. See Exercise 8.D.1.

Craft. Assume a position on the hands and knees, with the knees directly under the hips and the hands under the shoulders. Bring one knee in close to the chest and bring the head down. Then extend the leg as far as possible, straightening the knee and lifting the head. Repeat the exercise three to eight times on each side or alternate sides.

Back extension on hands and knees

Science. See Exercise 8.D.4.

8.F. Standing at the Barre

Stretching exercises performed with the aid of a ballet barre increase range of movement and flexibility, helping to develop height and control in standing extensions without the added difficulty of balance. These exercises should not be used for the short beginning course. For such classes, the movement exploratory exercises and locomotor combinations are more important.

8.F.1. Sliding stretches

Art. See Exercise 8.D.1.

Craft. Stand facing the barre with the hips parallel to it. Both legs should be turned out equally and as far as individual control permits. The heel of one leg should be on the barre; the hands should hold the barre a shoulder width apart, or wider. They should not be crunched in close to the body. Keeping both knees straight, slide the lifted leg along the barre as far as individual flexibility allows, then return to the starting position.

Sliding stretches

• = Barre

Science. Be efficient. Keep the stretching muscles relaxed. It is easy to tighten up slightly and resist the stretch when first trying the sliding stretches.

The barre should be used as an aid, not as a prop. Never hang the leg on the barre; this will cause a strain at the back of the knee. Keep enough tension in the thigh to partially support the leg, both for knee safety and for strengthening the leg toward eventual elimination of the barre. Maintain turnout on the standing leg so as not to roll over on the arch of the foot. If there are two barres at different heights, the student with limited flexibility will progress more rapidly by starting with the lower barre.

It is very easy to lean on the barre, which causes loss of back alignment and control. Students need to check back alignment frequently when working at the barre.

The hand should just rest on the barre; avoid holding onto it with a death grip. The supporting leg will require constant checking to be sure a perpendicular line is maintained. It is easy to press backward or to the side of the standing leg so the standing leg is in a diagonal line. This angle can cause a strain on the back of the knee and eventually a hyperextension of the knee.

8.F.2. Sliding stretches: Variations

Art.   See Exercise 8.D.1.

Craft.   These are variations of sliding stretches:

1. Start with a *plié* on the standing leg, taking care that the knee bends over the toes. Using the straightening of this *plié* as the impulse to slowly slide out as far as possible along the barre, as described in Exercise 8.F.1. Return to place with both knees straight.
2. Keep both knees straight and slide out as in the basic exercise. After reaching the maximum stretch, *plié* on the supporting leg, watching knee alignment. The straightening of the knee should instigate the return to place. When returning to place, be sure to go to the spot just over the supporting foot. Do not go beyond it.

Sliding stretches: Variation 2

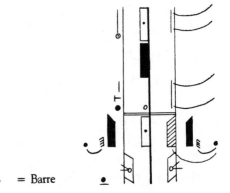

•   = Barre

Science. It is vitally important to maintain back and torso alignment without producing a strain in the lower back. Retain turnout in the lifted leg. Be sure the lifted leg does not rotate to hook the toe on the barre or to club the ankle. Maintain a perpendicular line with the standing leg. Also, see Exercise 8.F.1.

8.F.3. Side bend and beginning back extension

Art. See Exercise 8.D.1.

Craft. This exercise can be combined with sliding stretches by hopping to the place for this exercise without taking the foot off the barre. Stand with the side toward the barre and the heel on the barre. Maintain the lifted leg at right angles to the barre. Be sure there is equal turnout in both legs. Raise the arms sideways. Using a lateral bend, tip the torso toward the barre, and let the outside arm curve overhead. Return to the upright position. Bend the torso away from the barre and try to arrive at a line parallel to the floor. The leg on the barre, the torso, and the arm should all form one straight line. Without straightening up, rotate the face to the floor. Swivel the standing foot to reach whatever turnout you can control, and rotate the lifted leg to an equal turnout. Cautiously lift the torso and head as far as individual flexibility permits without straining the small of the back.

Science. See Exercise 8.F.1.

8.F.4. Forward extension with contraction and release

Art. See Exercise 8.D.1.

Craft. Stand facing the barre with the hips parallel to it. Place one foot on the barre, keeping both knees straight and equally turned out and holding the arms in a long curve overhead. Take a preliminary stretch by bending the torso forward over the lifted leg. Next, stand erect in good alignment with the arms extended overhead. Without permitting the standing knee to bend—and taking care not to sink into the standing hip—perform a small, localized contraction in the midsection. Release, elongating the torso and pulling up out of the supporting hip and knee. Keep the shoulders down. Repeat this two or three times before changing legs. This may appear to be a simple exercise, but it is one of the best for discovering a relationship between the torso and the hip area and for contributing to increased control of the areas. This needs to be tried to be understood.

Forward extension with contraction and release

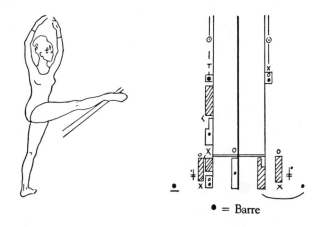

• = Barre

Science. The actual movement is very subtle but important. The alignment of torso and knees and of shoulders and arms is vital for the total result.

8.F.5. Front and back extension

Art. See Exercise 8.D.1.

Craft. Stand with one side close to the barre, the hips at right angles to the barre and the inside hand resting easily on it. The outside leg is placed forward on the barre with the knee straight. Both legs are equally turned out. Bend the torso forward and try to touch the head to the knee. Return to the upright position. Bend the torso back, starting with a lift in the upper torso (not a drop in the small of the back), and try to see the floor. Return to the upright position. Lift the leg off the barre, circle it to the back, and place the heel on the barre in the back, maintaining turnout in the hip. Bend forward to touch the floor with the free hand. Lift the torso as high as individual flexibility allows without straining the lower back. When moving the leg from front to back, try to maintain a level; it is easy to drop the leg down at the side and then lift it again to place the foot on the barre.

Front and back extension

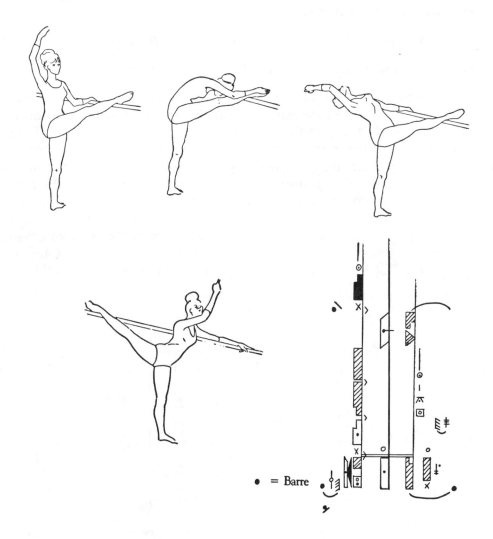

● = Barre

Science. See Exercise 8.F.1.

8.G. Leg Extension Against the Wall

8.G.1. Leg extension against the wall: Front

Art.   See Exercise 8.D.1.

Craft.   This is for advanced students. Stand facing the barre with both hands on it. Place one foot on the barre with that knee bent. Place that foot on the wall. To get the foot onto the wall, it may be necessary to lean the torso slightly back away from the barre and to *plié* on the standing leg. Slowly slide the foot up the wall until the knee is straight. Straighten the back and the standing knee as the leg moves up the wall. As extension improves, move closer to the barre. To bring the leg down, swing it to the side and lower it slowly, holding turnout in both legs and keeping the knees straight. Lift arms to fifth position high as the leg lowers.

Leg extension against the wall: Front

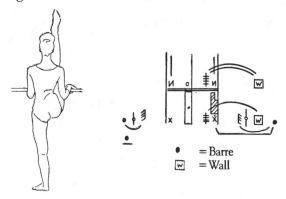

● = Barre
w = Wall

Science.   Be sure to maintain pull in the thighs and torso to prevent hyperextension or bracing back in either knee. This is more apt to happen in the standing knee. Do not force these extensions. Each individual will vary in degree of hip and torso flexibility, which can be increased, but it must be increased gradually.

8.G.2. Leg extension against the wall: Side

Art.   See Exercise 8.D.1.

Craft.   Stand at right angles to the barre, with one foot on the barre, the raised knee bent, and the hand nearest the barre holding it in front of the leg. Place the foot on the wall and slowly slide it up the wall. It may be necessary to *plié* on the standing leg and to bend the torso away from the barre to start the foot up the wall. To bring the foot down, swing the leg to the front. Lift the torso to an upright position as the leg slowly lowers. Keep both knees straight as the leg lowers.

Leg extension against the wall: Side

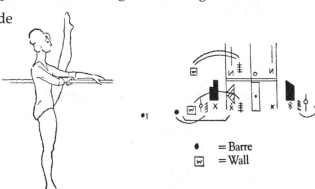

● = Barre
w = Wall

Science. Be sure to lift up in the torso and thigh as the leg swings to the front to come down. There should be no shoulder lift, nor should there be tension in the neck or arms. Find control in the torso and thighs so there is no resisting tension in the stretching muscles or the hip joint.

8.G.3. Leg extension against the wall: Back

Art. See Exercise 8.D.1.

Craft. This is for advanced students, definitely not for beginners. Stand with the back to the barre. Bend one leg with the knee and foot on the barre and the hands on the floor at each side of the torso. Bend the torso forward, parallel to the standing leg. Slowly slide the foot up the wall. It may be necessary to bend the supporting knee to start the foot up the wall. To bring the foot down again, swing it either to one side or to the front. Lift the torso to an upright position as the leg slowly lowers, keeping both knees straight.

Leg extension against the wall: Back

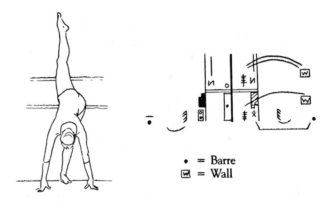

• = Barre
☒ = Wall

Science. See Exercise 8.G.2.

8.H. Standing Knee Lift

Art. See Exercise 8.D.1.

Craft. Stand with good alignment, bend one knee, and lift it high in front. Grasp it with both hands and pull it as near the shoulder as possible. In doing so, keep the back straight and feel as though the rib cage is pulling slightly toward the lifted thigh. Keep the hand that is on the same side of the body as the lifted knee in place, but release the other hand. Carry the knee out to the side, rotating the leg at the hip joint. Keep the foot of the lifted leg pointed directly under the knee. Keeping the hand on the knee, carry the leg to the back, rotating the hip joint so that the lower leg is parallel to the floor and the foot crosses the torso behind. The foot should not drop below the level of the knee. Do not permit the torso to tip or bend forward as the leg goes back. The pelvis should not tilt, nor should the knee of the standing leg bend.

Science. See Exercise 8.G.2.

8.I. Standing Leg Extensions: Away from Barre

In all standing extensions, the alignment of the back and the standing leg and the relationship among the back, hip, and thigh are of vital importance. The bend must come at the hip joint and not at the waist. A bend at the waist will permit the pelvis to tip.

There must be no sinking into the hips or loosening in control of the standing knee. Feel the lifting knee going toward the torso, not the torso going toward the lifting leg. On the other hand, the torso should not move away from the lifting leg. The height of the leg is determined by the height of the knee, so be very conscious of knee placement.

8.I.1. Extension from knee lift

Art. See Exercise 8.D.1.

Craft. Stand in parallel position. Lift the knee in front, grasp the thigh (not the knee or lower leg) with the hands, and try to straighten the knee without lowering the leg. Let go of the thigh with the hands and try to maintain the level of the leg. Lower the leg to the floor by reaching for the floor with the toes. After the toes touch the floor, brush this foot into place beside the standing foot. The leg should feel very long when it is lowered to the floor. For variation, repeat to the side or repeat to the back.

Extension from knee lift

Science. See exercises 8.G.1. and 8.G.2.

8.I.2. Extension from knee lift without holding thigh (developpé)

Art.   See Exercise 8.D.1.

Craft.   Stand in fifth position with arms extended sideways. Repeat exercise 8.I.1., but without holding the thigh with the hands. Experiment to see how high the knee can be lifted without lowering as the leg extends. Gradually try for a higher lift.

Science.   See exercises 8.G.1. and 8.G.2.

8.I.3. Leg extension followed by knee bend (enveloppé)

Art.   See Exercise 8.D.1.

Craft.   This is not for beginners. Reverse the knee lift and extension in Exercise 8.I.2. Start in fifth position with arms extended sideways. Brush the foot out, trying to raise it level with the hip. Keep the thigh in place (don't drop it), bend the knee, and bring the foot in to the standing leg. Keep the toe well-pointed so the toes, not the heel, are close to the standing leg, and lower the foot to close in fifth position front. Maintain the turnout during the movements. The starting brush should be a sweeping lift of the whole leg. As the knee bends, keep it turned out and to the side. Repeat to the side and to the back. On closing from the side extension, the foot may be placed in fifth position either front or back. The back movement will be the most difficult. The difficulty comes from keeping the moving knee turned out, the torso and thigh well-lifted. In all three directions, guard against dropping the thigh as the knee bends.

Science.   See Exercise 8.G.1.

Chapter 9

Turns, Falls, and Recoveries

In this chapter, we have exercises for two movements that create excitement in dance compositions: turns and falls. We also have exercises in recovering from a fall. This last movement is complementary to the fall, and they should be practiced together.

Turns (*Tours*)

In most turns, the motivating force is a lift to half-toe with rotation around the central shaft of the torso. There are other sources of propulsion, however. An arm, a leg, a hip, an elbow, or even the head may be used to lead into a turn. One propulsive force often neglected is the opposite of the rise to half-toe: a pushing down into a *plié*.

Some of the most exciting turns appear to be off balance. Actually, this appearance is an illusion. The act of turning demands the establishment of a center of balance between two compensating pulls.

An important aspect of turning is focus. A sight focus, usually called spotting, is frequently used. Another kind of spotting, found in Oriental and Middle Eastern cultures, is an internal focusing of the whole self. Actually, this is a form of concentration.

Many beginning students seem to be afraid of turns. This fear may be overcome by starting work on turns early in dance training. At first, present the exercises in small doses and encourage the discovery of how easy it is to turn. The circular patterns listed in Chapter 2 can be used as a lead into turns.

There are so many kinds and styles of turns that it is impossible to list them all, but some of the more basic ones are described here.

9.A. Preparatory

9.A.1. Change of direction

Art. Turns need a serene center, psychologically as well as physically. There must be sureness in alignment: a control in the ability to balance one part with another. As a dancer, your concentration should be so strong that you feel you are the center of the universe and that it turns around you.

There should be a feeling of immediacy and a sense of excitement in facing the new direction. Perform the step as though launching yourself into space. There should be a sense of suspension on the step.

Craft. This is a good preliminary exercise for adjusting to space, focus, and immediacy of action. It consists of a series of quarter-turns. Step into the new direction on half-toe with the knee straight. Immediately close the free foot to the stepping foot. Make the step into a new direction as large as can be controlled. Use a strong focus in the direction of the step. The eye focus and the turn of the head should precede the step into the direction. Make a complete circle on one side with four of these steps, then repeat on the other side. Increase the tempo of the turns as proficiency permits. However, a very fast tempo will not be possible with this turn.

Science. Keep a close check on the ankle and back alignment. There should be a straight line at the front of the hip joint and waist areas; the shoulders must stay over the hips. The step directly onto a high half-toe, often called a *perch*, must be clean-cut with the knee straight. Do not step with the knee bent and then straighten it.

Turn the whole torso in one piece. Do not let the shoulder or hips lead or turn separately, with the rest catching up later. Guard against a slight bend or give of the knee or waist just before or at the moment of the step. Also, do not step onto the whole foot and then lift up to half-toe; this can cause a recognizable rocking motion.

9.A.2. Paddle turn

Art. See Exercise 9.A.1.

Craft. The paddle turn gives the feeling of turning in place. The weight is kept primarily on one foot, but a quick catch-step is taken briefly on the other foot to supply a turning impulse. Try this using three of the catch-steps to make one complete turn; hold; change feet; and repeat on the other side. If turning to the right, the fast catch-step is on the left foot.

Science. See Exercise 9.A.1.

9.A.3. Three-step turn

Art. See Exercise 9.A.1.

Craft. Many dance teachers prefer to start with the three-step turn. Others prefer the hop turn (Exercise 9.A.8.) as the best introduction to turns. This is a matter of individual preference. Each teacher should experiment to discover what works best for his or her way of teaching; different classes may demand different approaches.

Starting either left or right, make a complete turn in place using three definite steps. Hold one count, then repeat the turn in the other direction. Keep the steps small and almost in place. (If dancers start with large steps, it will be difficult to acquire any degree of speed in the turn.) Be sure to keep shoulders directly over the hips, the head straight (not tilted), and to turn in one piece without separate arm or torso movements. Use a strong eye focus directly to the front. Try not to see anything but that spot directly in front. This is an important factor in preventing dizziness. Increase the tempo as proficiency, which usually comes quickly and easily, allows.

Science. See Exercise 9.A.1.

9.A.4. Double turn

Art. See Exercise 9.A.1.

Craft. The double turn is a variation of the three-step turn. Instead of stopping after one three-step turn, do two complete turns before pausing to change direction. This will require five steps and a pause before repeating to the other side. Increase the tempo. Some beginners quickly develop the ability to do very fast double turns. When introducing this, it may be necessary to keep reminding the students to keep feet close together with small steps.

Science. See Exercise 9.A.1.

9.A.5. Step-leap-step turn (tour jeté or jeté en tournant)

Art. See Exercise 9.A.1.

Craft. This exercise is also a variation of the three-step turn. Rather than using three steps to turn, change the second step to a small leap. When first introduced, use a very small leap. Later, this can become the most important part of the turn, becoming as high and as big as possible.

Science. See Exercise 9.A.1.

9.A.6. Step-leap-step turn: Variations

Art. See Exercise 9.A.1.

Craft. These are variations on the step-leap-step turn:

1. Change the tempo either by increasing or decreasing speed.
2. Increase the range of the leap both in distance and height.
3. Vary the leg movements. For example, use a straight knee on the leg leading into the leap or bend both knees when in the air.
4. Vary the level by extending the leap while keeping close to the floor or by going as high as possible.
5. Employ a ballet, folk, or jazz style. (In ballet, this exercise may lead into the *jeté en tournant*, and in jazz dance it may lead into a butterfly or camel spin.)

Science. See Exercise 9.A.1.

9.A.7. Jump turn (tour en l'air)

Art. See Exercise 9.A.1.

Craft. This can be used as the first exercise to introduce turns. It is especially successful with men.

Jump, taking off and landing on both feet at the same time; turn while in the air. Maintaining torso and leg alignment is vital. Start the exercise with four quarter-turns; then do four half-turns. Be sure to repeat on the other side. The half-turn should be mastered before attempting a full turn (this is easy for most beginners). Mastery means that the turn can be accomplished with great ease while maintaining alignment. Sustain control long enough to finish with balance and proper alignment. Discover how little energy is needed for even a full turn. Most beginners throw themselves off balance by using too much energy and by slinging the arms to start the turn. It is not necessary to use any arm movement for one full turn. Eventually work for double and triple turns. Some arm movement will be necessary for these.

Science.   Many beginning students twist the shoulders away from the direction of the turn, then use a lot of energy in a big heave into the turn, which throws them off balance. Other frequent mistakes are: bending forward at the waist to prepare for the turn; throwing the shoulder as a turning impulse, which throws the torso out of alignment and destroys balance; and turning in segments (for example, the shoulders before the hips or the hips before the shoulders) instead of moving all in one piece. Also, see Exercise 9.A.1.

9.A.8. Hop (sauté) turn

Art.   See Exercise 9.A.1.

Craft.   The hop turn is particularly good for practicing focus and for building a sense of turning all in one piece. Stand on one leg with the other leg raised in front, the knee bent, the arm on the same side as the raised leg curved in front, and the other arm overhead. Use a very small hop and a *plié* as a turning impulse. The feeling is up, down, hold. It should be counted ''a one, a two, a three.'' Turn in the direction of the lifted leg. Perform four quarter-turns, change feet, and repeat on the other side. Perform four half-turns on each side, then four full turns on each side.

Develop this into a spin on the supporting foot, instead of using the hop for the full turn. Many students discover this spinning variation without being told. More advanced students may progress into double or triple turns using this variation.

Hop turn

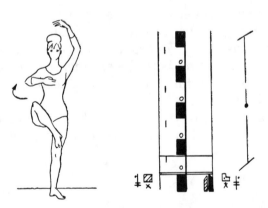

Science.   Guard against permitting the arms and the raised leg to move during the turn. It is very easy to let them pull in the direction of the turn and to pull out of alignment, thus destroying balance. This is particularly applicable to the full turn.

Do not drop in the center on the *plié*. There is a sense of slightly sitting into the *plié*, but be sure to maintain the lift in the center. Also, maintain a strong eye focus; really see the new direction every time. This habit should be established at the beginning with the quarter-turns: See the new direction.

9.B. Other Leads for Turns

9.B.1. Spiral turn with arm lead

Art.   See Exercise 9.A.1.

Craft.   Take small steps while turning, swinging one arm across in front as the impetus for the turn. Be sure to use a true arm swing as the turning impulse. It is important to move as a complete unit. Once the turn is under way, do not permit the arm to move in a swing that is independent of the rest of the body.

After getting a feeling for the arm really leading into the turn, make the turn a spiral by bending low at the start of the arm swing and then gradually lifting during the turn to finish with the arm overhead. Even beginners usually can take this movement into a double—and sometimes a triple—turn.

Science.   See Exercise 9.A.1.

9.B.2. Spiral turn with arm lead: Variations

Art.   See Exercise 9.A.1.

Craft.   The following are variations of the spiral turn with arm lead.

1. Increase the tempo.
2. Reverse the turn by swinging the arm in back instead of in front. (This is more difficult and should not be given to beginners until they have attained some facility in total coordination and in combining movements.)
3. An even more difficult variation is using both arms in a parallel motion as a lead into the turn.

Science.   See Exercise 9.A.1.

9.B.3. Turn with leg lead

Art.   See Exercise 9.A.1.

Craft.   Use a leg swing as the impulse to turn. Swing the leg back with the knee bent. There should be a feeling that the thigh of the lifted leg is exerting the pull. Permit the leg swing to pull the whole torso into a back turn. At the end of the turn, lift very high in the back and midsection. Lift the knee very slightly with a sense of a subtle pull between the chest and the knee.

Science.   See Exercise 9.A.1.

9.B.4. Turn with leg lead: Variations

Art.   See Exercise 9.A.1.

Craft.   These are variations of the turn with leg lead:

1. Use the leg swing for a forward turn. Start with a swing out to the side, then across in front.
2. Vary the level of the swinging leg; try a low swing or a very high swing.
3. Vary the level of the foot of the standing leg. Try a very high half-toe position. Instead of a half-toe position, try with the heel close to the floor. Try turning on the heel. This requires very strong control in the center of the torso and in knee alignment.

4. Change alignment by bending or tilting torso before, during, or after the turn.

5. Vary the degree of turn. Try a quarter-turn, a half, a three-quarter, a third, a two-third, a one-and-a-half turn, and so on, in order to learn to control the energy needed for each degree of turning and to experience the different feelings of yourself in relation to space.

Science. See Exercise 9.A.1.

9.B.5. *Pivot turn (pirouette)*

Art. See Exercise 9.A.1.

Craft. The propelling impulse in the pivot turn is a lift to half-toe with the whole body turning in one piece around a central shaft. Maintaining true alignment and keeping the standing knee straight but not locked are vital. It is easier for most beginners to start with a back turn (turning away from the supporting leg). Stand in a turned-out position with the free foot pressed against the front of the ankle of the standing leg and with the knee pressed out to the side. Maintain this pressed-out position of the knee throughout the turn.

It is best to have beginners discover how easily they can turn before they try for virtuosity. First try to learn the least amount of energy needed to accomplish the desired degree of turn. It should be possible to perform a quarter-turn, a half-turn, and a single full turn without the help of arm movements or a preceding *plié*. Experimentation can occur in a preliminary exercise, begun in fifth position. Quickly rise to a high half-toe (or perch) on the back foot, and at the same time lift the front foot to press against the ankle of the standing foot, with the knee pressed out to the side. Discover how to hold a balance with this fast perch before attempting the turn. Then repeat the fast lift to half-toe, going into a quarter-turn. Next, go into a half-turn, then a full turn. Work for ease in performance. Do not yet add a *plié* or an arm movement as preparation for the rise to half-toe. (Later, to go beyond a single full turn, it will be necessary to add a *plié* in the preparation and an arm movement to start the turn.)

Pivot turn

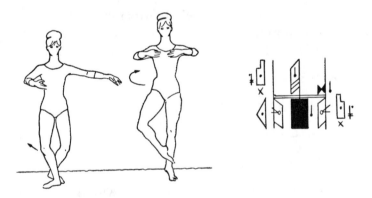

Science. Maintain alignment of the torso with the shoulders over the hips so that the turn is in one piece. Check to be sure there is no give in the small of the back on the rise to half-toe. A stiffening in the wrists or neck is usually an indication that control has been lost in the center.

9.B.6. Pivot turn: Variations

Art. See Exercise 9.A.1.

Craft. The following are variations on the pivot turn:

1. Reverse direction; do the exercise as a forward turn.
2. Change the standing foot. Instead of performing the pivot turn on the back foot, use the front foot for all variations.
3. Vary the position and preliminary movement of the free foot. That is, instead of holding the foot at the ankle of the standing foot, discover what happens if the foot is extended front, side, or back; try these variations either with the knee bent or with the leg straight. These all take different controls and have different feelings.
4. Vary the positions and movements of the arms.
5. Increase the degree of turn to double and triple turns.
6. Instead of maintaining an erect torso position, vary the torso position and add torso movements during the turns. This is definitely for more advanced students.

Science. See Exercise 9.B.5.

9.B.7. Turn from downward push (press-turn)

Art. See Exercise 9.A.1.

Craft. This is for more advanced students with sure control of knee alignment. Exert a downward pressure into a *plié*, lifting the heel slightly to turn on the ball of the foot as a source of propulsion for the turn. Perform this first in a turned-out position with a forward turn, lifting the free leg to the side. Be sure to hold the free leg to the side throughout the turn. Do not permit it to swing forward.

Turn from downward push

Science. Keep close watch on the knee and ankle alignment of the standing leg during this turn. Think of the heel as a steering wheel that almost leads the movement. Permitting the heel to lag behind can twist the knee.

9.B.8. Turn from downward push: Variations

Art. See Exercise 9.A.1.

Craft. These are variations of the turn from downward push:

1. Vary the degree of turn. Try full turns, double turns, or one-and-a-half turns. This last turn is often more difficult than a double turn.
2. Vary the direction, going into a back turn instead of a forward turn.
3. Vary the arm positions both in preparatory movements and while turning.
4. Vary the torso position to side tilts.
5. Try torso, arm, and leg positions that appear to be off balance.
6. Experiment with additional movements while turning.

Science. See Exercise 9.B.7.

Falls and Recoveries

Falling, like turning or jumping, creates a special excitement. In a dance composition, care must be exercised that there is a reason for going to the earth—that the movement does not become a mere acrobatic feat—unless, of course, displaying acrobatic skill is the intent of the dance theme. For technical training, as much importance should be given to the recovery from a fall as to the fall itself, and falls and recoveries should always be practiced together.

Some individuals have a genuine fear of falling. Usually, with movement exploration and a visual image to follow, they will learn to concentrate enough on the visual image to forget their fear. Actually, they are not really falling but rather transferring weight from one part of the body to another.

9.C. Falls

9.C.1. Exploration of falling

Art. Explore the feeling of a fall performed as a statement of fact, as a positive accent similar to a stamp of the foot or a clap of the hands. Also explore controlling a fall to emphasize the feeling of weightless suspension, as though the fall occurs in slow motion. For contrast, experiment with a fall performed with the impression of giving up, which creates a feeling of death or disintegration.

Craft. Watch a feather or a light scarf fall to the floor. Notice that there is no sound. Think of imitating that fall. Be careful not to land on the knee, the elbow, the coccyx, or the tip of the shoulder. Discover how to fall without making any sound. Again drop the feather or scarf, and go down with it, trying to duplicate the action. Go to a complete lying position, not just a sit. The first attempt may have some sound. However, succeeding attempts should be soundless.

Science. Falls have definite points of danger. The principal safety factor in falls is to avoid landing on joints—primarily the knees, the elbows, the coccyx, or the tip of the shoulder—or catching yourself with a straight arm. To lessen the jolt of impact, dancers should take four basic precautions. First, control the weight so the mass of the body is as close to the floor as possible, and attempt to slide into the floor instead of landing hard on one spot. Second, lessen the impact by dissipating the force through a sequential bending in a series of joints similar to the use of the *plié* in landing from a jump. In falls, the timing of the sequential bending action is of vital importance. Third, try to land on padded parts of the body rather than on points. Fourth, to assist in these controls, use the weight of the body to pull in opposition to the direction of the fall.

As a special safety note: Do not land on the kneecap. Also, do not take the impact from a fall on a straight, stiff arm, thus forcing the strain into the shoulder. This can dislocate the shoulder.

9.C.2. Exploration of falling: Variations

Art. See Exercise 9.C.1.

Craft. Because different feathers and scarves will fall in varying patterns, several objects may be used to stimulate further explorations in falling. Some will slip from side to side in the descent, and some will turn. Experiment with several, find the different directions, ways of falling, or ending positions. Continue to try for no sound on landing and to protect the joints. Repeat the above variations while increasing the tempo.

Science. See Exercise 9.C.1.

9.C.3. Front fall

Art. See Exercise 9.C.1.

Craft. Precede this fall with a few push-ups, which establish the feeling for bending the elbows as the body is lowered. This exercise will also indicate the arm strength of the students so you can judge whether or not they are ready for the fall.

Stand in first position and let the feet slide apart sideways to a wide stride. At the same time, lean forward, reaching for the floor with both hands. As the hands touch the floor, the elbows should bend (an elbow *plié*), thus cushioning the impact. With a little practice, the fall can be done with no sound on impact. Hold a straight line in the torso from the heels to the top of the head. Avoid bending at the waist; then, after the hands touch the floor, bring the hips down.

Front fall

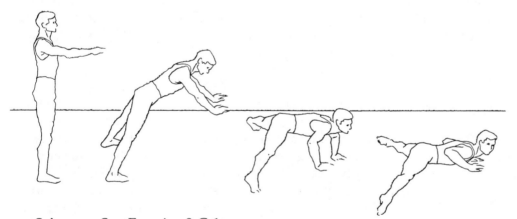

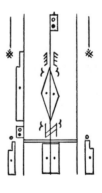

Science. See Exercise 9.C.1.

9.C.4. Front fall: Variation

Art. See Exercise 9.C.1.

Craft. Try the front fall on a diagonal. Keeping the torso straight, slide one leg out on a diagonal with the arm on that side reaching out parallel with the leg.

Science. It is important that the elbows bend and that the arms not be stiff on impact. However, there must be enough resistance and control in the arms to prevent hitting the chin on the floor. The stride should be wide enough so that the body and hands are close to the floor before impact. The back should be kept straight, with no forward bend at the waist or hips during the fall. The diagonal fall is not for beginners.

9.C.5. Back fall

Art.   See Exercise 9.C.1.

Craft.   Stand in parallel position. Start down with a *plié*. As the *plié* increases, let one leg extend forward along the floor. Continue down to sit on the heel of the supporting foot and then sit on the floor, carrying the weight of the torso forward with the shoulders reaching forward to control the descent. After the buttocks touch the floor, roll backward to a complete lying position. This should be a smooth, soundless rolling down on a rounded back.

Back fall

Science.   The sit should be on the underside of the buttocks; it should not be a hard sit on the coccyx (the end of the spine). The forward control of weight for the sit and the rounding of the back when continuing to the floor are important. Do not plop down to the floor on a straight back.

9.C.6. Simple side fall

Art.   See Exercise 9.C.1.

Craft.   This fall is described as a standing position start. However, for beginners, introduce this from a kneeling position first. When correctly performed, this fall is basically a slide into the floor. To fall to the left, stand on the right foot with the left foot off the floor behind the right foot and the left knee bent. Bend the torso to the right, exerting a pull to the right strong enough to counterbalance the fall to the left. *Plié* on the right leg deep enough to bring the left thigh very close to the floor. The kneecap must not touch the floor. The impact is taken on the side of the lower leg and thigh. As the leg touches the floor, extend the thigh from the hip joint so that it will slide to the floor instead of dropping straight down. Continue the pull of the arms and torso to control the rate of fall. Going to the floor should be smooth with no jolt or bump. To finish the fall, bring the left shoulder to the left knee, then slide out on the shoulder until the torso is extended. Either one or both legs may extend.

Simple side fall

Science.   The impact must not be taken on the kneecap but on the side of the leg. After landing, be sure to bring the shoulder to the knee before extending the torso. From the sitting position, guard against dropping straight out to the side to land on the tip of the shoulder. Wearing tights and long-sleeved leotards will help prevent floor burns during slides.

9.C.7. Side tilt fall

Art.   See Exercise 9.C.1.

Craft.   This is a variation of the simple side fall. Start with the torso well aligned in a straight second position. Start with a back-and-forth sideways rock of the torso, keeping the back straight. Shift weight from one foot to the other, lifting the free foot from the floor on each shift. Gradually increase the degree of the tilt. Suspend the last tilt as long as possible, then add the *plié* and shift of weight described in the side fall. These should occur very quickly at the last moment. If the weight shift and *plié* are performed quickly enough, the audience will not be aware of them and will be given the impression of a straight side fall with the back still straight. This effect is increased if the legs and arms extend quickly after reaching the floor.

Side tilt fall

Science.   See Exercise 9.C.1.

9.C.8. Roll fall

Art.   See Exercise 9.C.1.

Craft.   Bend forward and sideways while doing a deep *plié*, thus bringing the whole torso to the floor and landing on the entire side of the back. The impact must be taken on the broad area on the side of the back, not on the tip of the shoulder or on the elbow. Roll over onto the center of the back, keeping the knees bent and well over the torso. Continue the roll to the other side of the back and come up to one knee, pressing through with the hip and reaching out with the top foot. Place the sole of the foot on the floor ready to sustain the weight, and then come to a standing position swinging the torso slightly forward and up to help carry the weight onto the forward foot.

In preparation for landing on the back, the initial *plié* must be deep enough to be very close to the floor. For an easy recovery to a standing position, take the roll quickly, using the velocity of the roll as the energy source for the rise.

This fall can be taken from a kneeling position first if students need more preparation.

Roll fall

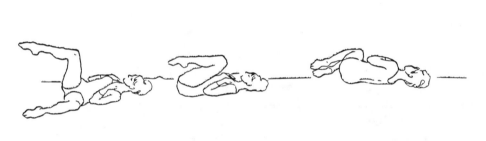

Science.   See Exercise 9.C.1.

9.C.9. Circular fall

Art.   See Exercise 9.C.1.

Craft.   This fall is for advanced students, as it is a complicated fall with many parts. Stand in a narrow second position. Leave the feet where they are and turn halfway around to the right; this will cause the legs to cross. Keeping the legs crossed, sit on the left buttock, contracting in the torso and keeping the shoulders over the knees.

Continue turning to the right and bring both legs parallel with the soles of the feet on the floor. Place the side of the right leg on the floor, continuing the turn. Bring the right shoulder to the right knee and then to the floor, and slide the shoulder out on the floor to lead into the next part of the fall.

Turn onto the back as the torso straightens. Continue into a side curve in the torso, bringing the arms overhead and slightly toward the feet. Keep the knees bent. There should be one continuous curve from the toes through the torso to the hands. All of these positions and movements should blend so smoothly that the audience does not see the separate parts. The impression should be of a continuous, descending spiral. Reverse the whole procedure to rise and finish in the starting position.

Circular fall

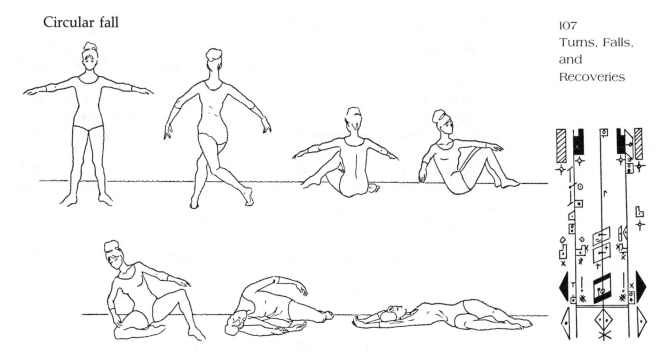

Science. See Exercise 9.C.1.

9.C.10. Front slide fall

Art. See Exercise 9.C.1.

Craft. This is not for beginners. The front slide fall should be executed from a run, but the fall must be learned and thoroughly practiced before the run is added. *Plié* and bend forward, reaching for the floor as far forward as possible. Keeping the abdomen very taut and the back well arched, bring the hands and diaphragm to the floor. At the same time pull back with the hands, causing the torso to slide forward on the floor. By correctly timing the pull with the hands, it is possible to slide some distance.

Front slide fall

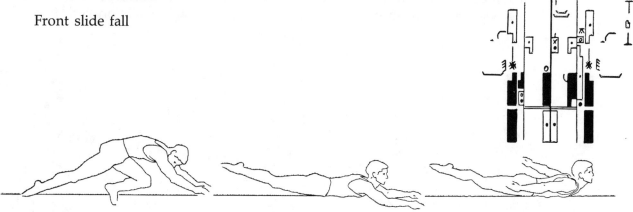

Science. Take care to be very close to the floor before dropping. Too precipitous a drop will cause a serious jolt and will stop the slide. Keep the back well arched so that the landing will be up on the torso. This will prevent bruising of the hip bones.

9.C.11. Falls: Variations

Art. See Exercise 9.C.1.

Craft. The following are variations of falls:

1. Vary the tempo. As proficiency and control develop, increase speed. Also, decrease speed to perform falls in slow motion, but keep all components in the same relationship or proportion.
2. Vary the accent and make various parts the important point or climax. The accent may be placed in the starting movements, the middle portion of the fall, or the ending movements. Or make the recovery the emphasis, using the fall as an upbeat into the recovery.
3. Execute the fall as a statement of affirmation or as a challenge, as though stamping the foot. Or use a fall as a giving up, a collapse into death, or a change of mood.
4. Develop a series of different falls. Recovery movements should lead into the next fall.
5. Add other elements such as a jump, leap, hop, or run, either before or after a fall.

Science. See Exercise 9.C.10.

9.D. Recoveries from Falls

Recoveries should be practiced along with falls. It is worth noting that the rise to one knee and the step onto the other foot as described in the roll fall (Exercise 9.C.9.) can be used for recovery from other falls.

9.D.1. Front prone position

Art. The feeling and effect of recoveries from falls should be consistent with the style or purpose of the fall and with its purpose in the total composition.

Craft. From a front prone position, roll to the back and come to a sitting position with one leg bent in front and one leg bent behind. The front foot should be in a walking position and ready to sustain weight. Lift up in the center of the torso and the lower back while pressing down with the thighs and feet. Come to a standing position in fourth position with weight distributed equally on both feet.

Front prone position

Science. Watch the alignment of the knees during rises on recoveries from falls. Be efficient in the use of your weight to assist in rising.

9.D.2. Back prone position

Art. See Exercise 9.D.1.

Back prone position

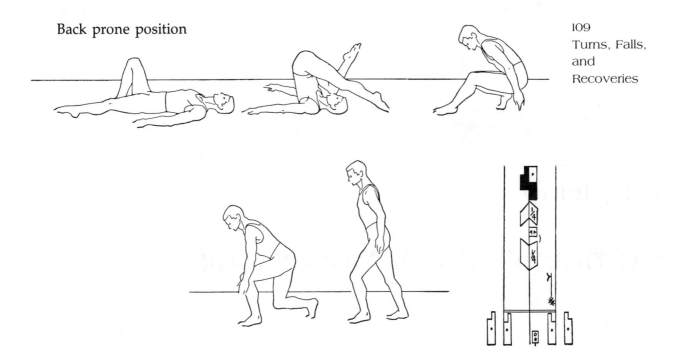

Craft. From the back prone position, bend one knee, bringing the foot on the floor as close to the hip as possible. Swing the torso up fast enough to bring weight onto the heel of the foot, reach forward with the other foot, and step forward onto it. To get a stronger impulse for the rise, swing one foot over the torso and swing the torso up as the leg lowers.

Science. See Exercise 9.D.1.

9.D.3. Sitting position

Art. See Exercise 9.D.1.

Craft. From a sitting position, bend one leg in front and place the other foot across this leg, with the foot as close to the hip as possible. Keeping the torso very straight and forward over the legs, lift up in the torso and press down with the thighs and feet as one might press on the floor with the hand to assist in standing.

Sitting position

Science. In the recovery from a sitting position, it is important that the top foot cross the other thigh with the foot close to the hip. If the foot is close to the knee or in front of the knee, it will be impossible to shift the weight onto the foot to rise. When the foot is across the thigh and close to the hip, the rise can be either straight up or with a half-turn, as described in the circular fall (Exercise 9.C.9.).

Chapter 10

Combinations Of Movements

The exercises in chapters 3 through 9 are important for tuning the dancer's instrument. However, the realm of dance lies in transitional movements: what happens between positions; in the combining of the myriad types of movements; in traveling through space; in a subtlety of timing in dynamics; and in the flow from one movement to another.

Movement combinations can be taught and performed merely as physical exercises. With such an approach, there will be some sense of accomplishment and enjoyment in improved coordination. However, for an expanded dance experience and a heightened awareness, other factors must be included. It is important to recognize such natural phenomena as gravity, the laws of inertia and momentum, and centrifugal and centripetal forces. The awareness and use of these forces should become a part of all movement. This added awareness may take the form of overcoming or denying these forces, or may be used to assist and expand the movement. If these phenomena are incorporated into a movement, the dancer will need to explore for the particular timing, flow, placement of accents, and for a sequence of movements that will permit the forces to become an integral part of the action. This exploration will have the added value of increasing the dancer's movement vocabulary.

The dance course should not be planned so that students learn all the separate tools first and then start on combinations of movement. All experienced teachers, however, develop their own particular progression in teaching combinations. Some feel that it is more logical to develop many combinations based on one particular step, such as a walk or slide, before progressing to another step. Or you might start with an axial movement, such as folding and unfolding or swings, and let this lead into traveling across the floor and into an introduction to other combinations. An effective way to start is with simple locomotor combinations, introducing several different types of locomotion without concentrating on just one type of step. Variation and enlarged vocabulary seem more important for beginners than discovering all the potentials of one area. You can delve more deeply into each type of movement in succeeding courses.

For all locomotor combinations involving traveling through space, a feeling for the air must be stressed. Students should develop an appetite for the air. In leaps, hops, and jumps, they should try to deny or overcome gravity and inertia. They should try for a sense of coming back to earth because they *choose* to, not because they *have* to. All this goes beyond counts or a basic beat. Students will need to discover in their own instruments the subtlety of timing, directed use of energy, and the particular flow in coordination of torso, arms, and legs that is necessary for sustaining the movement from takeoff to landing. The teacher can help by providing a carefully planned progression, offering individual suggestions, and by allowing time for individual experimentation.

For all of the easier locomotor combinations, start with a moderately fast tempo. Many inexperienced teachers feel that they must go very slowly with beginners. Combinations of walks, runs, leaps, and hops taken at a slow tempo can be deadly dull. At too slow a tempo, beginners may have problems with balance. Also, beginners will not be able to sustain movement and might develop the habit of stopping between movements, a difficult habit to overcome later. Take the combinations at as fast a tempo as the class can manage while maintaining some sense of alignment and style.

Although students do not need a slow, detailed analysis of how to walk, run, leap, jump, slide, and skip, they may need a quick review for identification or recall. Later, after the initial introduction, beginners will need much practice maintaining alignment of torso, legs, and arms while performing these steps.

It is doubly important to stress correct alignment of back, knees, and ankles when combining movements, particularly those using turns and going into the air. The movement combinations will demonstrate how well the students have mastered control of the basic techniques you have included in your course.

The rest of this chapter contains a number of movement combinations for the locomotor techniques and axial movements listed earlier. It is hoped that this will serve as a guide and a start to help the beginning teacher and dance student develop their own movement combinations.

The movement combinations have been divided into two categories: locomotor combinations; and combinations with other movement areas such as axial movements, use of energy, and change of level. In actual teaching, these combinations should not be so rigidly separated; both types should be intermixed in practically every lesson.

Teach some movement combinations as technical exercises, but for other movements try to allow time for students to explore and work out their own combinations.

Locomotor Combinations

The following locomotor combinations are listed in approximate order of difficulty.

Walk And Run

The combination exercises in this section involve basic walking and running.

Forward and backward walk and run

Using a moderately fast walk, take four steps forward and two slow steps backward. The number of steps is not important, but four to eight will probably be easiest for most beginners, especially for the first class. This should not be repeated more than two times as it is not very interesting, but it introduces adjusting to changing direction and tempo.

Walk and run variations.

1. (a) Walk forward, then turn to face the opposite direction for the backward walk, progressing in the same direction as the forward walk.
   (b) Combine a forward walk with a sideways direction instead of a backward direction.
   (c) Combine the forward walk with a diagonal direction.
   (d) Use diagonals, making a zigzag floor pattern.
2. Vary the number of steps taken.
   (a) Change the number of steps to three, five, six, etc.
   (b) Use a different number of steps for the forward walk and for the other directions, such as three forward and five backward.
   (c) Use an accumulative pattern by adding one more step for each change in direction: two forward, three backward, four sideways, and so on.
3. Vary the tempo.
   (a) Start with a moderately fast tempo.
   (b) Go twice as fast or run.
   (c) Go half-time to the original tempo.
   (d) Vary the tempo within the combination while changing directions.

Skips

One step and a hop is a skip, although there are many variations that will not feel like the traditional skip. Beginners will need to start with a step-hop to get the feeling of taking off and landing on the same foot. Most will have no difficulty. Once across the floor should be sufficient; you might even add the element of increasing the tempo as they proceed. The following combinations involve varying the rhythm:

1. Start with an even rhythm, allowing the same amount of time for both the step and the hop. Be sure to take this as fast as the students can manage, and continue to another combination.
2. Use an uneven rhythm. Take the hop immediately after the step so that the two actions become inseparable. Allow more time for the step and hop into the air. Use a short beat for the landing, moving quickly to the next step-hop.
3. Vary the position of the free leg in the hop.
   (a) Hold the free leg in front with the knee bent.
   (b) Hold the free leg in front with the knee straight, the ankle extended, and the toe well pointed.
   (c) Lift the free leg to the back. Try this both with the knee bent and with the knee straight.
   (d) Lift the free leg to the side.
   (e) Perform a combination in which the free leg position is changed on each step-hop, for example: forward, side, back; or forward, back, side. This will be more confusing than physically difficult. It requires concentration.
   (f) Step-hop, lifting the free leg behind; without taking another step, hop again on the same leg, swinging the free leg forward; repeat on the other foot.
4. Vary the dynamics.
   (a) Make the hop very big, trying for height, distance, or both.
   (b) Make the step-hop extremely fast and small.

5. Vary the number of steps between hops. When you use three steps and a hop on an even rhythm, remind the class that this is a schottishe step.
6. Vary the direction of facing and traveling. Travel sideways lifting the free leg to the side. Uneven numbers of steps will alternate sides. Even numbers of steps will use the same side each time. Develop a sequence using several changes in directions.
   (a) All of the listed combinations for skips should be performed moving backward as well as forward.
   (b) Most of the listed combinations for skips should move sideways. Keep hips facing directly forward. This will require a controlled turnout of the legs and a step across for some of the steps. This is a somewhat tricky combination for many students, and they may need some practice before they feel secure.
7. Combinations of hops, turns, and leaps are listed with these activities in Chapters 3–9.

Leaps

Start with developing an ease in the leap before adding increased dimension or technical aspects of style. A few beginners may be afraid of going into the air, but this seldom lasts. Most students thoroughly enjoy the leaping section of the class period. Some men may be carried away and try for greater height or distance than they can control. Be sure that students use both legs equally for both the takeoff and landing. Watch for those who always use only one leg. From the beginning, emphasize back, knee, ankle, and arm alignment and the use of the *plié* in landing and takeoff. The height and distance of the leap should always depend on the individual's ability to control both its takeoff and landing. .

The following combinations involve varying elements in the leap and combining the leap with other steps.

Vary the number of steps between leaps. It is not advisable to go beyond four steps and a leap. Class time is needed for other areas.

Vary the range and dynamics. As quickly as possible, get the class to extend themselves in leaping, trying for both height and distance. Stress trying to hold the leap in the air to develop a sense of sailing or soaring through space.

Vary the rhythm. It may be necessary to start beginners on an even rhythm, with both the step and the leap taking the same amount of time. However, as an even rhythm is apt to produce a heavy landing and stilted leap, do not stay with this. Quickly progress to using an uneven rhythm. Use the step for the takeoff as part of the leap. A quick beat is used for the landing. If you are using a drum, do not give a separate beat for the step into the takeoff, the actual leap, and the landing steps. Count the step into the leap and the leap as one.

Vary the leg positions in the air.

1. Bend both knees while in the air.
2. Keep the front leg straight but bend the back knee.
3. Bend the front knee and keep the back leg straight.
4. Keep both knees straight.
5. Start with both knees straight, but after going into the air, bend the front knee. This is sometimes called a "stag leap." This variation should not be used with beginners. Without proper control, it can strain the lower back.

6. Horizontal leap: Holding the torso and one leg extended parallel to the floor, with the standing leg in *plié*, and the arms extended sideways, leap, changing legs without raising the torso. The legs scissor by each other in the air. This will not travel as will conventional leaps. At first, it will take some courage to lift the standing leg before the lifted leg comes to the floor. Guard against lifting or tightening in the shoulders, arms, or neck. At first, the students may need to be reminded to *plié* when landing.

Horizontal leap

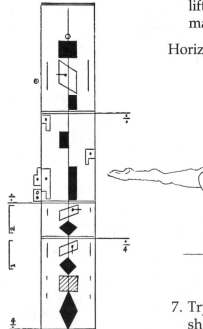

7. Try these variations in groups of two or three, with hands on each other's shoulders. The trick here is to hold oneself up and not press down on a neighbor's shoulders.

Vary the direction of facing.

1. Perform the steps and leaps sideways instead of forward. Do not push for height or distance on the side leap until a reasonable control of the turnout can be maintained. Be sure to maintain the turnout on the step across. If the toe leads on the step across, the student will soon be leaping forward instead of sideways. Also, the step across should be small.
2. Use a zigzag floor pattern.
3. Use a varied combination of steps and leaps in a circular formation.

Combine leaps with hops.

1. Try for distance on the leap and height on the hop.
2. Perform the leap forward and the hop backward or sideways.
3. Combine one step and hop with one step and a leap. This is not technically difficult, but it is tricky for beginners, and they will need a little practice adjusting to the coordination. Actually, this is a syncopated rhythm, but the syncopation is internal, in the transition between movements, not in the sound of the beat. Some students have said that it feels like a hiccup.
4. Leaps can be combined with other steps such as triplets, slides, and turns. These will be listed in the following exercises.

Jumps

Before combining jumps with other steps, review the basic controls for jumps as presented in Chapter 7. Instead of performing one step and a jump, it will be easier for most beginners to take three steps, close (taking weight on both feet), and then perform two or four jumps. This uses a takeoff from both feet for the jumps. Using four steps without the close will use a one-foot takeoff for the first jump. The following are variations and combinations using the jump:

1. Vary the number of steps and jumps.
2. Vary the direction of the steps and the jumps.
   (a) Use the four steps forward but have the two, three, or four jumps go forward, sideways, and backward.
   (b) Use two steps forward (or backward) with two jumps, one forward and one backward. On repetition, the first jump can be backward and the second forward or sideways.
   (c) Jump sideways. This can use one step crossing in front for the takeoff. It can be performed as a continuous progression across the floor, always stepping across with the same foot or as a side-to-side movement alternating feet. Because the landing is on both feet, the weight can be shifted to either foot for the next movement.
3. Vary the range and dynamics.
   (a) Try for height and distance.
   (b) Experiment with very fast and very slow jumps with various numbers of steps.
4. Combine jumps with runs, hops, and leaps.

Slides and gallops

These were introduced in Chapter 1. A short review may be needed when using them in combination with other steps. The following exercises are variations involving the slide and gallop:

1. The main variations presented under jumps may also be used with slides and gallops. For example: Vary number, direction, range and dynamics, tempo, and floor pattern.
2. Combine slides with half-turns.
   (a) Perform two slides and a half-turn. The direction will remain the same, but first one side leads, then the other.
   (b) Perform two gallops and a half-turn. The first two will be forward, and after the turn the next two will be backward. It will be easier to hop on the turn. This combination becomes a polka step.
   (c) Later add a full turn. Perform two slides and a half-turn; repeat; then perform two slides and a full turn. Try this with gallops as well as slides. On the slides, the movement is sideways and will keep the same line of direction. When a gallop is used, the dancer will start facing the line of direction, and after the half-turn, the dancer will be facing the opposite direction. To maintain the same line of direction, the next gallop will need to be taken backward. If the second gallop is again taken forward, it will travel in the opposite direction. This produces a back-and-fourth pattern, and the dancer stays in the same place.
3. Combine slides and gallops.
   (a) Perform two gallops forward and two slides to the side.
   (b) Perform three gallops forward and two slides to the side. Repeat three times; then perform just the three gallops and a step, followed with a jump to both feet and a hold. Repeat, starting with the other foot.
4. Other combinations of slides and gallops with jumps, hops, and leaps can be found later in this chapter under ''More Specific Movement Combinations.''

Triplets

The triplet, or *waltz run* (see Chapter 1), has become one of the most basic steps used in modern dance. There may even be a tendency to overuse it. It is important to stress the even quality of this step—even both in time and in the distance covered by each step. The basic beat is an even three counts. Count one is accented with a slight *plié*, while counts two and three are taken on half-toe. Most beginners tend to take a big step on the *plié* and small steps on the half-toe; they will need practice taking reaching steps on half-toe. This requires lifting up in the thighs and torso. They should feel that their legs are very long and should move the leg from the hip joint, not just from the knee. There should be a lift in the whole torso, not just the shoulders, when rising to half-toe. If the lift is maintained in the torso and legs when this step is taken quickly as a run, the feet will barely touch the floor on counts two and three. This should be practiced alone before it is combined with other steps. The following exercises are variations on the triplet:

1. Vary the tempo.
    (a) First practice triplets at a moderately fast tempo.
    (b) Perform the triplet fast, like a run. Later try for an extremely fast tempo.
    (c) Go slowly, emphasizing the down-and-up and sustaining the movement through the counts.
2. Vary the accent. Perform three triplets. On the first triplet, accent count one; on the second, accent count two; on the third, accent count three. Keep repeating the combination. The tricky part is in starting the repeat, which entails accenting count three and immediately accenting count one.
3. Combine the triplet with a step-hop.
    (a) Perform two triplets followed by two step-hops with the free leg lifted straight behind.
    (b) Perform two triplets with two step-hops. On the step-hops, lift the free leg forward on the first and backward on the second.
    (c) Perform two (or three) triplets forward, then one step and two hops sideways; repeat the step-hop-hop to the other side.
    (d) Perform two (or three) triplets forward, but take the step-hops to the side, first to one side then to the other.
    (e) Repeat, but turn to face the side of the room and perform the step-hop-hop in an arabesque position instead of sideways. Try to hold the lifted leg in place so it does not bob up and down.
4. Combine the triplet with a step-leap.
    (a) Perform two triplets followed by two step-leaps.
    (b) Perform three triplets and one step-leap.
    (c) Perform the two triplets forward but take the step-leaps sideways. Vary the leg positions on the leaps.
    (d) Perform one triplet and one step-leap; repeat, then add three triplets and one more step-leap.
5. Combine triplets with other steps.
    (a) Perform two triplets, a step-hop, and step-leap. This will alternate sides.
    (b) For a slightly longer combination, perform two triplets forward and two three-step turns (one to each side). Vary the number of each instead of performing two of everything.
6. Other combinations with triplets can be found later in this chapter under ''More Specific Movement Combinations.''

Three-step turn

The three-step turn was described under turns in Chapter 9. Before incorporating this into combinations, it may be advisable to review this turn, emphasizing alignment, turning in one piece, and maintaining eye focus (spotting).

Combine three-step turns with step-hops.

1. Complete two step-hops forward and two three-step turns (one to each side). At first, pause before repeating the three-step turn to the other side.
2. Perform variation 1 without the hold between the turns.
3. Perform variation 2, but add a hop at the end of each turn. Try various rhythm patterns.
4. Perform variation 3, but, instead of doing the three-step turn to the side, complete the turns progressing forward in the line of direction.
5. Perform one three-step turn sideways and two step-hops sideways (one to each side). Complete this traveling across the floor lifting the free leg to the side with knees straight.

The preceding combinations can be performed with step-leaps instead of hops.

Locomotor steps combined with other areas

These combinations are offered to suggest possibilities for combining movements to the beginning teacher and to the student for practice outside of class. For their own development, teachers and students must constantly experiment in making their own combinations. The emphasis in this section is on the locomotor patterns, but you should experiment with various torso and arm movements with these sequences.

Many of the following combinations are not for beginning students:

1. Perform an easy, light run, picking the feet up behind, arms extended to sides but below shoulder level, with no tension in the arms or neck.
2. Perform a moderately slow walk backward, using a long reach for distance. *Plié* on the standing leg to permit a longer reach. Experiment with your arms to find a position that helps in performing the exercise.
3. Perform a fast sideways run. Keep this completely sideways without turning to face the direction of traveling. This run may be taken with the trailing foot crossing in front or crossing in back; or it may be taken like a grapevine step, alternating the front and back crossing. For the grapevine variation, the steps taken may be very small with no turning of the hips, or they may incorporate as much turning of the hips as can be controlled. It may be taken on a very even beat or on an uneven rhythm.
4. Take two slow steps forward, then four steps forward twice as fast. Prances or jumps may be used instead of the fast steps. Or this may be performed with a turn in place on the four fast steps, prances, or jumps. All of these may be combined in one combination.
5. Take four moderately fast walking steps forward; make a half-turn and take four steps backward and another half-turn to walk forward again. Keep this smooth and even.
6. Take five walking steps forward, make a half-turn, then take three steps backward. (Vary the number of steps.)
7. Step-hop, lifting the free leg behind with the knee straight.

8. Take two steps forward and then four steps in a small circle, keeping in the line of the starting direction. Step sideways, step backward, cross over in front, step forward. Vary the direction of the four steps along with the tempo and torso and arm involvement.

9. Traveling forward: step-hop-hop-hop; step-hop; step-hop. The step and three hops can be taken sideways with the single step-hops forward. Or one step-hop can be forward and the other backward. There are many possible variations with this.

10. Take two steps and a hop. The hop can be taken either for height or for distance; the free leg may be held straight or bent and to the front, the back, or the side.

11. Take two steps and a hop. On an even rhythm this is a schottische step. Many variations of this combination are possible. The free leg may be in front, at the side, or in back; it may be held straight or bent. This combination can be taken traveling forward, sideways, or backward.

12. Traveling forward, step-leap; go for distance or for height.

13. Try two steps and a leap; three steps and a leap.

14. Moving sideways, take two steps and a hop. There are two variations of this.
    (a) Start by stepping out in the direction of traveling. The free leg will lift in the direction of traveling.
    (b) Start by stepping across in front with the trailing foot. The free leg will then lift away from the direction of traveling.

15. Take three steps and a hop traveling sideways. This will alternate the lifting leg. It is like a combination of (a) and (b) in the preceding combination exercise. This can also be performed with a half-turn on the hop.

16. Perform two triplets and two slow walks. Keep them as smooth as possible, as if you were gliding over the floor.

17. Perform two triplets and two step-leaps.

18. Perform one step and two hops with a leg swing. On the first hop, swing the free leg behind. On the second hop, swing the same free leg forward. The hops will be on the same foot with the same leg swinging back and front. However, on repetition, the beginning step will alternate sides. Travel as much as possible during this.

19. Perform slides and gallops for height, touching the trailing leg to the other leg while in the air. Keep the legs straight.

20. Perform two slides and a half-turn. This can also be performed holding hands with a partner. Partners will alternate face to face and back to back.

21. Take two slides and a half-turn, two slides and a half-turn, two slides and a full turn. Keep traveling in the same direction.

22. Step-leap, traveling sideways. Start by stepping across in front with the foot away from the line of direction. Bend the leading knee and feel that this knee is pulling into the leap. The back leg should be straight.
    (a) If this is performed for distance rather than height, it is possible to develop great speed and power. There must be an immediacy to the lift and reach of the leading knee coordinated with the push of the takeoff of the other foot.
    (b) At a slower tempo, try for height instead of distance.

23. Take four step-leaps, with the first two traveling sideways and the last two traveling forward. There must be clear changes of facing while maintaining line of direction.

24. Alternate a step-hop and a step-leap. Try for height on the hop and distance on the leap.

25. Take two slides traveling sideways, then two step-leaps traveling forward.
26. Perform three triplets, then one step-leap. Do not count the landing from the leap as the first step of the next triplet.
27. Perform two triplets forward, then a step-hop-hop to one side and a step-hop-hop to the other side. There should be no hold between the two step-hop-hops.
28. Take one or two triplets forward, then two three-step turns, alternating sides. The turns may be taken sideways or forward in the line of direction; or the sideways and forward turns may alternate.
29. Increase the tempo of the preceding combination exercise.
30. Take two polka steps forward, then four step-hops turning in place. Set positions of arms, legs, and style of the movement; or have students set their own style.
31. Traveling in a large circle, perform each of the following four times: two steps and a leap; three steps and a leap; four steps and a leap; then end with eight straight leaps.
32. Perform front scissors, traveling forward with one step into each scissors.
33. Perform back scissors with one step into each scissors. Try this first traveling forward, then try traveling backward.
34. Take two triplets forward, then a side jump. Step across in front for the takeoff into the jump. Either keep going with no hold at the end of the jump, or add extra counts to rise to half-toe after landing and suspend before repeating.
35. Step-hop (with the free leg back), step-leap, step-back scissors, step-leap. There is only one step between each of these.
36. Perform one triplet, then step-leap, step-hop, step-hop. On the step-hops, the free leg can be either front or back, or front and back can be alternated on the two step-hops. Also, the direction of the step-hops can be varied.
37. Take four step-hops with the free leg lifted in front and the knee bent. Perform the first three step-hops traveling forward. On the fourth, take a full turn holding the hop position. Perform the hops for height and good alignment in the air. Try the turn both toward and away from the lifted leg.
38. Try a movement theme and variation while holding a rhythmic pattern of two counts of three and three counts of two (one, two, three; one, two, three; one, two; one, two; one, two).

   (a) Take two triplets forward (the two counts of three) turning to face the side, step into a perch on half-toe, lifting the free leg behind (count one), come down taking the weight on the free foot (count two), repeat this to the back and to the other side (the other two counts of two).
   (b) For a second variation, perform the triplets in place, starting by stepping across in front (count one) and then taking two steps in place (counts two and three). Repeat, starting with the other foot across. For the two-count phrases, turn in place by stepping on half-toe behind the supporting foot. Pivot toward the lifting leg. Do one full turn in place with the three counts of two.
   (c) For a third variation, perform two triplets traveling forward (on the two counts of three). For the two-count phrases, take a big step across in front with a *plié*, permitting the torso to turn with the step; take a small step with the back foot by the side of the front foot; at the same time, straighten the torso to face front so it can again turn with the next step across. This will have a twisting action. Do three of these.

39. Combine the leap with the torso parallel to the floor (see the illustration on page 114), with a straight perpendicular jump on both feet. Start with a straight jump, for height, tilt the torso while in the air to land on one leg with the other leg lifted behind in a straight line with the torso. The torso and lifted leg should be parallel to the floor. Do one, two, or three leaps in this position (these do not travel like conventional leaps); then, while in the air, straighten the torso to repeat the straight jump to start over. This is not for beginners.

40. Stand on one leg in a small *plié* holding the free foot at the ankle of the standing leg with the toe pointed and the knee well turned out. The arm positions can be varied. Hop into the air, straightening both legs and holding them tight together while in the air. Return the free foot to the ankle before landing as in the starting position.
    (a) Try this with the free foot in front; then in back.
    (b) Start with the foot in front but end with it in back and vice versa.

41. Combine the preceding combination with triplets and leaps. Here is one combination: Do one triplet, a step-leap, and two hops, holding two counts in the air.

42. Facing front, jump off of both feet, making a quarter-turn to the right in the air to face side; land on one leg in *plié*, with the other leg lifted behind and its knee bent. Hop off the one foot taking a quarter-turn to the left in the air to face the front; land on both feet. The landing *plié* is also the take-off *plié*. At first, perform several of these combinations to one side; rest and repeat on the other side. Later, alternate sides.

43. From a slow, smooth, straight-leg walk, step into a controlled back extension with both legs straight and the torso tilting forward so the torso and extended leg are approximately parallel to the floor. Holding the extension, rise to half-toe. Keep a strong lift on the supporting leg and, still on half-toe, perform a quarter-rotation of the torso carrying the lifted leg into a side extension as high as possible. Swing the leg into a forward extension as the torso faces the original line of direction. Repeat the walk.

Axial and Other Movement Combinations

The combinations presented in this section are much less tangible than loco-motor movements and cannot be arranged in a neat list of exercises ranging from easy to difficult. There is much greater diversity among schools and teachers as to just where to start the movements, what progression is best, and what methods of teaching are most productive. And there is almost as great a variance in terminology. The order in which these movements are presented is not vitally important. However, no matter how short the course, it is important for students to be introduced to all the kinds of movement listed in this section. Whatever the order of the exercises, some work and practice on alignment should be involved. As a general guide, the areas should be intermixed, for example: explorations, directed technical study, combination with other areas, and compositional studies. Just how these are used and how much of each is incorporated in a particular course will depend on the length of the course and on the particular needs of each class. No two classes are ever alike.

In the first part of this chapter, the emphasis is on acquiring a feeling for the use of space. Awareness and use of space seems to be one of the primary contributions of American dance. Through all the following movements, maintain a sense of using space. Think of carving space or of displacing air in much the same way as a swimmer moves water. Feel the air as you move it in space. Feel air as a supporting force.

Axial movements are introduced in Chapter 4. Allow time for individual, partner, and group explorations to discover controls for balance. To extend these explorations, offer the following suggestions:

1. Find an easy balance while standing on both feet. Be efficient, holding no unnecessary tension in any part of the body.
2. Maintain this ease while rising slowly to half-toe and then returning slowly to the whole foot. (Avoid using the term "flat foot.") On the rise, deny gravity in the legs, but pull up against it in the torso. Sense energy going in two directions: into the floor through the balls of the feet and up to the ceiling through the top of the head.
3. When lowering, permit gravity to pull the torso down into a collapse.
4. Use different arm positions with these variations.
5. On one foot, move the free leg around in various directions and positions. Be aware of necessary changes in relationships to other body parts.
6. Try all this on half-toe.
7. On the whole foot and one leg, try moving the torso with bends and twists in various parts of the body.
8. Try some of the preceding variations with a fast rise to half-toe instead of a slow rise.
9. With all of the preceding variations, try changing the focus of the eyes and head.
10. Try moving into and out of these balances with various locomotor steps.

Circular movements

Review or introduce the basics of alignment (Chapter 4). Allow time for individual, partner, and group explorations to acquire a feeling for centripetal (center-seeking) and centrifugal (center-fleeing) forces. The following suggestions may help with these explorations:

1. Stand in a good alignment, without moving the feet.
2. Make a continuous circular movement from this position. Be sure to try both directions.
3. Vary the tempo of this circular sway: medium; slow; fast; very fast.
4. Keep the sway going, but increase the size of the circle so that steps are necessary. (Be sure the torso movements make the steps necessary. Do not start with stepping.) Keep facing the same direction and increase the size of the steps or the number of steps needed.
5. Keep the sway going but direct the steps and range to make a spiral pattern on the floor. Spiral out and spiral in.
6. Move in a small circle facing the line of direction. Maintain awareness of the center point of the circle.
7. Repeat this circle with variations of size and speed, permitting the torso to tilt in slightly with the centripetal pull.
8. Try tilting out against the centripetal pull.
9. Move in a small circle but move backward in the line of direction.
10. Move in a small circle but alternate moving forward, backward, and sideways (face in and out from the center of circle) while maintaining the size of the circle.
11. Explore rolls on the floor in various positions: torso straight, extended; doubled up; moving in one piece; with one part leading.

12. Explore forward and back rolls. (Mats should be used for these.)
13. Try many of these variations with a partner or in groups of three or four. The play of centripetal and centrifugal force will change according to the number of dancers involved, their positions, and the size of the circle.
14. Try some of these variations with various locomotor steps.
15. Use these circular explorations as a lead into turns.

Flexion, extension, and rotation of joint areas

Review or introduce material discussed in chapters 5 and 6 on flexibility with control, flexion, extension, and rotation. The following suggestions may aid in individual, partner, and small-group explorations:

1. Examine each joint area to discover all movement possibilities. Some do not rotate (for example, the knee and the elbow). Experiment with each joint area separately. Do not forget fingers, toes, jaw, eyes, tongue, even ears (if possible).
2. Experiment for sequential action from one joint to another. Try for a feeling of movement flowing from one area to another.
3. Find the axis around which various parts rotate.
4. Examine the different feeling when two or more joints alternate or combine in a movement.
5. Combine these separately or put them together with balance, circular movements, and various locomotor steps.
6. Use these explorations as a lead into falls.

Shape, dimension, energy, accent

Review or introduce basics listed in Chapter 1. Allow time for individual, partner, and small group explorations of shapes. The following suggestions may aid in these explorations:

1. Try making yourself into two-dimensional shapes: square; circle; triangle; etc.
2. Work with the concept of three-dimensional shapes: orb; cube; cone; and so on.
3. Work with the concept of molding space into the shapes mentioned.
4. Mold space using mixed floor and space shapes and paths.

Experiment with dimension and size of shapes and use of space:

1. Use the whole body; use only one or two parts.
2. Work in terms of very small and slow; small and fast; large and slow; large and fast; etc.
3. Work in terms of amount of energy used or needed for each type of movement. Discover how accents are used to assist in the movements. Repeat some of the patterns or shapes, consciously using accents to help execute the various movements or to make the movements more interesting.

Direct the use of energy and accent to produce the following quality of movement both as total movement and as movement in separate body parts:

swinging	suspended
sustained	vibratory
percussive	combinations of all or some of these
collapsing	

Localized leads

Review or introduce flexion, extension, rotation; and shape, dimension, energy, and accent. Allow time for individual and partner explorations to discover how one part of the body can lead the movement with the rest following. In all of these explorations, be sure to use all directions: forward; backward; sideways; diagonal; up and down. Combine them with variations in the use of energy, accent, dimension, and shape and with various locomotor steps:

1. Experiment with each of the extremities (legs, arms, head), starting a movement that pulls the rest of the body into following.
2. Try the preceding with different areas of the torso: chest; midsection; lower torso.
3. Experiment with shoulders and hips separately and combined.

Levels and planes

Review or introduce basics of falls, recoveries, and leg lifts discussed in Chapters 8 and 9. Lifts, discussed at the end of Chapter 11, can be included for more advanced classes. Allow time for individual and partner explorations with different ways to go to the floor and recover to a standing position. Through all of the following explorations, it is important to be well aware of alignment and safety factors:

1. Try to find completely new ways of going down and up: use forward, backward, and sideways actions; vary torso, arm, and leg positions and shapes; go part way down; go all the way to the floor and up.
2. With a partner, experiment with unusual, different, and interesting lifts.
3. Try with different body parts leading.
4. Extend the falls and lifts by adding leaps, jumps, and hops.
5. Repeat some of these explorations, concentrating on the use of a specific plane: horizontal; perpendicular; and slanted.
6. Repeat some of the preceding exercises, adding various locomotor steps.
7. Repeat some of the preceding variations, combining them with ideas discussed in the sections on shape, dimension, energy, and accent.

Rhythmic patterns

Review or introduce basic music information (Chapter 2). Allow time for individual and partner experimentation with keeping a basic, even beat based on $\frac{4}{4}$, $\frac{3}{4}$, and $\frac{6}{8}$ musical signatures or meter.

1. Start walking, following a drumbeat or music. Continue the walk, holding the beat after the drum or music stops. Make a strong accent on the first beat of each measure. Guard against speeding up or slowing down after the drum or music stops.
2. Individually, practice developing a rhythmic pattern based on one of the musical signatures given.
3. Repeat these explorations using other musical signatures. Experiment with syncopation.

More specific movement combinations

The following movement combinations involve balance. Review the exercises in Chapter 4 on this subject:

1. Stand on both feet with the torso in alignment and the feet in parallel position. Slowly rise to high half-toe. Use four counts to rise and four to lower the heels. Keep the arms down but slightly open to the sides with a feeling of air between the arms and the body. Keep the up and down movement very smooth, sustained, and continuous, maintaining good ankle alignment. Without stopping, make a transition to repeat in other positions.

2. Repeat on one foot with the free leg extended just off the floor and the toe pointed. Try this with the free leg in front, to the side, and to the back. There must be equal energy going out through both legs. It is easy to feel that only the standing leg is important, but equal energy going through the free leg is just as important for balance. For an added variation, straighten or flex the knee of the free leg in varying degrees.

3. Repeat, holding the free leg at other levels: medium; high; and very high.

4. Repeat this exploration, lifting the free leg at the same tempo as the rise to half-toe. Have both arrive at the highest point at the same time. This requires a fine localized control between various parts of the body so that the lifting leg does not pull the body out of alignment and off balance. Lowering of the leg should be timed with the coming down from half-toe.

5. Instead of the rise to half-toe on the standing leg, step forward into a perch on half-toe with the free leg extended behind. Also, try this with a step to the side and with a step to the back. Use a brush, with the leg taking the weight. Students will need to experiment to discover just how much energy is needed to arrive at the point of balance on a high half-toe with no extraneous movement.

6. Repeat, but vary the position of the free leg. When stepping forward, brush the free leg forward with the knee either bent or straight. When stepping sideways, brush the free leg across in front with the knee bent. When stepping backward, brush the free leg back with the knee either bent or straight. Vary the arm and torso positions with this perch.

7. Use some of the above balance exercises as a coda, or finish, when practicing combinations of various kinds.

The following combinations involve circular movements:

1. Lie on the floor with the torso, legs, and arms extended in a long line. Holding a medium tempo, roll two or three times. Roll while pulling the knees and arms in toward the waist, forming a closed, rounded shape either on the knees or on the side. Lift the torso and come to one knee while the other leg steps forward. Extend to a long *arabesque* position with the lifted leg straight and the standing leg in a *plié* (experiment with possible arm positions). Circle the lifted leg around to the front as high as possible while lifting the torso to an upright position. Rise on half-toe. Suspend as the lifted leg pulls forward with a counter pull into a high, controlled back bend in the upper torso. Step forward on the extended leg. Contract and *plié*, going into a roll fall. Straighten out to repeat the exercise.

2. Use six steps for a circle walk. Keep facing front and step the right foot to the side; step the left foot diagonally behind the right; step the right foot diagonally behind the left; step the left to the side; step the right diagonally

in front of the left; and step the left diagonally in front of the right. This can be repeated several times on the same side. Or add a small catch-step after the sixth step and repeat on the other side.

  (a) Repeat the circle walk, but after one circle, step to the side into a press-turn, first to the right and then to the left.

  (b) Add the fast catch-step and repeat on the other side.

3. Facing the line of direction and moving in a small circle, walk four steps forward, take a half-turn, and walk four steps backward. Make this continuous with no extra counts for the turn.

  (a) Repeat this pattern, but use two steps instead of four, with an uneven rhythm. Make the first step quick with a small *plié* and the second step slower with a rise to half-toe for the turn. Try for a suspended feeling on the turns. Also, try this with three steps.

  (b) Repeat, making a larger circle by using four runs instead of steps, and a hop instead of the rise to half-toe.

  (c) Repeat the larger circle with a partner. Have partners face opposite directions so that one is traveling forward as the other travels backward. Inside hands should be joined; partners should change hands on the turn. Also, try this with a jump instead of a hop on the turns.

  (d) Repeat this but have the partners change places as they go into the turns.

4. Use the idea of traveling in small circles. Alternate moving forward and backward in the line of direction, making many small circles in different places on the floor.

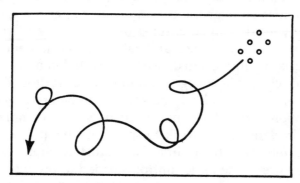

5. Repeat some of the above with different torso positions and shapes.

Combinations of the various areas of axial movements must be intermixed; they cannot be isolated into specific combinations using only one area. Combinations of movement for flexion, extension, and rotation will involve some degree of localized leads; of variations in use of energy; change of level, shape, size, and rhythm. These cannot be completely isolated in movement combinations.

These exercises and variations in no way exhaust the possibilities for movement combinations. Those listed here are offered as a springboard to help both the student and the new teacher in the creative development of their own movement combinations. As student or teacher, think in terms of making the combinations as interesting as possible and adapting them to the correct developmental or technical level of the dancers performing the combinations.

Chapter 11

Men in Dance

Through the ages, men have been the principal dancers in folk dances of all countries. In the United States, the participation of men in dance decreased for a while. However, interest in dance among men is growing. There is an increasing number of men (and women) participating regularly in square dance and folk dance group activities all over the country. There is also a great increase in the number of men involved in all other types of dance: as participants in classes and performing groups in modern, jazz, and ballet, and as audience for dance performances. This increasing interest in dance has resulted in more and more men participating in dance classes in colleges and in private studios. Despite this current situation, however, it will probably be some time before prejudice against men in dance—the notion that dance is not for men—will be completely dispelled. All of us interested in dance must work to speed up this process.

There is no difference in the technical and artistic training needed for men and women, no difference in the basic controls needed to prepare the instrument for genuine freedom and expressive movement. All the exercises in the preceding chapters are for both men and women. Nevertheless, in spite of sundry unisex movements, there is a difference between the sexes. The differences in build, strength, and interests should be recognized in dance classes and respected in compositions and performance. The dynamics, range, and style in performing the techniques should vary. Adjusting to these differences may induce more men to enter dance classes. Urge men to try a class; most men who try a good class once are sold, but they must experience the physical activity as participants, not as spectators.

Men's Objections to Dance Class

Men object to dance class for two basic reasons: (1) They dislike the classroom attire; and (2) they are afraid of failure.

Many men object to wearing tights. (Incidentally, dancers borrowed this garment from wrestlers as a practical way to keep the legs and hips warm without restricting movement.) There are probably two reasons for the objection. First, they may encounter ridicule and snide remarks from nondancers. Second, and perhaps the most important, most find the dance belt worn under the tights to be very uncomfortable. Another factor affecting men is that most dance classes are taught

126

by women (although this is changing). They are afraid of being required to move like the women in the class.

Most men are afraid of looking ridiculous, of not being able to do the steps and exercises correctly and smoothly. Care must be taken to convince men that they will experience difficulties but that everyone in the class, women as well as men, will be going through the same learning process. Everyone will make mistakes, but no one will look ridiculous.

Teaching Pointers

Allow men to wear T-shirts and trousers loose enough to permit free movement. Blue jeans should not be worn; they are too tight and restrict movement. If their finances permit, men can buy stretch trousers worn by gymnasts; these are ideal. The usual gym shorts worn by men are not good for floor exercises, but they might be permitted for the first few classes. With no hassle, the men will soon decide on their own to wear the regulation dance clothes.

Because most women in dance class have had some previous experience with dance movement, they often progress more rapidly at first than the men through the basic dance techniques. If possible, arrange a few extra practice sessions for the men in the first two weeks of the course. It will be time well spent. However, most men who enter dance class are strongly motivated; they are prodigious workers and soon catch up with the women.

If you are not used to having men in a dance class, do not be surprised if the stretches and work on flexibility induce a vocal reaction. Men are apt to be much more vocal about the discomfort in some of the exercises.

If you are a woman teacher, do as little demonstrating as possible. When you demonstrate, tell the men that they must not copy your specific mannerisms, but that they must make their movements stronger and bigger, discovering their own way to perform the movements.

Everyone in the class should get a complete physical workout. Give the men a chance to show off in such exercises as jumps and leaps. Have the men perform the exercises at a slower tempo, giving them an opportunity to exhibit their ability to leap and jump higher. Do not be disturbed if at first they do not have any style while performing the leaps and jumps; this will come. However, you may have to hold them down a bit for safety reasons.

Be very careful in the stretching and flexibility exercises. Most men (though not all) are more tightly knit in the joint areas, especially in the hips. Do not force the stretching. Eventually their flexibility will increase, but the process must be slow to prevent injury. They will find many of the floor stretches extremely difficult and uncomfortable. Most men will need extra work on ankle movements. Pointing toes is particularly difficult. Impress on them the importance of ankle control, urging them to work on this outside of class.

If tights are required, either for class or for a performance, men new to this garment may not know how to put on the dance belt correctly. You should be prepared to instruct them on this.

In addition to the exercises listed previously in this book, other exercises can be given to the men if they are able or interested. After the men have learned the sequence of standard basic exercises in your course, some of the following gymnastic exercises and movement variations for men can be used, incorporated as part of the other exercises, or added as a coda at the end of the other exercises. If these can be included, they will help increase the strength and movement vocabulary the men will need when performing lifts.

Gymnastic Exercises

The exercises in this section are gymnastic activities. Some will require the use of mats, at least while the students are learning them; thus, you may not be able to use them in your class. Many of the exercises can be performed by the women as well as men. Several are not suitable for a beginning class unless the men have had previous gymnastic training. They are listed here as suggestions to add interest for the men and to increase their movement vocabulary. However, they are to be used at your discretion after you determine the ability and interest of the men in the classes. The exercises should be used sparingly. Be sure your classes do not turn into gymnastic classes instead of dance classes.

11.A. Push-ups

11.A.1. Simple push-ups

Craft.   To perform a simple push-up, assume a prone position with the toes turned under and the hands on the floor at chest level. Keeping the torso straight, straighten the arms to lift the torso from the floor. Bend the elbows to lower the torso, but do not go low enough to rest the weight on the chest or torso. Perform this up-and-down movement from two to eight times.

Some form of push-up can be added as a coda for the men after many of the floor exercises or at the end of the floor work, just before standing. The women can join the men in this.

Push-up

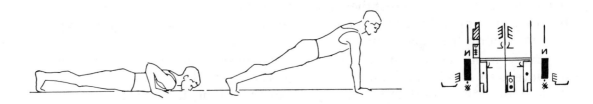

Science.   There are many variations of the standard push-up exercise that can be added to other exercises. Care must be taken that the torso is held straight, otherwise the value of the exercise is lost. It is better to perform one push-up correctly than several incorrectly. Some physical education teachers seem to feel there is value in the ability to do 50 to 100 push-ups. However, quantity in this respect is greatly overrated and can be dangerous or a least counterproductive. When overdone, push-up exercises can tighten muscles in the shoulder girdle so that an undesirable inflexibility results. For dance classes, these should be limited to four or eight and used only occasionally as codas or extra accents.

11.A.2. Simple push-up: Variations

Craft.   There are two main variations of the simple push-up: (1) Extend the ankles so the weight is carried on the top of the instep instead of on the toes; and (2) push-up hard enough so the hands leave the floor. Clap the hands one or more times in front of the chest before returning to the floor.

Push-up variation: Extend ankles

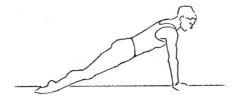 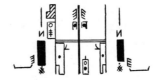

Push-up variation: Clap

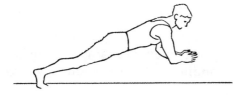 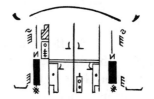

11.A.3. Side push-ups

Craft. Start in a side sit with the lower knee forward and the higher knee bent and pointing up so the foot is flat on the floor. The hand on the side of the forward leg is placed on the floor as far out to the side as possible without tipping the torso. The other arm is extended out to the side. Push against the floor with the foot on the side of the raised knee, extending the torso and knees to a straight line from feet to head. At the same time, shift weight to the toes of the lower foot. The shoulders should be straight over the supporting arm with the other arm extended straight toward the ceiling. The legs should be parallel to each other.

Side push-up

In the exercises performed while sitting on the floor, when changing sides (see Exercise 11.H.3.), the men could use this push-up and swing the legs to the other side while changing arms instead of swinging the legs with the hips on the floor.

11.A.4. Side push-ups: Variations

Craft. Three variations add interest to this exercise:

1. Raise the top leg while maintaining the extended torso position supported on one hand and one foot. This may be used by itself or may be continued into the next variation.

Side push-up: Variation 1

2. Turn to face the floor, taking the weight on both hands and one foot while keeping the other leg raised. The legs may be changed in this position to stretch both legs as a lead into standing or this variation may be continued into the next one.

Side push-up: Variation 2

3. Add one or more push-ups with the same leg still raised so the push-up is on two hands and one foot. Add a torso turn, lifting one hand and arm, then returning the hand to the floor on the other side and ending with the back toward the floor. The raised leg will swing under the torso but without touching the floor. Return to side, sit on the other side from the starting position, ready to repeat the total exercise, or, if used to change position for a floor exercise, continue with the floor exercise. This variation can also be used as a separate exercise for both men and women.

11.B. Rolls

11.B.1. Forward roll

Craft. A mat should be used when learning and practicing the forward roll. Stand at the edge of the mat and bend the knees so that the weight is over the toes. Place the hands on the mat approximately in front of the feet, bending the knees. Tuck the head down (feel as though trying to look through the legs). Keep the back well rounded and press equally with the hands and feet. Supporting some weight on the hands to protect the head, roll over onto the back of the shoulders—not the top of the head—keep rolling to the buttocks, and then roll to the feet and to a standing position. Make the roll one continuous movement so the velocity of the forward motion helps in coming to a stand.

This roll can be used as a variation for coming to a stand at the end of floor exercises when starting from a sitting position.

Forward roll

11.B.2. Back roll

Craft. A mat should also be used when teaching a back roll. Start in a standing position with the back to the mat. Bend the knees and sit with the buttocks as close to the heels as possible. Keeping the back well rounded and bringing the hands up by the ears, with the fingers pointing toward the shoulders and the palms of the hands to the back, sit and then keep rolling back. Bring the knees close to the chest, roll onto the shoulders, and place the hands on the floor. Use a strong push of the hands to continue the roll to the feet and to a stand. Make this one continuous action so the velocity of the roll helps in the stand. Be sure there is equal pressure on both hands to prevent a roll to one side.

This can be used as a variation for coming to a stand at the end of the floor exercises or for rising from falls.

Back roll

11.C. Kip

Craft. This is not for beginners; it is for those who have had some gymnastic training or for those who wish to work outside of dance class in order to perfect the movement.

To execute a kip (sometimes call a ''neck spring'' or ''snap-down''), start as though doing a back roll, but keep both knees straight and swing the legs back toward the starting position. With a strong push of the arms and by arching the upper back, bring the feet to the floor and come to a standing position. Hips must not be allowed to collapse.

Kip

Science. Use a spotter when teaching this or until the men are very proficient. The spotter stands beside the dancer, ready to place his or her hands under the dancer's shoulders to help on the lift forward to the standing position if the dancer does not give enough push to land on his feet.

II.D. Handstands

These exercises, when correctly performed, are useful in helping both men and women increase awareness of body alignment and increase arm strength.

II.D.1. Basic handstand

Craft. A handstand (sometimes called an "inverted balance" or a "hand balance") should be performed on a hard surface, not a mat. Start by facing a wall. Place the hands on the floor about one foot from the wall. First kick one foot up, then quickly follow with the other to place both feet against the wall. Keep the torso well extended and the knees straight. Come down in control by first bringing one foot and then the other to the floor. After becoming familiar with the feel of this inverted position with the feet against the wall, pull the feet slightly away from the wall to discover how to balance in this position.

This exercise is more than a stunt; it can be an aid to understanding control and awareness of the torso.

Handstand

II.D.2. Handstand: Variations

Craft. There are several variations of the handstand:

1. Practice controlling the handstand away from the wall, without using the wall as a starting prop.
2. Walk on the hands. Try walking in various directions and around in a circle to learn to control changes in direction.
3. Move the legs to different positions while in a handstand. Move the legs to a wide split with one leg opening forward and one backward; or open the legs sideways to form a V shape; or bend one knee and bring the toe to the other knee.
4. Lower and raise the torso by bending and straightening the elbows in an elbow *plié*. (This is a very advanced version for those with well-established control and with very strong arms.)

Handstand: Variation 2 (opening front to back)

Handstand: Variation 3 (opening and bending one knee)

11.E. Cartwheel

11.E.1. Basic cartwheel

Craft. A cartwheel, like a handstand, should be practiced on a hard surface, not a mat. Start facing the direction of progression. Place one hand on the floor and kick the feet high overhead. Place the other hand on the floor and lift the first hand. Bring down one foot and then the other. Try to travel in a straight line with the hands and feet staying on the line. There should be an even rhythm in the touching of the hands and feet to the floor: an even one, two, three, four. In the first attempts, the knees will stay bent, and it will be difficult to bring the feet into a straight line with the hands. Work to completely extend the arms, legs, and torso. Be sure to practice in both directions.

11.E.2. Cartwheel: Variations

Craft. There are a number of cartwheel variations:

1. Increase speed to perform fast, continuous cartwheels.
2. Travel in a circle.
3. Practice one-handed cartwheels, keeping the free hand out at the side or on the hip.
4. End a series of cartwheels with a round-off (a jump to both feet making a quarter-turn to face the starting spot).
5. Walk briefly on the hands before bringing the feet down to complete the cartwheel.
6. A syncopated walk can add an interesting rhythmic variation to the cartwheel.
7. Perform any of these variations, but instead of finishing on both feet, finish balanced on the leading foot with the other leg in a high side extension. Or, this can be a moderate side extension with the movement continuing by raising the leg as high as possible as an upbeat into the next movement.

11.F. Chest Roll

Craft. A chest roll should be practiced on a mat at first. As preparation, rock in a front prone position with a long arch in the back. Be sure this is not just a giving in with compression in the small of the back. To continue preparation, face the floor, supporting the weight on the hands and toes. Kick first one foot, and then quickly follow with the other so they meet. Bend the elbows. With the head well lifted and with a controlled elbow bend, lower the chest to the mat. Keeping the torso well arched, roll down to the floor. The feet should be the last part to touch the mat.

Chest roll: Preparation primary

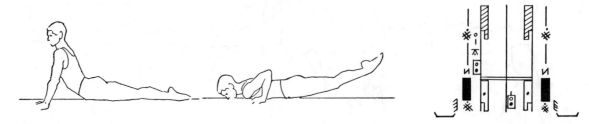

For the chest roll itself, proceed as before but assume a handstand position before starting the roll. If going to the floor for exercise after standing, this could be used as a way to go to the floor.

Chest roll: Preparation secondary

Chest roll

11.G. Jump Through from Front to Rear-Leaning Rest

Craft. Start in an extended position, facing the floor and supporting the weight on the hands and toes. Pull the knees up to the chest and, without moving the hands, swing the feet through between the arms and extend the legs and torso to a straight line, with the back toward the floor.

Movement Variations for Men

The following exercises illustrate how some of the basic dance techniques can be extended and varied especially for men. This section can serve as a guide for developing other variations in the techniques described in Chapters 3–10.

11.H. Variations: Previous Exercises

11.H.1. Side chest arch

Craft. Although the side chest arch is for torso flexibility, a contrasting control for strength can be combined with it. After performing the side chest arch (Exercise 5.C.2.) two or three times, add the side push-up (Exercise 11.A.3.).

Side chest arch

11.H.2. Shoulderstand

Craft. Have the men add a scissors movement of the legs, forward and backward, while standing on the shoulders. A number of other variations are possible:

1. Open the legs sideways to a wide V, then bring the legs together for two fast beats before opening them again.
2. Instead of rolling down, bend the knees, and slide the legs out on the floor; then add a kip to land on the feet.
3. Instead of returning to a prone position on the back, perform a back roll either to a standing position or to a front-leaning rest with a lateral roll to the back-lying position.
4. Start the shoulderstand with a back roll, but finish with a push-up into a handstand. This is a very advanced version and should not be attempted until the dancer is very sure of control in rolls and handstands.

Shoulderstand

11.H.3. Change of sides in sitting position

Craft. When sitting with one foot in front and the other behind, the usual way to change sides is as follows. Straighten both legs out to the side; then swing the legs across in front to the other side. Open the legs in a scissors action, with the under leg going forward. Bend the knees to sit in a position ready to repeat the exercise on the other side. While the women perform this version, have the men complete another shift: extend the torso to a side push-up position; swing the legs to this position on the other side; and lower the hips to the floor to perform the scissors opening in preparation for the knee bend to the sit position.

Changes of sides in sitting position: Women's version

A still more spectacular variation is to swing the legs completely around twice in a fast pinwheel effect and then to end as described. This change will be a fast, sweeping swing of the torso and legs, with first one hand and then the other as the center of the circle. The change will require a quick shift of weight from one hand to the other as the legs swing under them. There will be a split second when neither hand is on the floor. (This is a standard movement found in many of the more difficult Russian folk dances.)

11.H.4. Transitions to stand

Craft. After finishing floor work, a transitional movement is often used to come to a standing position to perform standing exercises. While the women are stretching first one leg and then the other to the back as the preparation to stand, have the men perform four to eight push-ups—with claps if possible—before joining the women for the standing exercises.

Transition to stand: Women's version

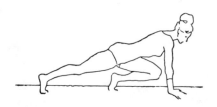

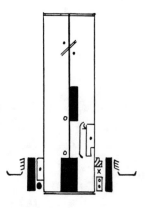

Transition to stand: Men's version

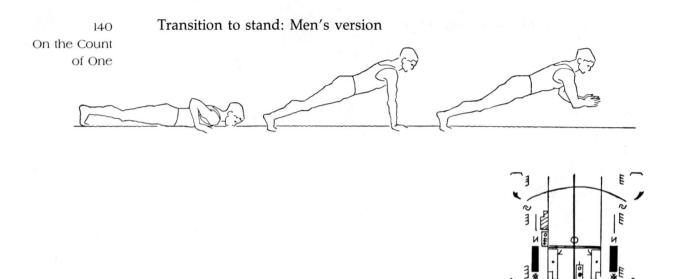

11.1. Variations with Leaps and Jumps

11.1.1. Jumps with falls

Craft. Perform six to fourteen straight jumps, add a roll fall, come to the feet, and continue with another set of jumps.

11.1.2. Horizontal leaps with centered jumps and half-turns

Craft. Jump into second position, pull up to half-toe in first position, and drop into a *plié* in second position. Jump again, turning half around in the air. Repeat the sequence three more times (four half-turns in all). Add a leap to the side, taking off from both feet and landing on one. Perform three or four horizontal leaps (either in place or traveling slightly). Return to a centered jump and repeat the pattern either on the same side or on alternate sides. On the horizontal leap, be sure the legs pass in the air; also try for a momentary position with the legs and torso horizontal on the floor. Work for complete center control with no tension in the shoulders, neck, or arms. The sections of this exercise will need to be practiced separately before combining them.

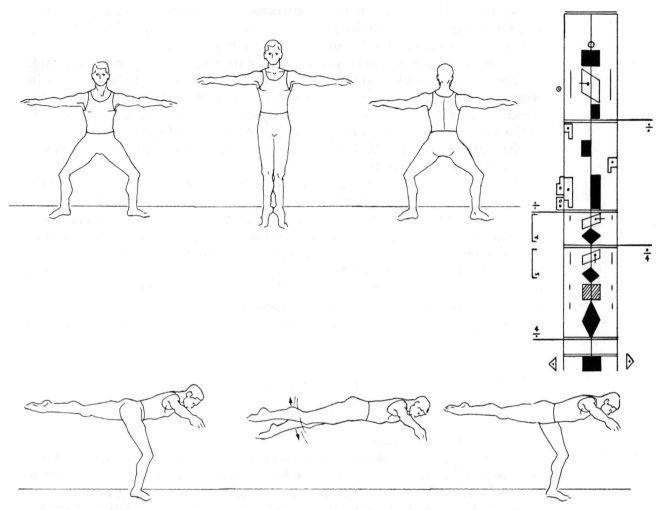

There is no limit to the possible combinations of leaps, jumps, turns, and falls. In addition, the degree of turning, the elevation achieved in the jumps, and the direction of traveling during leaps may be varied. The movement possibilities are exceptionally diverse.

Lifts

Lifts can be an exciting factor in dance. However, as in falls, there is a temptation to let the movements become stunts instead of recognizing them as integral, expressive statements in dance. One possible approach that may help students resist this temptation is to use lifts as one might use leaps or jumps. Think of them as extensions of leaps or jumps. Or, experiment with using lifts as rhythmic accents. Most important, careful experimentation is necessary to discover new lifts that are genuinely expressive of the idea of the dance.

The following are basic and standard lifts. Practice these in technical training just as you do *pliés* and brushes. They should be part of the dancer's vocabulary. With control of these basic lifts, dancers may experiment with other variations and devise completely original lifts. Working on lifts is fun for both men and women, and lifts can add interest to class work and dance club activities. When incorporating lifts into a dance theme, however, experiment with improvisations to discover lifts that are appropriate for the mood or theme of the dance.

When practicing lifts it helps if the woman wears a belt, preferably an elastic belt about one and a half to two inches wide that fits very snugly. This helps prevent the leotard from slipping up as the man lifts.

There are certain dangers involved in learning and practicing lifts. Safeguards are needed. Always use spotters (one or two helpers ready and able to catch the woman and at times the man, if there is danger of falling). The man must use the standard safety factors involved in lifting weights. These are: (1) Use the legs instead of the back as the principal lifting force; (2) keep the lifted weight (woman) over the base of support; and (3) time the application of the lifting force as a continuation of the woman's jump.

The woman must also work and not expect the man to do it all, although the audience must receive the impression that the man is performing the lift unassisted. In most lifts, the woman must jump. She performs a *plié* as preparation. The man must *plié* at the same time, and the straightening of their knees must be timed together. The woman then jumps into the air and the man continues the lift from the height of her jump. This timing is essential. If he is late and tries to lift as she is coming down, he is in trouble. For both, a small, fast *plié* is better than a slow, deep one. The lift must appear to be effortless.

In any lift, the most important factors are timing, weight placement, and alignment.

11.J. Front Lifts

11.J.1. Front lift: Man and woman facing

a. Basic position: Man

The man places his hands at the woman's waist, below the rib cage, with the main part of the lift coming from the heel of the hand, not the thumbs. His thumb should be on a line with his fingers, not pressed into the woman's back or abdomen. (If he presses his thumbs into her back or front, this tends to tip her, making it difficult for her to hold her alignment. Also, this pressing is apt to leave bruises.) His elbows must be kept down and close to the body, not out. The woman must be very close to him so the lift can be straight up over his own base of support. This basic position of the man's hands and arms is the same whether the woman is facing toward or away from him.

b. Basic position: Woman

In many lifts, the woman helps support herself with her hands on the man's shoulders. The hands must be on the solid part of the shoulder, never out at the tip of the shoulder or on the throat. She must press down as she goes into the air. However, she must keep her shoulders and shoulder blades pulled down. For this lift, she performs a small *plié* with a fast straightening that carries into a straight jump. As she goes into the air, the press down on the man's shoulders and the straightening of her arms must come as a continuation of the jump. The timing is important.

c. The lift: Man and woman together

Craft. The actual lift combines the basic positions. The man and the woman face each other, standing close together, the woman's hands on the man's shoulders and the man's hands on the woman's waist. Both *plié* at the same time and

the woman jumps, pressing down with her hands and trying to lift high enough
to straighten her elbow. At the same time, the man lifts the woman, continuing
the lift from her jump and trying to straighten his elbows to obtain maximum height.

Front lift: Man and woman facing

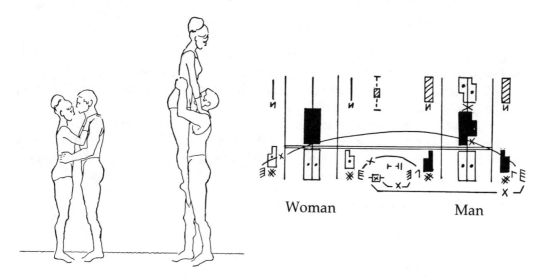

Woman · · · Man

The man can control a slow descent by resting the woman on his chest and
letting her slide down his torso. It is the man's responsibility to know how close
the woman is to the floor and to control her landing. The woman must help cushion the landing with a small *plié* upon touching the floor. The proper timing of
this requires much practice.

For the first introduction to the lift, both should practice the timing of the *plié*
and the straightening with the woman jumping, but they should do so without
performing the actual lift; this will enable them both to get the timing for continuing into the lift. Try this two or three times before attempting the lift.

The first time the woman is actually lifted, she may feel an unexpected fright.
It will probably feel terribly high. There will be a tendency to collapse in the middle. This is the worst thing she can do. It will make her very heavy and the man
may not be prepared for the added weight.

Take time to have the men practice lifting each other so they will know what
the woman is experiencing.

Science.   The man must keep the woman very close and lift straight up over
his base of support. He must keep tight control of the center of his torso and not
go into a back bend, which can severely strain the small of the back. The woman
must maintain a straight line through her torso and must never bend either forward or backward at the waist. If she breaks at the waist, it will be very hard for
the man to hold her. If the woman lets her shoulders lift as she presses down,
control will be lost, the energy of her push will be dissipated, and she will be much
heavier.

11.J.2. Front lift: Variations

Craft. Here are two variations of the front lift: (1) The woman can be slightly to the side. On the lift, the man can pick her up from one side and put her down on the other; (2) the man and woman can start facing each other, but the man can turn one or more times before putting her down.

11.J.3. Front lift: Man behind woman

Craft. The woman stands in front of the man with her back to him. The man has his hands on the woman's waist, with his elbows in. She holds his wrists. Both *plié,* and she jumps pressing down with her hands on his wrists and keeping her shoulders down. The woman should arch her back slightly, keeping her chest high. She must maintain alignment in her torso and hip areas, and she must control her legs so they do not swing forward. At the same time, the man lifts as a continuation of her jump, trying to straighten his elbows for maximum height. The woman must maintain her position until she returns to the floor.

Front lift: Man behind woman

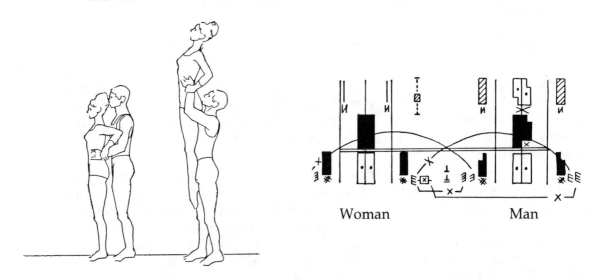

Woman   Man

Science. See Exercise 11.J.1.

11.J.4. Front lift: Man behind woman: Variations

Craft. After acquiring control of timing and alignment, with the woman holding the man's wrists, begin the variations:

1. Instead of holding onto the man's wrists, the woman lifts her arms into a high fifth position as she goes up. When first learning this lift, the woman should keep her feet in fifth position and lift her arms forward and up, not sideways and up. Later she may experiment with the various arm and foot positions. However, be sure to tell the man what the changes are before trying them. There should never be surprises in the middle of a lift.

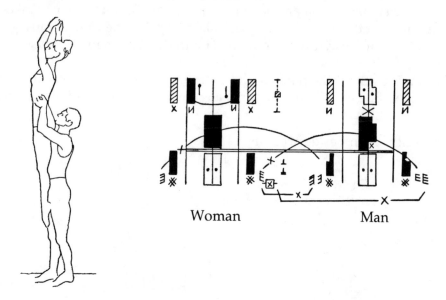

Woman   Man

2. The man lifts the woman high enough to sit her on his shoulder. The woman must keep her back very straight, and just as he places her on his shoulder, she must bend enough at the hips to be able to sit on his shoulder. One foot can curve behind the man's back for added control. They must decide beforehand which shoulder he will use. The woman must not bend forward as she sits.

Front lift: Man behind woman: Variation 2

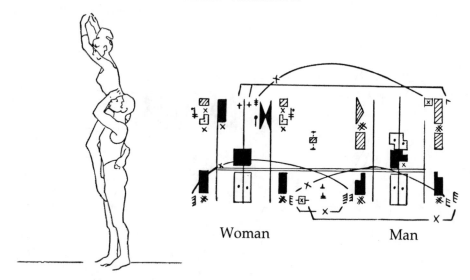

Woman   Man

3. As the woman is lifted, she opens her legs and arms as though leaping. The woman must be careful to go straight up and not to really leap away from the man.

11.J.5. Front lift: Man beside woman

Craft. The man and woman stand side-by-side but with the woman very slightly ahead of the man. Proceed as for Exercise 11.J.4., variation 3, but instead of standing in place, the man travels while the woman is in the air. For the beginning practice of this lift, both take three (small) steps at the same time. Start by stepping across in front, then to the side, and again in front. Keep the steps small. On the third step, the woman *pliés* for her jump into the air. The man takes a small *plié* but continues the walk. This will look like a leap, but the woman must go straight up, and not leap away from the man. The man must keep her over his base of support.

In coming down, the man should tip the woman slightly, placing her on her forward foot. She must maintain torso alignment and leg position until returning firmly to the floor.

Front lift: Man beside woman

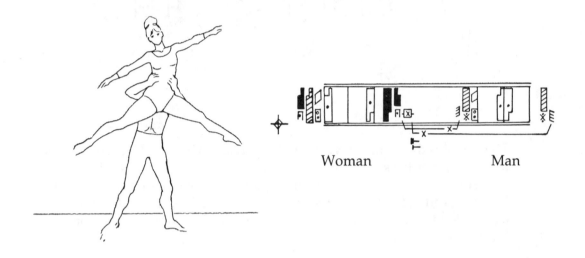

Woman   Man

Tilt to recover

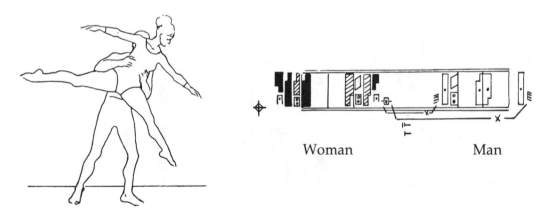

Woman   Man

11.K. Sit to Hip

11.K.1. Basic sit to hip

Craft. The woman stands at the side of the man, her arm around the back of his neck and his arm around her waist. She presses down with her arm on his shoulders and, at the same time, jumps to sit on his hip. When first trying this, most women are surprised at how high they must jump. The man should not have to lift her. He should pull her into his side at the height of her jump. He should stand in a medium-wide second position.

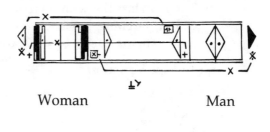

Woman   Man

Science. The woman must maintain the downward pressure of her arm, keeping her shoulders down. She must be sure to jump high and to sit on the side of the man's hip and not slide forward in front of him. Her arm must be well up on the shoulder and not out on the tip of the shoulder. Also, she must not reach so far around to the other side that she is pressing on his throat. The man must be sure that he is holding her onto his side, not pushing her forward, with enough lift so she does not slide down on his thigh.

11.K.2. Sit to hip: Variations

Craft. The following are some variations of the sit to hip:

1. Instead of standing at the man's side, the woman can start a short distance away and run to the man. However, the takeoff jump must be at the man's feet and go straight up; she must not hurtle into him from a distance.

Sit to hip: Variation 1

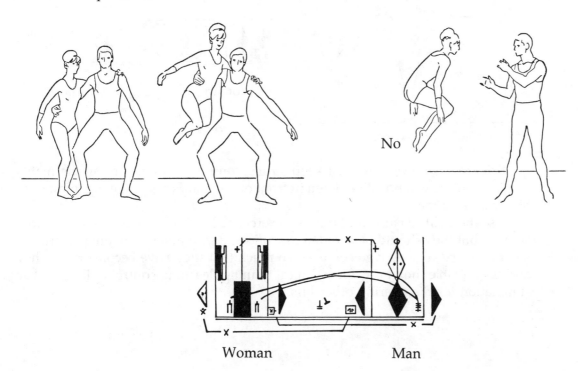

Woman   Man

2. The man turns with the woman on his hip.
3. The man lifts two women, one on each hip. The women must practice timing the jump so both land at the same time.
4. The man performs a turn with this double lift.
5. The man lifts the woman to a hip sit, and then she swings both feet in front of him, arching her back and rotating slightly so her back is toward the man. This is easier to do if the man is turning.

Sit to hip: Variation 5

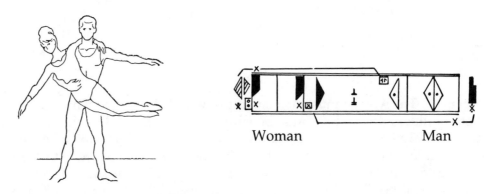

Woman   Man

6. The man and woman start as for the sit to hip, but he helps lift the woman, pulling her higher on his torso. At the same time, he tilts his torso away from the woman and lifts his leg sideways. She lifts her outside leg to parallel his leg. The man must take the woman with him as he tilts his torso.

Sit to hip: Variation 6

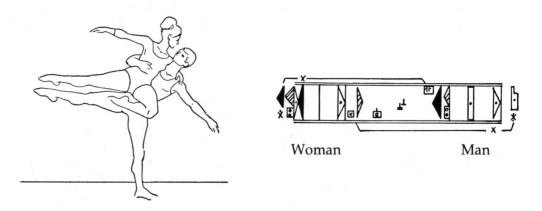

Woman   Man

Science. The woman must keep strong control with her arm on the man's shoulder so she will not slide down in front of the man's hips, making it impossible for him to move.

Use these lifts as technical training exercises. The lifts may be used for studio studies, but they should be avoided for concert dance unless you are performing a period piece. They have been used so much that they have become trite. They are still valuable, however, for technical training, learning control of lifts, and as stimulation for discovering other lifts.

Chapter 12

Creative Approach to Technique

By the time students reach junior high, high school, and especially college and enroll in their first modern dance class, they have acquired a myriad of poor postural and movement habits. Also, each student will have a different concept of the meaning of "dance." Very few will have seen a live professional modern dance concert (although this is changing). Some will be familiar with the current stereotyped modern jazz dance on television and will have seen some ballet. Most likely, some students will have had tap, ballet, or jazz lessons as young children, and others will be familiar with disco dance. Some students will think that modern dance teaches the latest social dance steps. However, do not discount disco and other newer forms of social dance as they develop—and they do change constantly. Such dances are improvisational, thus creative. This is one of the main values of current social dance. Also, participation in social forms of dance is an important phase in maturation. Students who do not participate in the current social dance are missing out on an aspect of their youth, something that they can never catch up with later. Incorporate the rhythms and movements of this current dance into your lesson plans. However, be sure to direct these rhythms and movements toward specific ends in the course outline; the class should not become a straight disco session.

Student Diversity

In this diverse mass of beginners, there will be students with quite natural, unspoiled movement. Some will have deep-seated, psychological certainty of their inherent awkwardness. Very seldom will this feeling be based on real lack of physical coordination. Some students may have had varying degrees of dance training in private studios; often these students will cause the biggest headaches. A few may have had excellent training, but others may be rigidly set in an external, decorative, often "sexy" type of movement. They prefer to limit their movements to poorly aligned *arabesques*, *tours jetés*, and off-balance *pirouettes*. They prefer the security of these known areas to the uncertainty of creative explorations—untried and new areas.

Fortunately, there are increasing numbers of classes in creative movement in elementary schools and in private studios. There should soon be an increasing number of students entering high school and college classes with the basics in movement and the ability to use movement creatively.

Suggestions for a Creative Approach

It is the teacher's responsibility to guide, lead, stimulate, and, at times, coerce these aspiring dancers to some degree of self-confidence and creative activity. By careful planning, the students must be permitted to discover and experience the difference between localized and total movement, awareness and use of space, and awareness of quality and meanings in movement. The students must increase their range of movement and learn the many ramifications of time and rhythm. Assure students that in movement explorations there is no right or wrong; everyone can move differently and be "right." This is one, if not the most important, value in a creative approach to teaching.

The use of movement exploration as a teaching technique is difficult for many teachers. One reason for this difficulty is that they were not taught this way, and it is easier to echo one's own teacher than to try new techniques. Also, when using this method, it is difficult to evaluate students' progress. I know of no way to grade creativity objectively: There is no formula. But more important than any of these reasons is the fact that the movement exploration method demands a degree of creativity on the part of the teacher. This method of teaching must be tried to be understood. Teachers who break through the barriers and experience the results never return to a straight technical approach. In some ways, this method is more tiring, but it is also self-nourishing and sustaining for both the teacher and student.

A note of warning: Currently, "Be creative" is a popular expression in educational circles, which does not mean that you tell the students to do what they want and then offer no direction or help. "Be creative" does not mean merely playing a record and saying: "Make up a dance." There must be a planned sequence of directed explorations before students are ready for this step.

In the straight teaching of technique, there is very specific instruction on how to perform movements. In the creative approach there is instruction on *what* to do within the definite limitations of certain areas of learning, but there is not instruction on *how* to do it. However, both methods are necessary for sound dance training. Using a creative approach does not mean eliminating the teaching of all specific techniques.

The more regimented the school, the more discretion is needed in the initial challenge to students to think for themselves. The first attempts must be planned to ensure a feeling of success. In the early stages, avoid instructions such as "Be creative" or "Improvise." In teaching any of the arts, some aspects need to be experienced first, then analyzed and labeled; other aspects need to be analyzed first, then experienced. Both methods are necessary in teaching dance, depending on the material being taught.

Beginning Explorations

For teaching purposes, it is often necessary to separate a whole into parts. However, during this process of separation, one should continually return to examine the relationship of these segments to the whole. Because it is much easier to teach the tangible aspects of the craft of dance, many beginning teachers slight the aspects of performance, particularly in elementary classes. Similarly, to some teachers the psychological factors involved in dance may seem unimportant compared with the great technical need. Other teachers who have had inadequate technical training may find it easier to structure all of the course around improvisation and creative studies; the end result may be fun in movement and possibly some freeing of the individual, but no real growth or development in dance. Technical training and creative experience must go hand-in-hand.

First, there must be an exploration of movements and of the self. Without an inner understanding of one's own capabilities, technical achievement is inherently meaningless. Essentially, each student must discover a personal awareness of movement: a sensitivity to the meanings of movement. But the teacher must set the stage and lead the way, proceeding from small, limited areas to a carefully planned, sequential expansion of ideas and areas of movement, and finally to the composition of a full-length dance.

At the beginning, dramatic adjectives and complicated artistic theories are apt to increase students' discomfort. They will think: "This is beautiful. I like the sound of it, but how can it help me?" First, students need tangible directions. Each person is unique, and we should recognize and accept this. A person's name is part of this uniqueness; this can be a tangible starting point.

Self-introduction

Self-introduction can be started on the first day, when students are often not dressed for active work. Each student, in turn, moves to a position in front of the class, faces the class, stands still without fidgeting or giggling, speaks slowly enough to be understood and loudly enough to be heard, and says, "I am (name)."

It is important to say "I am" and not "My name is." This may seem a very small and unimportant distinction; however, to say "My name is" can be impersonal. It implies that the speaker lacks involvement or certainty. For the time being, the class is the student's world. To be able to face that world and say "I am" with poise and assurance is a meaningful achievement.

If a student is too painfully shy to do this on the first day, do not force the issue. Try to assure the student that he or she will be able to do it next time. The shy student needs to be aware of the teacher's confidence.

Many students hesitate to try new things for fear of making mistakes. Tell them that the class is the place to make these mistakes, that occasional errors are usual in the learning process. If they could do it all, there would be no point in their being there. However, many mistakes may be avoided if the students concentrate completely on what they are doing. Concentration is also one of the best ways to avoid self-consciousness. It is an important brick in the individual's foundation for future development. Students must try to find the kind of concentration that focuses on what they are doing rather than on themselves as persons.

Beginning concentration exercises

A beginning concentration exercise can be done the first day of class, even if students are not dressed for active work. Concentration studies are designed to help beginning students overcome the shyness and self-consciousness that most feel. Concentration exercises will also help students develop a fuller understanding of the meaning of concentration, which can be a useful tool for all that follows.

As a beginning concentration exercise, have the students stand on the floor, as far apart as possible. Ask each to visualize a room at home, including the furniture, doors, and windows; the disorder or neatness; and the walls separating that room from the others. Have students look for a misplaced book, pencil, or some such familiar object (the article is not important as long as it is familiar and frequently used). Add a note of urgency. They have to take the article to school, and it is almost time for class. They do not want to be late. If the students have to work fast, they will not have time to think about themselves.

Instructions to the class should include such statements as: "Do not put on an act." "Do it for real as though you were alone at home with no one watching." "There is a wall between you and all the others in the class; you cannot see them, and they cannot see you." Have a definite signal such as a hand clap or drumbeat to end the search.

Keep the time short for this exercise. Beginning students will not be able to concentrate for long. At the outset they will benefit more from several short sessions in successive class periods than one long session. Most students will need at least two practice periods to be successful in maintaining concentration.

The need for successive practice periods applies to most dance activities. It takes time for ideas to be absorbed, to be digested to the point where mind and body can coordinate them as wished.

Practice in self-control

"Breaking up" is a theater term. It is used when a person loses concentration and becomes giggly. For this exercise, students work with a partner. One of the pair repeats the previous exercise as though alone with no one watching. The partner tries to distract the searcher, tries to cause a loss of concentration. The searcher must not let on in any way that the other person is there. This can succeed only with complete concentration on the search. It requires complete visualization of the place and the object and includes awareness of color, texture, odor, and sound. The partner may talk, make faces, or try any kind of gesture or motion but cannot actually touch the searcher. The exercise should be repeated so all students try both roles.

This exercise is fun for beginning students. The distractor must use his or her creative imagination to find ways to break up the searcher, especially after the searcher has had enough practice in maintaining concentration well. A note of warning: At times during this exercise the class may be noisy. Actually, this can be an indication of wholehearted participation. Be glad, not disturbed, if this happens.

For a six- to nine-week course, which is usual in many high schools, this is the maximum amount of this type of activity that should be included. For a longer course, variations of these exercises may be included at intervals throughout the term.

Variations of concentration exercises

You may vary and complicate the concentration action by adding another definite activity such as wrapping a package, setting a table, or some familiar activity. Use imagination or have students suggest activities. Have definite obstacles such as a table, a desk, or a large rock with certain dimensions in specific locations, which two students must remember. Have both adjust their actions to the location, size, shape, and height of the obstacles.

In this sort of exercise, as in the compositional studies discussed later, some students may suggest ideas that are too complicated. Be prepared to guide students into selecting the essential parts of an idea or just one part of the idea. Be sure that no feeling of censorship arises. Students offering their own ideas, especially for the first time, are very vulnerable and their creative impulses can be easily squelched. Strive for delicate skill in guiding the students' first sortie into thinking for themselves.

In some cases, class laughter may be a sticky problem, especially in junior high and high school. Laughter at the wrong time can seriously thwart some students and can establish a poor atmosphere for the class. Some students may strive for undeserved laughter. Eventually, all should learn to deal with it. Occasionally the teacher will be tempted to laugh at inappropriate times when something unexpected happens. If the situation deserves laughter, join in enthusiastically.

Movement Exploration

A highly trained, skilled performer may feel that these exercises are too simple for the beginner. However, they form the foundation needed for the more complicated activities that follow. Do not spend much time on the simpler exercises; they are for recall and for identification of the movement tools students already have at their disposal but may not recognize as such.

It is best to introduce all of the basic elements as quickly as possible, thereby increasing the students' movement vocabulary. The larger the movement vocabulary, the freer students will be in improvisation. How much is introduced and how quickly depend on the age, developmental level, and previous experience of each class. Some teachers prefer to introduce one element or area at a time and to explore all its ramifications for an extended, in-depth exploration before continuing to the next area. Beginning students, however, are unable to extend explorations or to delve deeply into the other related elements in their first attempts at creative movement. Therefore, it is best to quickly introduce many different elements to help them develop a usable movement vocabulary. Each teacher should experiment and discover what works for him or her; different methods may be necessary for different situations.

Introduce new elements as rapidly as the students can grasp them. Keep returning to the earlier explorations, adding variations, enlarging the area, and combining the earlier movements with other elements. This return and re-exploration will heighten and stabilize the students' understanding while keeping their interest. The art and craft of dance will be unified in the dancers' development.

Basic locomotion

This exercise should be completed very quickly. It is not necessary to teach students how to perform the steps; they should be thoroughly familiar with all of them. It should be included merely to remind the student that these steps are tools they already have at their disposal.

Have students stand in a large circle, all facing one direction. It is not necessary to stop after each step and explain the next. Call out the next step while they are still performing the preceding step, and change the tempo or rhythm with a drumbeat. Eight of each kind of step should be sufficient. Start with a moderately fast walk; run; leap; jump (some may hop, and if so, say, "Land on both feet at the same time"); hop (one foot); change feet; change to first foot and hop backward; change feet, still going backward; face center of circle and slide to the right; change to slide left. (There may be slight confusion in starting backward or going right and left, but they soon straighten it out. It still should not be necessary to stop in most cases.) It may be necessary to pause briefly before the slides to have everyone face toward the center of the circle. To continue, again have students face the line of direction in the circle (tell the class which way to face), then gallop (keep one foot in front); change the front foot; gallop backward; change feet; go forward again with a skip; skip backward. It should be possible to review all these basic steps in a few minutes.

These movements can be followed by improvising to music. For most beginning classes on this first day it is better not to tell them that they will now "improvise.'' After they have finished, tell them that they were improvising. Select music with a fairly fast tempo and with an uneven rhythm suitable for slides and skips. Tell the class to go in any direction they wish and to see how many of the different steps they can do to the music. You have given them something to work with: a starting point. For some classes, it may be necessary to say ''Change'' at intervals or to suggest steps to try.

Direction and time

This is another exercise that should take very little time. You do not need to teach students how to do it. The exercise is to remind them of tools they already have at their disposal. Have the students scattered on the floor—not in straight lines—and establish a moderately fast tempo by using drumbeats or music. Tell them to go forward (six to eight steps are sufficient), backward, and sideways. (Do not say which side. Say that it is all right to be different from their neighbors. Such a small decision as this can be the opening wedge for important decisions later.) Instruct the class to move in the opposite direction, still sideways, then turn in place (again, let each choose which way to turn), and turn in the other direction. While this is going on, maintain a steady, moderately fast tempo. Next, set a beat twice as fast and repeat the instructions for moving in the different directions. It may be necessary to remind students to stay on the beat. Then double the tempo to make it extremely fast, and repeat the instructions for moving in the different directions. Again, it may be necessary to remind students to stay on the beat. This exercise goes very quickly and takes very little class time while allowing you to introduce two important tools for future use: tempo and directions in space.

There is no need to explain beat, tempo, or other music terms at this time. Go into these details when you reintroduce these concepts later in the course or when you use them as a separate unit. There is a tendency for young teachers, fresh from theory classes, to talk too much. You do not need to tell them everything you know in the first class period. Guard against dance classes becoming talking classes rather than doing classes.

Variations of steps

Combine the elements of basic locomotion, directions, and time. Again call out the directions to move, but have each student choose a different step for each direction. Allow a little more time for each direction. They can all be different and yet all be right. Use music or a rhythmic beat suitable for a skip or a slide. Some classes will go right into this without hesitation, but a few may need suggestions for steps to get started.

Variations of directions

In the first exercise, the directions of front, side, and back were in relation to a place called ''the front of the room,'' as well as the dancers' own front and back. If students are moving sideways, oriented toward the front of the room, suggest that they change and continue that direction backward, or try turning while moving in any of the directions. Introduce the other possible directions of diagonals and level (up and down). Have the class experiment with combining these new directions with tempo and locomotion. Have the class work on short movement studies using these three elements, making the studies as interesting as possible. Have half the class show these studies to the other half.

Use of Energy

Have students explore the use of energy in movement. Remind them to be aware of how they are moving. They should be sensitive to the feeling of the action, of the relationship of one part to another, and of what happens when changing from one activity to the other.

Pushing and pulling

For the first explorations of energy in movement, each student should work with a partner of approximately the same size. With hands joined, the students both push, then both pull. Next, have one push while the other pulls. Alternate this push-pull action.

Direct the partners to experiment with other parts of the body, using a pushing and pulling action. Both do not need to use the same body parts. If necessary, suggest shoulders and hips, heads, and so on. Students do not need to stay on their feet; they do not need to be symmetrical. Suggest that they find as many combinations and ways of pushing and pulling as possible. Do not forget the directions of up and down. Change the amount of energy used: weak; strong; or medium. Have each partner use the same or different amounts of energy. Spot some particularly interesting experimentation and have the whole class try it. Discovering that the teacher approves of real explorations and unusual movements is one of the best stimulants for future creative activity. This is also an introduction to performance.

Imaginary use of energy

Have students work alone and repeat some of the two-person actions, remembering the amount of energy that they used when they were working with their partners. The student should try for the same feeling and the same sequence of movements in the various parts of the body and be convincing in this movement of using imaginary energy. Saying: "That was convincing"; "I believe you"; "That was not convincing"; or "I did not believe you" is better than saying: "Good"; "Bad"; or "Wrong." Variations that might be used are: "Make it convincing"; "Make me believe you"; "I couldn't quite believe that"; "Try it again."

Variations in type of activity

1. Without a partner, experiment with actions of lifting and carrying. How does the movement change with a change in the weight or size of an object? Be aware of the amount of energy needed for these variables. If the class needs help, be prepared to suggest that students use something extremely heavy, very light, very large, very small, very valuable, very fragile, and so on. These early explorations are more effective if the suggestions are paired with opposites. This is not necessary for further explorations later in the course. Students should clearly visualize definite objects.
2. Explore or experiment with actions such as striking, throwing, kicking, and catching. Again, visualize an object with size, weight, and texture. Students should select their own object. The same suggestions listed for variations in size and weight may be used. Also, use body parts other than hands. Be sure to include the resulting action or movement, not just the initial strike, catch, etc.

3. A further variation that may be used with all of these exercises is to change time or tempo. Try the actions in slow motion, keeping all elements in the same relationship.

4. After trying these explorations based on literal movement of an actual object, experiment with movement based on the feelings and ways of moving already experienced, but abstract them into dance movement. This early in the course these should be short studies, not full-length dances.

Further explorations

The following suggestions may be used in place of some of the other variations listed, or they may be used later in the course when this area is reintroduced or when more extended studies are used:

1. Do the actions of striking, catching, kicking, and lifting produce an emotional feeling? Does an awareness of this feeling change the way of moving? Does an emotional state produce the desire for any of these actions? Explore both approaches.

2. Use these same ideas and types of actions in localized areas. Without letting any other part of the body move, experiment with hands, elbows, feet, or head. Vary the amount of energy used.

3. Starting with the localized areas as in the preceding variation, let the movement progress sequentially to another area of the body or into total involvement. This process can also be reversed: Start with total involvement and progress to localized movement. Further variations can be explored by changing the level of the starting position by sitting, kneeling, or lying in various positions on the floor.

4. Now, add a time element to your explorations. Move quickly, slowly, and in extreme slow motion. Then vary the tempo during the activity, such as starting in one tempo and then gradually changing it to end in another tempo.

5. Try changing the direction or amount of space used. How does the amount of space used change the actual movement and the feeling the movement produces?

There is no end to the possibilities of movement exploration. How many of these suggestions are used in a single term depends on the length of the course and on the creative level of the class. No two classes are ever the same. Remember, this is one small element to cover. It should not take up too much time in the total course.

Regardless of how many of the exercises are used, take time at intervals to have students demonstrate some of their studies to the class. At first, have half the class show the other half. Later, divide the class into four sections so that fewer are performing at a time. Gradually decrease the number until students are able to perform alone.

Improvisation

Strictly speaking, all of the previous explorations constitute a type of improvisation. The following devices lead to freer dance movement and a wider use of space and level. Keep in mind that a beginner needs the security of something definite to hold on to. Remember also to tell the students *what* to do but not *how* to do it.

When you introduce improvisation, do not tell the students what is coming.
Most beginning students perform better if they do not know. Of the following exercises, the circle dance and the square dance are for use very early in the course, possibly on the first day. Use music with a catchy rhythm that is fairly fast. Give definite instructions until the class is in time with the beat of the music; then offer suggestions that permit individual choice.

Circle dance

After the music has started, give the following types of directions: Start moving to the left, stepping on the beat. Reverse, moving right. Pick up a slower, half-time beat and step toward the center of the circle. Pick up the beat again and move away from the center of the circle. Do a slow turn in place and end facing in. Pick up a faster, double-time beat, move to the opposite side of the circle, and end facing out. (There will be a momentary jam-up in the center, but it should not bother anyone.) Move to the left again on the basic beat. Break the circle formation to move anyplace on the floor; cover as much space as possible. Stay in one place and change level. Vary the tempo at will: sometimes on the beat, sometimes slow or very fast. Travel again, covering space; make it big; change your level by stooping, leaping, and so on.

End this improvisation by slowly turning down the volume of the record or by having the piano become softer and softer until the music cannot be heard. At the same time, talk the class into smaller and quieter movements. Have students stop and hold the position when they can no longer hear the music.

Square dance

The square dance is a variation on the circle dance and may be used in the first or second lesson instead of the circle dance. Music may be of a folk type with a skipping or syncopated rhythm.

Again, start with very definite instructions and gradually open the areas of choice. This time use a square formation. Designate one side as side 1, and continue in sequence to numbers 2, 3, and 4. Start with sides 1 and 3, have them do four skips toward each other and four back to place. Then have sides 2 and 4 do the same. Starting with side 1, have students do some kind of jump and a turn. The whole side does not have to do the same jump and turn; each person can do his or her own. Proceed around the square, with each side doing its own jump and turn. Have sides 1 and 3 slide across the square to change places. Repeat for sides 2 and 4. This move can be repeated, with sides returning to original positions. (Whether it is done will depend on the phrasing of the music used.) Go around the square again with each side, in turn, doing the jump and turn (or suggest a new activity). Repeat the slide with sides changing places, but this time continuing into space away from the square. Continue with suggestions similar to those used with the circle dance. Give the students something to hang on to while letting them exercise a degree of choice of activity within a limited area.

If necessary, remind the students of the tools they have at their disposal: many kinds of locomotor steps; many directions and levels; and different tempos.

Improvisations based on sound

Use a percussion instrument such as a gong or a woodblock. Instruct the students to make their movements last as long as the sound continues and to change movements and direction each time the instrument is struck. Because a woodblock produces a completely different quality of sound from that of a gong, most students will automatically move differently to these sounds. Beginners, though adjusting to the differences in quality of the sounds, may need to be made aware of what they are doing. Short class discussions after demonstrating studies will help students clarify and improve their improvisations. Care must be taken to guide students by making constructive rather than destructive comments. Find something, no matter how small, to compliment or praise, but keep in mind that the compliment must be legitimate.

Improvisations from floor pattern

If emotional expression is expected from beginning students without carefully preparing them, the result will be distressing to the student and disappointing to the teacher. The following is a device that may be used as a lead-in to such expression.

Establish an uncomplicated floor pattern. It should be simple, something easy to remember, but using several different directions. For example: four steps moving forward; two slow steps back; six steps and a hold sideways; four or eight running diagonally back; and some kind of a turn or a circle.

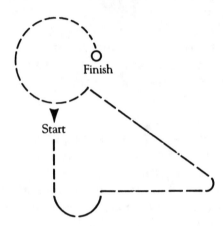

Have each student work out his or her own variation. Keep the basic directions, but use steps other than walks, and change the direction of facing. After each student has worked out a movement variation (the "something to hang on to"), have all students dance their own variation at the same time, moving as though they were terribly hot and tired. (They may make some changes in their movement pattern if they feel it is necessary.) Use this basic floor pattern for several mood or feeling variations.

Or, the variation in mood or feeling may be stimulated by using music with definitely varied moods. Tell the class to move with the feeling of the music.

Improvisation from slow motion

Slow motion offers an excellent opportunity for gaining a heightened awareness of movement. Start with any previously established movement pattern, or work out a new one and repeat it in extremely slow motion. It is important to keep the movement complete and the flow of energy sequentially accurate. (Students may be interested to learn that in ancient Greece, the Olympic athletes practiced their athletic events for the Olympic games in slow motion.)

Improvisation with eyes closed

Moving with eyes closed is an excellent device for increasing movement awareness. This may be used as a variation in performing an established pattern, or the following device may be used:

Divide the class into groups of four or five. The groups need not be the same size. Have the students position themselves so they are touching someone else in their group with some part of the body other than their hands. Have each group work out an interesting design with variations in level, position, and direction of facing. Tell students to close their eyes. This will seem very strange at first. Occasionally, students may exhibit fear of not seeing where they are going. Reassure them as you talk them through the exercise. Tell them that you will not let anyone run into anything that will be harmful. Instruct the class to move slowly. Very soft, slow music may be helpful.

It is normal to giggle when faced with an unusual situation. Also, the more insecure students will want to peek to see what others are doing. You must stress that the purpose of this exercise is for each to experience a new feeling about movement and that there is nothing to see. If they peek, they will be missing out on the experience and, if they giggle or talk, they will be interfering with the experience of others, which is not fair.

It may be necessary to remind them, at intervals, to keep the eyes closed. The following are suggestions for procedure:

Keep eyes closed and start moving slowly; interweave with others in your group; keep eyes closed and change level as you interweave; keep in contact with someone in your group; keep changing the contacts; the contact need not be with the hands; make the group slightly larger; keep eyes closed and keep interweaving, but do not try to keep actual contact with others though contact is all right. Keep eyes closed and, still moving, slowly try to move to another group. Do not open eyes to find another group. See if you can make yourself so sensitive that you can sense when you are close to someone. (When you feel this has gone on long enough, add the following.) Open your eyes and see where you are.

Often, students will end up in one group in the center of the studio with a few scattered out in the studio. It is a good idea for you to keep moving as you give instructions so students do not choose their directions by moving in relation to where you usually stand.

A variation of this is to have students move in the dark, if it is possible to darken the studio. Even if the room cannot be darkened completely, students like the sensation of moving in the dark and may have a more secure feeling about movement when they feel that no one can see them. Others like this exercise because it is "mysterious." If the room blacks out completely, arrange a small, shaded light some place so it is possible to know where others are and to prevent collisions. It is not necessary to keep movement slow in this situation.

Additional ideas for early creative studies or improvisation

The following are for beginning students, early improvisations, and early dance studies. These are not for more advanced students ready for a separate composition course. Some students may wish to experiment with some of the ideas outside of class. Allow relatively little time for these exercises.

1. Move without sound. This may be added at the end of the exercise involving moving with eyes closed or moving in the dark, mentioned in the previous section. Gradually lower the volume of the music until it is completely off. Tell the class to keep moving. They probably will not be able to continue for very long, but it is worth a try.

2. Vary the starting position. Consider positions such as sitting, lying (facing front, back, or side), kneeling, etc. Or, if the class is secure in making choices, use less definite instructions such as: Start in a low position, in a high position, or in a position halfway between low and high. Make the position as interesting as possible.

   Some variation of the following may be used to get the class moving: Start in some kind of sitting position. Start a swaying movement in the torso; try swaying forward, backward, and side-to-side. Keep this going and let the arms join the movement. Let these movements change your sitting position and direction of facing. Now let the movement lead you into a standing position and then to traveling around the floor. Keep changing your direction and facing.

3. Localized leads may be used as a starting point by giving instructions such as the following: Start one arm moving in as many ways as possible. Let the rest of your body follow where the arm leads. Change arms. Let the resulting movement from the arm lead, carrying into another part leading. Keep changing leads.

4. New ways of moving may be suggested. Starting in a lying position, find new ways to travel across the floor. If needed, be prepared to suggest rolling, crawling, wriggling, and possible combinations of these. Another useful device is to mention ways of moving that you see students using themselves instead of offering suggestions yourself. This gives recognition to the students initiating their own ideas, while at the same time providing suggestions for those needing help.

5. Suggest variations in use of dynamics. Instruct the class to start with very strong, sharp movements in one place; then to use the same or similar movements while traveling. Contrast this with slow, smooth movements; with strong and slow movements; with smooth and fast movements. Try a gradual change from smooth to sharp; from strong to weak; or vice versa. There are dozens of possible variations.

6. Another useful device is to say, "Move as though you were: very tired; very aggressive; uncertain; facing a strong wind; going with a strong wind"; and so on.

7. As soon as students have some confidence and ease in improvisation, they should be given frequent opportunities to move freely to music. Give suggestions only when they are needed to broaden movement experience or awareness. Wide variation in types of music should be used. Early in the course, this should be kept short. You do not need to play a whole piece.

8. Develop short movement studies starting from the movement, feel, or sound of a heartbeat; breathing; laughing; crying.

9. Develop short movement studies with a prop. Several approaches are possible with this.

   (a) Use a prop while moving.
   (b) Examine the prop for shape, texture, quality, feel, weight, and its own movement possibilities. Then develop a movement study based on these properties but without actually using the prop.

(c) Use the prop in three or more ways other than the actual purpose of the object. For example, for an umbrella: Do not use it as an umbrella, but use it as a pan for panning for gold, as something to hide behind, or, closed, as a gun. A stick might be used as a fan, a mirror, or a tree branch to swing on.

(d) The props can be used for literal pantomime or for abstract movement.

(e) Props can be used for solos, duets, or large group studies.

(f) One or more props might be used in the same dance study.

Students are most creative in devising uses for props. Keep a box of odd objects in the studio for use in these studies and add to it constantly. It might contain objects such as: a large piece of plastic; old umbrellas; long pieces of elastic; handles of old broken badminton and tennis rackets; many odd-shaped pieces of fabric of various weights, textures, and colors; egg cartons; various sizes, shapes, and weights of boards and sticks; ropes of different length and sizes. A long length of elastic (4 to 6 feet) offers many possibilities for small group improvisations.

When using props, stress that familiar objects are not to be used for their intended purpose. For example, chairs are not to be used for sitting. Of course, these are only guidelines. For all creative work, there can be no absolute rules. It is possible that a very interesting dance study can be composed involving a student sitting on a chair.

(g) Use furniture (such as tables, folding chairs, ladders, and the like, or any other object in the studio) as a starting point. If necessary, remind students that these can be turned on the side or upside down.

(h) Watch the way someone you do not know walks or moves. Try to copy the movements exactly and see what tensions and feelings these movements produce in you. Develop this into a short dance study.

(i) Move in different paths: curved; zigzag; straight lines with sharp corners; spiral; and so on.

(j) Use focus as the main point of study. Experiment with holding the focus with some part of the body other than the eyes or face. For example, the back, an arm, or a leg may be pulled toward or away from a definite spot on the floor or wall.

(k) In groups of three, develop interesting designs from the concept of: symmetry; sequential line; or oppositional design. In the oppositional design, another area can be included, that of energy. In addition to an opposition in line of the various parts of the bodies, be dependent on each other for maintaining position in the design or for maintaining balance. Each dancer can be leaning on another in such a way that, if the person moves, position or balance is lost. Let opposition of energy between people sustain the positions.

(l) Improvise with fast reaction to action works. A device that may be helpful is to say a word, allow a short time for the movement reaction, then have students just walk for a few steps before saying the next word. Here are a few suggestions: ooze; cling; melt; bounce; slink; barefoot on hot cement; coiling; sailing; rush hour; rocking chair; molasses; gimmee!; sandpaper; popping corn.

(m) Make sounds (not music) and have students adjust their movement to fit the sounds. Or have students create their own sounds.

(n) Move from a tactile experience. Feel an object in a sack or with eyes closed, then try to move from this feeling. Try to select objects that cannot be identified by touch.

(o) Develop short studies (either solo or small group) from a visual design or from an abstract mobile.

(p) Develop a short movement study in which the movement, tempo, or use of space decreases or increases; enlarges and diminishes; or vice versa.

(q) Base a study on the individual or contrasting use of tension and relaxation.

(r) Develop a short movement study based on a set rhythmic pattern. Use a full phrase. The beats of the rhythm do not have to be carried by the feet.

The possibilities are infinite.

Chapter 13

Introduction to Dance Composition

It takes great self-discipline and honesty to work with movement objectively when composing a dance. Such composition requires both careful analysis of the subject matter to extract the essence of the subject and enough technical control of your instrument to be able to communicate your meaning to an audience. To be able to do this, there must be sincerity, sensitivity, completeness of movement, and a concentrated awareness of the idea of the dance. And, with all this cerebral labor, there must be an emotional expression: an objectified passion.

Dance is not easy. You must furnish your own drive, exuberance, and vitality. Examine the unfamiliar with the open mind of a child seeing something wonderful for the first time; search out the essentials, but do so without your prejudices or a set of contemporary patterns. Trying this will often be difficult, sometimes painful, but the result will bring rewards and satisfaction.

Transition into Composition

The creative artist must have a broad cultural background. Look at pictures and read as much as you possibly can in such fields as philosophy, social anthropology, and art history. Listen to all kinds of music. See all you can of the graphic arts. Observe people. Be aware of their movement. Ask yourself why they move as they do, what is behind certain tensions and postures or shapes they fall into. From a practical standpoint for students, you may be able to combine some background work for dance composition with research papers in other courses.

When composing a full-length dance, form is necessary, but the motivating force must always be the idea, mood, or content of the dance. Start with exploration of movement to find expressive and meaningful themes. You must always begin this way. Do not start by performing your favorite steps, repeating movements you've seen others do, or by listening to your favorite music. You must learn to work with the medium of dance, which is movement.

After the student has had experience in improvisation and has tried short movement studies in many areas, the studies should be increased in length and complexity so they become short dances in which more attention is paid to structure and compositional form.

Why bother about form? A statement often repeated in the classes of Louis Horst comes to mind: "Doing a dance without form is like trying to drink tea without a cup."

The understanding of and beginning practice in compositional form is part of the craft of dance. However, work on form alone can become so mechanical that the elements of expressive movement and communication are lost. This loss results when the experience in improvisation and short studies is omitted. However, if such experience is not omitted and is used to lead into the study of form, there should be no problem in retaining feeling and expressivity in the movement.

When an experienced choreographer works on a composition, each dance dictates its own way of starting and working. Each individual eventually develops an approach to choreography that works for him or her, and this may vary with each dance. For the student just beginning to study composition, here are a few guidelines to use as a checklist. At intervals throughout the choreographic process ask yourself these questions about your composition:

1. Did I thoroughly explore movement possibilities and select truly expressive movement themes that are appropriate for this subject?
2. Is the meter definite? Are the rhythm patterns and phrasing interesting?
3. Is there sufficient variation in dynamics and quality?
4. Is there interesting use of space (unless the subject dictates otherwise)? Am I using variation in level, direction, and stage areas?
5. Is there repetition as well as variation?
6. Is there a logical development of thematic material? Is development logical from one theme to another?
7. What form or forms does this particular dance demand?
8. Do I avoid overuse of trite or frequently seen movements and positions? (This should include the use of lifts.)
9. Is this type of accompaniment the best for this particular dance?
10. Is the title appropriate and interesting?
11. Can I remember the movement sequences? (If a movement sequence is almost impossible to remember, the chances are that there is something wrong with the sequence, and it should be re-examined for logical development or expressiveness.)

In their first attempts at actual composition, most students will need help from the teacher and the discipline of a deadline they must meet. Whatever the performance—whether for a class, an informal studio recital, or a concert—there is always a deadline that must be met with a finished, thoroughly rehearsed dance.

Compositional Form

Beginning composition students need to know and understand the traditional forms of composition. Of course, those who continue in this field of dance and become experienced choreographers should not feel tied to the traditional forms and may not feel any compulsion to use them. Each dance they compose will dictate its own form, which may or may not be recognizable by traditionalists. However, they should have the traditional forms in their background.

A possible progression for introducing compositional form is: (1) development of movement themes; (2) the form of beginning, middle, and end; (3) A-B-A form; (4) theme and variation; (5) rondo; (6) round; (7) composition for definite numbers (duet, trio, quartet, etc.); (8) composition by chance. These studies will introduce students to the most basic, traditional, compositional forms.

The average beginning composition class, especially the short courses, will not be able to go into all of these forms. Ideally, there should be a series of a minimum of three courses in composition, which is designed for increasing difficulty and complexity.

Movement themes

Several approaches can be used to provide practice in the development of movement themes. Some teachers include these approaches as part of their technique classes. Those who have had this type of technique class can consider the following:

1. Combine two or three movements in such a way that one movement flows into the next with a feeling that they belong together.
2. The theme might start with an arm movement, lead into a locomotor step traveling in space, and continue into a turn or a leap.
3. The theme might start with small swinging movements that increase in dynamics and range and carry into a hop, followed by a fall (with or without recovery to a standing position).
4. The theme can be developed on a low level, perhaps completely on the floor.
5. The theme can be developed from movements based on a feeling or mood.
6. A movement theme can be built on a rhythmic phrase.

Beginning, middle, and end

The form of beginning, middle, and end is often called a "literary form," although it is also a basic form for both dance and music. It can be applied to a long, extended composition in which other forms are used in the various sections, or it can be applied to a very short study or composition. Several approaches are possible. Whatever the approach or point of departure, however, a few basic guidelines should be followed. Be sure to have a very definite beginning and ending, with a (usually longer) middle section in which the main idea is developed. There should be a climax. This climax or special point of interest usually appears in the middle section (it can be at any point in the section), although it may actually come any place in the dance.

The following are some possible approaches to use for this form:

1. For beginners, try using the dramatization in movement of a tightwire act. Have a definite beginning, a middle section in which the tightwire act is developed, and a pronounced ending. Even though this movement is done quite literally, it still lends itself to dance movements. Students should be encouraged to perform in the exhibitionistic style of the circus.
2. Follow a simple story line. If the students perform this in literal pantomime, they should rework the composition in stylized dance movement. A simple story line might be as general as two people meeting, something happening, and the two people parting. The students will need to make several decisions. The meeting can be an expected event or an accident. The happening can be the giving of a gift, an argument, or something else. The parting depends on the happening. In addition, the students will need to decide on the type of characters, the relationship between the two, and the location of the meeting. All of these considerations will also affect the

direction of the movement when abstracting the literal pantomime into stylized dance movement. The method by which students abstract the literal pantomime into dance movement can be based on earlier short dance studies, or it can be directed into a new approach. If the students are far enough advanced, the movement can be formed in a primitive, balletic, jazz, or an ethnic style.

A-B-A form

The A-B-A form is fundamental in music and literature as well as dance. Basically, this form is the statement of a theme or idea, the introduction of a second theme or idea, and the return to the first theme or idea. The restatement of the first theme may be the same as the original, or it can be a variation. This form should incorporate the basic concept, or theme, and thematic development; it may or may not include the beginning, middle, and end form. The A-B-A form often has an additional ending called a coda.

As an introduction to this form, have students compose a short movement theme. This theme can originate from a mood or from abstract actions such as sustained movements starting on the floor, slowly rising, and ending with some kind of turn. After finishing this theme, call it "A." Then compose a second theme to start where A ended. The second theme might be built around locomotor movements traveling in space, perhaps with some swinging movements and steps that go into the air. This theme must end in the position from which A started, or in a movement that can lead into the beginning movement of A. Call this second theme "B." Now repeat A to complete the A-B-A form. The return to A may be a variation of the original A; it may be shortened, expanded, or reversed. There are other possibilities although, for the first experience, it may be advisable to keep it simple and just repeat the original A.

Theme and variation

Theme and variation is the most versatile form; the variables are innumerable. Basically, there must be some element that is established and remains. This holding base may be a floor pattern, a rhythmic pattern, or a movement pattern. If the floor pattern is the base, the movement and rhythmic patterns can be developed with many variations. The floor pattern can be enlarged, diminished, inverted, or doubled while still considered the holding base for the other variations.

If the movement pattern is established as the holding base, there may be many variations in the floor and rhythmic pattern and use of space. In addition, the movement pattern itself can have the same variations that were listed for the floor pattern: (1) diminished; (2) enlarged (repeat some parts before continuing with the next part, or use more space); or (3) doubled (add more dancers performing the movement in unison or as a mirror image, or whole sections can be repeated before continuing). The movement pattern can also be varied in tempo, style, or mood.

If the rhythmic pattern is the holding base, it is possible to develop many variations in the movement pattern, the floor pattern, the use of space or level, and in the mood. In addition, the rhythmic pattern may be varied in tempo and in musical signature, or it may be syncopated, to name a few possibilities.

Rondo

The easiest approach to the rondo form is to compare it with a song that has several verses and a chorus that is repeated between each verse. The rondo may also be considered a variation or an extension of the A-B-A form to A-B-A-C-A-D-

A, and so on. Theoretically, the rondo may be any length, but it is advisable for beginners to use some discretion in its development. This form is often more successful with small groups than a with a solo dancer.

An effective first explanation of the rondo form is to have a small group (not more than five) work together in developing the A theme. The group may work in duets, trios, or as a solo in developing the B, C, and D (or however many) themes that follow. Then, when performing, the whole group joins in for the repetition of the original theme, that is, the A that appears between the B, C, and D section as well as at the beginning and the end.

Any of the suggestions given in preceding sections on variations of a rhythmic pattern may be used as takeoff points in developing this form. Slight variations in the original theme are permitted as it is repeated, particularly in the final statement.

Round

The round in dance may be easily understood if the musical version is considered first. Nearly all school children have sung ''Row, Row, Row Your Boat'' or ''Good Night, Ladies.'' These are rounds using three groups of voices all singing the same theme, but each group starts at a different time.

In a dance version of a round, variations in direction and level may be used by the succeeding dancers as they join the theme. For the first exploration of this form, either of the songs mentioned may be used as a starting point if you do not have access to other music.

Practice composing simple rounds with a base of abstract movement of various moods, a floor pattern, or a movement quality. There are some basic guidelines that should be considered when composing a round. The movement of the different ''voices'' must harmonize when seen as a whole. The placement in space of the different sections is important so that all can be seen. The ending of the theme must lead into the repetition.

This form can be a very useful device for a teacher who is called in at the last moment to assist with the yearly school operetta or musical. All too often in these instances, the dance is added after all other areas are well along in their development. In such cases, it may be necessary to be inventive instead of creative in order to meet the deadline of the opening-night curtain. Further, there are extreme variations and limitations in mood, music, stage space, ethnic or historic style, and, above all, in the performers' lack of dance training. The round can permit a great deal of stage movement while keeping to a minimum the actual dance movement that performers must learn. They all learn one simple sequence, but different groups start at different times and possibly on different areas of the stage.

Use of groups

When most students attempt their first dance study involving more than one dancer, they usually set the movements in a unison pattern: All of the dancers are asked to perform the same movements at the same time. However, students should experiment with the variations possible when using two, three, four, or five dancers who are not all performing the same movement at the same time, though they may perform in unison at times.

Ideally, the movement pattern should reflect why a specific number of dancers is needed. Louis Horst conveyed this idea by saying that if one of the dancers were removed, the pattern would be incomplete and unbalanced, and if one were added, the pattern would seem cluttered or wrong.

Eventually, in composing full-length dances, the idea of the dance should always dictate the number of dancers used. However, this is not absolutely necessary in beginning composition studies.

Composition by chance

For more advanced students, or for a more contemporary experience, introduce composition by chance. One type of approach for this form follows, though there are others.

Have three sets of numbered lists: one list of rhythmic patterns, one list of mood or feeling situations, and one list of floor patterns (provide sketches if you wish). Have students pull numbered pieces of paper from a hat or bag. The first drawing will determine the rhythmic pattern to use; the second, the content of the dance; the third, the floor pattern to use. The students then put the three elements together for their dance study. This will take much more time to work out than most of the studies.

Use of Word Phrases

To retain the concept of combining expressive movement with the cerebral study of form, you may employ the simple device of having the students select a phrase from a list you provide and use that as the base for a dance study. If the students are simply told to find an idea for a dance composition, it may take half the class period for most to decide on a starting idea. Supplying ideas from which to choose can save time but also may serve as a springboard for later compositions. Choose phrases that offer many possible interpretations. If students do have their own ideas, by all means let them use these. But be prepared in case the class needs help.

The following are some possible phrases you might use. The students must be secure in creative exploration before being introduced to these. These are not quick little studies as presented in some of the early explorations. Allow time for students to work these out and to perform the studies in front of the class.

So what!

Scatter time.

No shadows here.

Command space!

Twisted rainbows all around.

That unfelt clasp of a hand.

Out of the wild darkness.

Encirclement.

I feel stapled, numbered, and spindled.

Where are you?

Interrupted laughter.

Storm warning.

Behind these walls.

The shimmering of the aspens.

Fasten your seat belts.

Too many people.

And all that jazz.

Walk alone.

Leave them a flower.

Take man as your companion.

The restless earth.

I am!

Defy time and the elements.

Ride the wild waves.

Step aside to give a caterpillar the right of way.

Ripple the air with quickening tempos.

The stranger in the house is myself.

Pale and shimmering.

Hands open in welcome, our welcomes blend.

Squeeze the universe.

The dull eternity of angels singing.

The sounds of insects fade.

In a vacuum.

Flight.

Changing vibrations.

Ever-silent spaces.

A place of mystery.
So long.
Ho hum!
Wrong way on a one-way
    street.
In ever-higher and wider rings.
Like suns that slide to the
    ocean floor.
I am surrounded by an infinity
    of giddy, laughing faces: all
    of them my own.

Silence is the shriek of life.
Across the plains, the endless
    trek.
Not with a laugh but a
    whimper.
The Pavane-like entry of a man
    who comes mysteriously and
    with ponderous gravity to
    say something ridiculously
    unimportant.

Performing Areas

Until recently, dances were composed for presentation on a conventional, proscenium stage. All this has changed with the advent of television and the current presentation of dances in parks, gymnasiums, streets, museums, and other places. In composing a dance for a specific location, you must consider the location in the shape of the composition, in the actual movement, the idea or content, and eventually in the costuming.

This is particularly true for television. Television is a very demanding medium. A dance composed for a conventional stage cannot be effectively transposed to television. The television camera has its own demands of space and time that can be confusing to the choreographer inexperienced with television techniques. Impression of distance is a fundamental problem. Three steps away from the camera look like the distance covered by ten steps on stage, and on television the dancer shrinks from a normal size on stage to a midget. On a conventional stage, the upstage area is smaller in width than the downstage area.

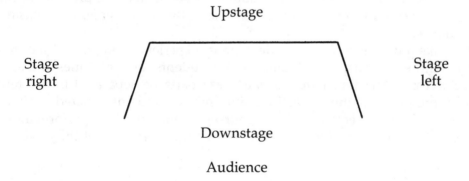

Upstage

Stage
right

Stage
left

Downstage

Audience

On television the opposite is true. The performing area is a triangle. The camera (the audience) is the point, but this can move. Anything happening outside the lines is not seen. Also, anyone too close to the camera blocks out everything else.

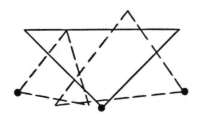

If you must present a previously composed dance for television, you must restage the dance. It may be difficult, but in most cases restaging can be done without changing the concept or purpose of the dance.

Dance for television is an area that needs much creative and concentrated work—studying television techniques, and being involved in editing the tape. Much of dance on television (except for the "Dance in America" series) has been so changed by the tape editors that choreographers are hard pressed to recognize their own work.

A note of warning: If you are involved in presenting a program on a local television station, check to be sure that the same director and floor manager will cover both the rehearsal and the performance. Try to choose a rehearsal time that permits this.

Performance

Even beginning students need a chance to perform. However, a formal program with paid admission should never be held after only six to to ten weeks in a beginning dance course. The first performance should be the showing of dance studies as they are developed in class. Later, an informal, studio performance for other classes, for parents and friends, or for an invited audience is fine. A lecture-demonstration program may also be suitable.

These programs must include all students in the class. The audience should understand that the students are beginners and that the studies were composed by the students.

There should be simple, inexpensive costuming even for an informal studio presentation. This may be a scarf draped around the torso, a sash, a head scarf, or a skirt. It must not be expensive or extensive. The costuming is for the benefit of the dancers more than for the audience, providing the feeling of a special occasion. Try to avoid the use of all-black leotards and tights if possible. There is something depressing for both dancers and audiences about an entire program in black. Simple colors can do wonders for the morale of the dancers and are pleasing to the audience.

To make progress in dance, students must experience a synthesis, a bringing together of the many aspects of dance in the students' own activities and awareness. Successful teaching requires that these parts be separated in a carefully planned progression, then practiced, intermixed, and interrelated in lessons throughout the total sequence of the course, culminating in a performance. Of course, the performance audience can be the other members of the class.

Part III

TEACHING DANCE

Students often decide to become dance teachers because dance is fun. This is great; it should be fun. However, some students do not recognize that responsibility accompanies the more enjoyable aspects. There is a tendency to forget the early stages of your own development and include exercises that seem easy for you now but are too difficult for beginners. Chapter 14 will help both the young teacher and the student about to become a teacher recognize the responsibilities associated with the teaching of dance. One of the most important responsibilities is understanding the relationship between the various areas of dance training and incorporating this into logical lesson plans that provide for progressive development of your own students. Chapter 15 shows how you can develop your own lesson plans. Sample lesson plans are presented for a six-week course. These lesson plans illustrate the progressive development that should occur in a dance course.

Chapter 14

Organizing and Evaluating Dance Classes

Your first teaching position can be exciting but at the same time frightening, and the amount of work is often overwhelming, especially at first. However, the responsible beginning teacher who plans lessons and courses carefully will soon learn the swing of teaching and begin to enjoy its rewards. Seeing your own students grow and develop in creativity and in technical skill—which in turn aid in their growth as mature people—is very satisfying and stimulating. Accompanying this will be your joy in recognizing your own maturation and capabilities as a teacher. The recognition that you have something to give, that you are also a creative person, is one of the greatest rewards.

Transition from Student to Teacher

Making the transition from student to teacher requires a new perspective, a new outlook. It can be a difficult time. Here are some tips for the beginning teacher that may make the transition somewhat easier:

1. Establish an efficient and organized filing system to organize all materials so you can find what you need when you need it.
2. Accept the fact that you are no longer a college student with the accompanying privileges of youth but an adult in authority, with responsibilities. Accepting this transition may result in: (a) a change of attitude toward dress style; (b) a change of attitude toward those in authority over you; and (c) a change in your way of approaching work.
3. Recognize that, while you do have a certain new authority, you are new to the situation and still have much to learn. Be willing to accept criticism objectively and gracefully. Although your first reaction to any criticism may be resentment and antagonism, give yourself time to think it through and find a way to respond tactfully.
4. Maintain a sense of humor; it can be a lifesaver.
5. Be friendly, but steer clear of cliques and antagonistic or negative groups.

6. Accept the fact that class schedules and assigned duties are not set for your convenience and outside interests. The school authorities feel that the school comes first and that you should have the same sense of responsibility. For example, you may be a member of a regional dance group preparing for a performance. An assigned school duty may interfere with a rehearsal that is vitally important to you. However, the school authorities could not care less about your other obligations and would rather not hear about it. Accept your responsibility to the school.

Class Organization

Varying the way a class is organized can help add interest to it. Such variations may include facing in different directions for exercises in place and incorporating many pattern variations for traveling exercises.

In addition to the specific objectives of the traveling exercises, they present opportunities and learning possibilities for both the teacher and student. For example, when the class is moving across the floor singly or a few at a time, the teacher can concentrate observation and give individual assistance. In addition, students may receive practice in leading. Because each passage across the floor should have a new leader at the front of the line, a pattern can be established whereby at the end of a passage across the floor the leader or leaders go to the end of the line and the next in line become leaders for the next crossing. At first, beginning classes will need to be reminded to do this, but most classes quickly fall into the pattern. Students should not hold back or act silly or apologetic when it is their turn to lead.

The traveling exercises also allow students to become more aware of, and to practice, phrasing and timing by giving them the opportunity to start across the floor at the correct time without being told. Again, beginners will need help at first. The teacher will need to help students learn to judge when to start. Work to reach the point where students start at the right time without help. This awareness requires that all students stay alert and concentrate.

The following are the most commonly used formations or class organizations:

1. Move from the corners of the studio. Most modern dance teachers use this formation. It offers the longest pathway and provides more room for movement. This formation has several variations.
   (a) Have one, two, three, or more (depending on the width of the studio and size of the class) cross the floor at a time. Have them cross on a diagonal path, then walk to the opposite corner for the return.

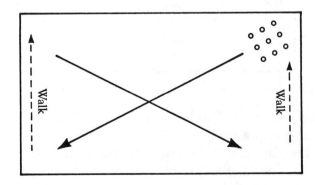

(b) Divide the class in half and alternate the corners.

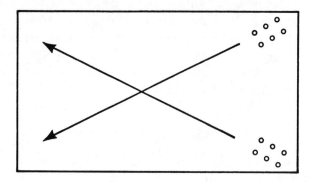

(c) Use a zigzag path. This formation can use either one or two corners. Groups can alternate moving, or both can move at the same time.

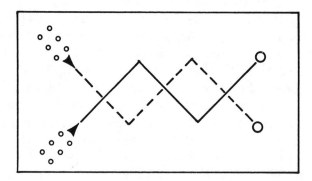

(d) Divide the class into three groups, each in a corner of the studio. Have each group travel a circular path to the open corners. All members of one group will finish traveling before the next group starts.

(e) Use a curving or random path across the studio.

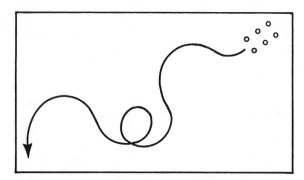

(f) Develop movement combinations with built-in floor patterns for solo, duet, or group action.

2. Organize the class into lines. Have the lines of dancers travel the length of the studio. The number of lines will depend on the width of the studio and the size of the class.

(a) Have students travel from one end of the studio to the other.

(b) Divide the class in half with half at each end of the studio, and have them cross to the opposite end.

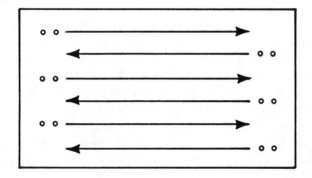

(c) If the studio is square or if it is wide enough, several variations are possible. Use a zigzag to end at an open side or to change places with those at the opposite end of the studio.

3. Use a circle formation. Have students form one circle, two or more concentric circles, or several smaller circles. The circles can all travel in the same direction or they can travel in opposite directions.

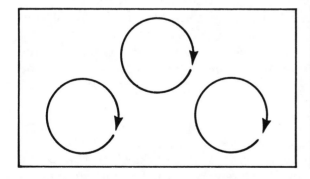 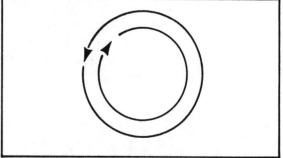

Evaluation

Assigning grades is one of the most difficult problems for teachers. In education circles, the debate over subjective versus objective evaluation continues, but in the arts a completely objective test or system of grading is not possible.

Most high schools have guidelines for grading that vary with the district or the school requirements. For years, physical education departments in high schools (and even some colleges) required teachers to check and grade (sometimes daily) such areas as: attendance and attitude (with no guidelines as to what was meant by "attitude"); neatness and cleanliness; whether students wore the required class attire; and whether a shower was taken after class. If your school still requires such rigid grading, you are stuck with it and must comply.

Preliminary planning

Fortunately, most schools are now less specific and leave the basis for grading up to the teacher. However, this places a vastly greater responsibility on the teacher. The teacher must decide:

1. What is important in each particular course (what activities, concepts, or movements are important enough to grade).
2. Exactly how to go about completing the actual grading.
3. How to prepare the students for the selected method of grading.
4. What method to use for informing the students of their grades.

The method selected for evaluation will vary with the subject matter of the course (technique, composition, teaching methods, and so on). For example, the grade for a technique class should not be based on a creative study assigned the last week or two of the course. This may be appropriate for a composition course, but a technique course should be graded on the techniques included in the course. There are also other variables. The kinds and number of tests will depend on the length of the course (six or eight weeks, full semester), for example. And the size of the class (12 or 15 students, or 40 to 50 students), level of the students, and length of the class (35 or 90 minutes) will affect both the method for evaluation and the number and kinds of tests.

Although the final grade will come at the end of the course, basis for grading must be built into the planning of the course. The teacher must decide in advance what points or areas of the course will be graded and how and when these will be introduced into the course. This is one reason why a course must be planned completely, not lesson by lesson (see Chapter 15).

Tests should also be planned in advance, because there should always be a review before a test (either physical or written). For a technique class, the teacher may review by choosing three principal points as a primary base for testing and checking these points informally over two or three class periods. Or the teacher may use a procedure similar to a regular test; this can serve as a rehearsal for the actual test so students will be more comfortable and, hopefully, less tense for the real test. However, teachers must stress that the review is not an actual test and will not be graded.

Information to students

Students should be given a handout sheet at the beginning of the course that lists dates of reviews and tests and gives a statement of the basis for grading. A simple device like this can prevent many of the complaints often encountered after grades are released. Most complaints stem from students not knowing what is expected of them, not understanding the basis for grading, or from receiving just a number or letter grade with no indication of where they were in error.

A basic outline of the course should be given to the students at the same time. This will help them see the relationships among the various areas of the course as these areas are introduced. Future teachers should keep these for later reference.

A decision must be made as to how grades will be distributed after a test and at the end of the term. If grades are posted, some method must be used to protect the privacy of the students. If individual conferences are possible, there must be a plan to schedule them. Individual conferences are desirable but not always possible with a heavy class schedule or a large student load.

The teacher must also decide whether to use a numerical system such as 1 to 10, or a letter grade such as A, B, C, etc., and what the qualifications will be for each. Most schools now use the A, B, C, D, F system for their permanent records.

Sharing meaningful grade information with students during the course is important. A number or a letter grade alone does not provide a very meaningful evaluation for them. Especially for a midterm exam or an exam early in the course, the number or letter does not tell students what areas need work for improvement. This can be very upsetting. Consequently, written tests should always be returned with notations showing mistakes or inaccuracies. Correcting tests in this way is time consuming and often a bore, but as a teacher your job is to help students learn, and they deserve this information. With practical tests, check sheets should be evaluated and results recorded, and then the check sheets should be returned to the students.

Let us look at an example of a practical test of a technique course. The test might include: a basic exercise, such as one on the floor or standing; an exercise including a *plié*; an exercise using brushes; an exercise traveling across the floor; an exercise involving leaps, hops, or jumps; and one or more combinations of movements. Several of these areas may be combined in one exercise. The actual exercises included will depend on the material presented in class. The test might be set up as follows with important points listed for quick identification:

(class number or day and time)

NAME _____ CLASS _____

IMPROVEMENT _____ DANCE QUALITY _____

ALTERNATE CONTRACTION AND CHEST ARCH

	Contraction	Arch
Control of center	_____	_____
Shoulders	_____	_____
Head	_____	_____

PLIÉ and *RELEVÉ*

	Small	Deep	*Relevé*
Back alignment; Hips	_____	_____	_____
Knees	_____	_____	_____
Ankles	_____	_____	_____
Arms; Shoulders; Head	_____	_____	_____

BRUSHES

	On Floor	Off Floor
Back alignment	_____	_____
Legs; Hips	_____	_____
Feet; Ankles	_____	_____
Arms; Shoulders; Head	_____	_____

JUMPS

Back; Center control	_____
Legs; Hips	_____
Feet; Ankles	_____
Arms; Shoulders; Head	_____

TRIPLET, SIDE HOP, FULL TURN

Triplet	_____
Leg and back control	_____
Turn: Degree, balance, smoothness	_____
Connecting movements	_____

ALTERNATE: STEP-HOP, STEP-LEAP

Connecting movements	_____
Alignment of back	_____
Landing control	_____
Knees: *Plié*, heel to floor	_____
Ankles	_____

How many exercises are included will depend on the size and length of the class.

When the test is given, try to establish an atmosphere that is positive and as free from tension as possible. You may be able to grade more than one student at a time. Each teacher will need to experiment to discover his or her observation capabilities. However, let's suppose you can grade three students at a time. The check sheets can be made up with three of the lists on one page to fit on a clip-board. Before starting the test, write the names of the students on the lists in alpha-betical order, then line the students up in alphabetical order. Start each exercise with a different group, so the same students do not always have the disadvantage of being first or the advantage of being last. In order to grade quickly and accurately, it is vital to think through beforehand what is involved in each exercise, what to look for.

After the test, the check sheet should be evaluated, results recorded, then the check sheets should be returned to the students. Post a schedule of days and times of office hours in a convenient place, along with a sign-up sheet for students who may want a conference.

Chapter 15

Guidelines for Lesson Plans

After acquiring both an understanding of many areas of dance movement and a technical facility that enables ease and authority in demonstration and performance, the beginning teacher is ready to consider a method of teaching. As a teacher of dance, it is essential to take time for careful planning of the total course and for each lesson within the course. This requirement means thinking in terms of progression, of how each exercise and lesson builds on earlier ones in both technical and creative aspects, so that the early lessons lay the foundation for the later ones.

This preliminary planning of the total course is vital for teaching, not only for dance but for all subjects. Too many schools omit or slight this stage in the training of the future teacher. Any student can plan one lesson, but to plan a complete progression for a total course is not so easy. Planning is a nuisance and it takes time, but it will actually save time later in the semester when all teachers are much busier. It will also make a significant difference in how far the class progresses and in the students' feeling of accomplishment.

Preliminary Planning

Before starting lesson plans, the teacher will need to answer the following questions about the specific teaching situation and the facilities to be used.

Teaching situation

1. What is the technical level of the students? Are they beginners or have they had previous dance experience? If they have had experience, what kind and how much?
2. How many weeks will the course last? How many lessons are there per week? What is the length of each class period? How much time is allowed for dressing both before and after class? Are showers required? Will the teacher be expected to supervise showers?

3. Will the class be all girls, all boys, or will it be mixed?

4. Will the students wear dance clothes or will they wear the regulation gym outfit? Are the clothes furnished by the school or do students furnish their own? If students furnish their own, where can they be purchased? If the school furnishes them, what is the distribution procedure, and is there an attendant in the dressing room to give clothes out, or are you expected to do it?

5. How many students are usually enrolled in the class? Is the teacher permitted any say in limiting the size of the class?

Facilities

1. What size is the room for the dance class?

2. What is the condition of the floor? Will it permit working in bare feet? Is the surface wood, tile, or cement? If it is tile or cement, it will be necessary to curtail the amount of leaping, jumping, and the like. Most school floors are so heavily waxed that they are a hazard not only for dancing but also for normal walking. If the dance classes are using a regular gymnasium, the floor will probably have what is called a gym finish. This type of finish was developed for rubber-soled shoes and works well for them. However, it is a hazard for dance; bare feet stick on it and ballet shoes slip on it.

3. What are the arrangements for keeping the floor clean? It can be very helpful to be on good terms with the school custodian. You must be considerate and thoughtful of the custodian's duties and time. (Many schools will not permit teachers to give suggestions or to make requests of the custodian. In such cases, all directions must go through the main office. Learn what the regulations are for your particular school. If they are oppressive or difficult, try to discover how to work around them tactfully and legally.)

4. Are there hazards such as posts, wall projections, or the like that need to be avoided?

5. What are the dressing room and shower facilities, and what is their condition? Are towels furnished? What are the laundry arrangements? Is there an attendant, or must the teacher handle and supervise these details?

6. What provision is made for music? What are the kinds and condition of percussion instruments, such as drums? What is the type and condition of the record player? What records are available and what condition are they in? What are the school regulations for purchasing new equipment and records, and for repairs if the record player needs it? Teachers cannot purchase items without the regulation form and school permit. If teachers purchase items without the regulation permit, they usually end up paying for them themselves. Many schools have yearly contracts with certain stores or supply houses through which all departments must buy. If the particular record or item needed is not carried by the contract firm, teachers must turn in a written statement to this effect when requesting permission to purchase the item elsewhere.

7. Is there a chalkboard and a bulletin board? If the bulletin board is glass enclosed and locked, find out who has the key and obtain a duplicate.

8. Do not hesitate to request new equipment or change in the existing facilities (such as a change from a cement floor or new records for those so old and scratchy that the music is hardly recognizable). Teachers never get all they ask for, but they do not get anything unless they request it. (The author once gave several workshops in a school in which some of the dance teachers

had taught for over ten years. They were constantly complaining about having to work on cement. When asked if they had requested that something be done to change this, they all said, "No, it wouldn't do any good." They knew no changes would be made. But that year they requested a raised wood floor be put over the cement, and the next year they had it. So do go after the facilities and records needed.)

School calendar

Obtain a school calendar that lists all school events—school assemblies, vacations, etc.—that may interfere with the regular class schedule.

Course Outline

With all these details in mind, you can begin planning your course. First, rough out a general outline of the areas to be included in the course plus others that might be included if time permits. Leave space under each heading for further details; this gives an overview of the total course. The following is an example of such an outline. Start out with this outline or something similar. As experience broadens and as class situations vary, you will need to change it. In fact, if you are a creative teacher, you will change it for every class each semester as long as you continue to teach.

1. Psychological aspect—belief in self
2. Movement vocabulary
   a. Dance positions
   b. Use of energy
   c. Time
   d. Use of space and direction
   e. Basic locomotion
   f. Basic axial movements
3. Specific techniques
   a. Alignment
   b. Flexibility control; increasing coordination and endurance
   c. Control of center
   d. Balance
   e. Flexion, extension, rotation of joint areas
   f. Feet, ankles, legs
   g. Hands, arms, shoulders
   h. Turns
   i. Falls and recoveries
4. Combinations of movement
   a. Locomotor
   b. Axial and other areas
5. Creative activities
   a. Preliminary explorations
   b. Compositional forms

How much is included under each of these headings, as well as the order and the specific exercises used, will depend on the ability of the students, the length of each class, and the length of the course.

Specifics for Lesson Plans

When planning lessons in detail, keep these guidelines in mind:

1. Each lesson should include: warmups, specific exercises for developing control and for increasing coordination and endurance; some vigorous activity such as locomotion traveling in space; and some creative activity.
2. As a general rule, review old material and then add new material.
3. For modern dance classes, it is customary to start on the floor, proceed to standing exercises then to combinations traveling across the floor, and finally to creative activities. Use this as a general format but vary it at times. Occasionally omit the floor work, using other, briefer warmups. At times omit the creative work, but then in other lessons devote the whole period to it. There is a tendency in some modern classes to spend too much time down on the floor.
4. Dance classes should be a minimum of 90 minutes long, with 25 to 30 minutes devoted to warmups and preparatory exercises. Unfortunately, almost all high schools and many colleges still have 35-minute (actual class time) classes, and we are forced to adjust to this. This time restriction is the main reason why the ideal format cannot always be used.
5. With knowledge of the class situation and the facilities available, and using the guidelines that were given, fill in details for the daily lessons. List the date for each class period in the course, and start sorting out and filling in specific exercises for the headings in the preliminary outline.
6. Experienced teachers usually develop their own format for lesson plans (although a few high school principals require teachers to turn in weekly lesson plans on a form they supply). Beginning teachers need a more detailed form than experienced teachers. The beginning teacher needs to learn or recall a great deal of information before each lesson. But learn to think of the lesson plans as a quick check or recall for the material to be taught that day. The plans should not consist of page after page of detail; use an outline form. It will save time and allow efficient use of the lesson plans. If detailed information about specific material is needed, go back to the textbooks.
7. It should not be necessary to write out every word to be used when teaching. However, the beginning teacher should practice before each class for the first lessons, saying aloud the actual words he or she will use (this includes practice in counting aloud). This practice is difficult for many new teachers, and it may seem a little silly, but it does make a difference. When things are said aloud, they come out differently and take a different amount of time than when they are just thought through. Also, beginning teachers should practice using the hand drum. Most need a lot of practice to be able to use the drum effectively.

Sample Lesson Plans for a Six-Week Course

The following lesson plans are only for illustration. There are other approaches, and many different exercises could have been included. These plans are for a six-week course of two lessons per week, with 35 minutes for each lesson. This format is used because most high schools (and still some colleges) use this scheduling. Approach these short courses as an introduction to dance; plan to provide experience in as many aspects of dance as possible. If a teacher decides, instead, to try to achieve facility in very limited areas, the following lesson plans would need to be completely changed.

For a longer course or follow-up courses, the areas introduced here would be reintroduced in greater depth, with more combinations, more technical drill, and longer and more creative studies. Note that many of the exercises used serve more than one purpose.

There is a great deal of material in the following lesson plans. Thus, time must not be wasted between exercises, and lessons must keep moving. Many high school and college dance classes move too slowly. When they do, the energy level, which drops between exercises, is difficult to recapture. Also, students may cool off too much; if so, they should warmup all over again. It is up to the teacher to generate energy and exhilaration in every class. Whether he or she succeeds in doing so depends partly on the progression planned in the lesson and partly on the length of waiting time between exercises. Long waits are usually found in classes where the teacher has no planned lesson; students stand around while the teacher tries to decide what to do next or to work out a combination. This waiting is inexcusable.

Teachers have various reasons or excuses for not planning lessons. Too often, the underlying reason is laziness. But another is that teachers become so overwhelmed with themselves as artists that they like to think they can create on the moment, and that planning ahead kills the creative spark. These individuals often excuse themselves by saying they do better by working spontaneously. Such self-indulgence deprives students of an uninterrupted class and a planned progression that provide technical growth and accomplishment.

Every class is different, so changes will be necessary no matter how carefully the lessons have been planned. Know what is most important in each lesson and be prepared to omit a less important exercise if time is limited. Also, do not hesitate to change a day's plans as varying situations develop in class. It takes experience to recognize class developments that require a change of plans.

Not specified in the lesson plans are details that should be automatic when teaching: Perform all exercises on both sides of the body; demonstrate with style and accuracy when introducing new techniques; and circulate through the class to help individuals and to make corrections as needed. For a beginning class, it is a good idea to announce that you will be moving around giving individual help and that this help may involve touching. Some students concentrate so completely that they are startled if they are touched when not expecting it. Also, some individuals do not like to be touched, and it may help if they have some previous warning. A note of caution: If you do touch or manipulate a student, be sure to do it gently and slowly. Roughness or speed will not help these students. Keep in mind that you are not making these corrections for punitive reasons. Rather, you are doing so to help the students teach themselves.

Detailed descriptions of the exercises named in the following plans can be found in Chapters 3 through 13. To further emphasize the importance of the relationship of one exercise to another, following most of the exercises (in parentheses) is the number of a lesson (1 to 12), and the roman numeral (and sometimes letter) in that lesson of a related exercise (for example 1-III-B refers to lesson 1, in which part III.B. gives an exercise in concentration). If the lesson number given is smaller than the current one, then the earlier exercise was preparatory to this exercise. If the lesson number is larger than the current one, this exercise is preparation for a later exercise.

Headings on Lesson Plans

One form for lesson plans includes the following headings: date; lesson; objectives; material to be taught; teaching pointers and safety factors; and formation and accompaniment.

1. Date and lesson are self-explanatory.
2. At the start of each lesson under "obj." there is a listing of the lesson's main objectives.
3. Material to be taught is listed in the order in which it will be introduced in class.
4. Teaching pointers consist of a word or phrase that will help students understand or learn the exercise. (How helpful such pointers are depends on how well you understand or have thought through the specific exercise.) The term "safety factors" refers to the way in which various techniques are performed to prevent injury. These two factors are listed under craft and science in the exercise explanations.
5. Formation is how the class is organized on the floor. Accompaniment is self-explanatory. Where there is no new listing for formation or accompaniment on the following lesson plans, it remains the same as for the preceding exercise.

OBJECTIVES, MATERIAL TO BE TAUGHT	TEACHING POINTERS AND SAFETY FACTORS	FORMATION, ACCOMPANIMENT
Lesson 1 *Obj:* To introduce students to course. To start developing vocabulary for dance.	Be friendly, but businesslike and as brief as possible.	

I. Introduction to class.
  A. Introduce self.
  B. Class costume.
  C. Rules, regulations, procedure for roll call.
  D. Procedure on showers, towels, and dressing rooms.
		Sit.
		Face teacher.

II. What is modern dance?
  A. General definition.
  B. Brief description of course.
  C. Hand out class calendar listing dates of reviews, tests, etc.		

III. Dance vocabulary. A. Belief in self—say names. (Check roll as students say names.)	Face the class and say "I am ____" and believe it.	Each goes to place in front of class.
B. Concentration (2-II).	Keep mind completely on what you are doing.	All scattered out on floor.

C. Space and time (2-IX).
    1. Medium tempo.
    2. Double time.
    3. Very fast.
	You are the beat. Be there at the moment the beat sounds.	Scattered, all face front.

D. Alignment. 1. Feet, thighs, between hip bone and lowest rib, chest and rib cage, neck, shoulder blades, buttocks (2-VI; 3-II, VI, X).	Be efficient. Use only the amount of energy needed, and only in the part you are using. Should be in perfect alignment and balance with no extra tension anywhere. Experiment with self, and find least amount of tension in all areas to accomplish alignment. Work on this outside of class.	Face teacher.
2. Rise to half-toe (*relevé*) (7-IV).	Hold everything and float up toward ceiling.	
E. Explore balance (7-IV). (Also, preparation for all exercises requiring balance and for turns.)	Experiment with yourself in different positions, trying to hold balance with ease. Try both feet, then one foot.	
F. Walk, run, slide, or skip until music stops.	Any step that fits the music.	Free use of space. Syncopated music.
IV. Resumé. You were introduced to some of the tools you have at your disposal; belief in self, concentration, use of space and tempos, alignment, balance.	Be explicit and as brief as possible. Do not ramble and repeat self.	Sit, facing teacher.

OBJECTIVES, MATERIAL TO BE TAUGHT	TEACHING POINTERS AND SAFETY FACTORS	FORMATION, ACCOMPANIMENT
V. Dismiss class; remind them to come to next class dressed for active work.		

Lesson 2

Obj. To deepen understanding and facility in use of dance vocabulary introduced in Lesson 1.
To increase dance vocabulary.
To introduce qualities of movement.
To increase facility and coordination in locomotion.
To introduce creative exploration.

OBJECTIVES, MATERIAL TO BE TAUGHT	TEACHING POINTERS AND SAFETY FACTORS	FORMATION, ACCOMPANIMENT
I. Review dance vocabulary from Lesson 1.	Ask class to name vocabulary.	Sit, facing teacher.
II. Review concentration. Variation: with a partner, trying to break concentration (1-III-B; 3-XIV).	One nearest me will do the concentration exercise as in Lesson 1. Partner tries to break concentration. Partner can talk, make faces, but cannot actually touch. As far as the one doing the exercise is concerned, that other person is not there. Keep your mind completely on what you are doing.	Scattered, standing in pairs.
III. Standing stretches: reach and bend; 8 counts each.	Reach for ceiling, first one hand then the other; stretch through your torso. Try to touch floor without bending knees. Bend from hips not waist.	Scattered, facing front. Drum.
IV. Twist and turn. Swing arms right, then left, then right again, taking you into a turn in place.	Swing arms way around; get a good twist in torso. Let the arm swing turn you. Do not let hips turn on the twist.	3 beats for each swing.
V. Swing and circle. Arms swing down and up to other side, repeat; swing continues into complete circle over head.	Start with arms extended to right (or left) side, swing way down and up, and circle way over the head to other side. Bend knees as your arms go down. (Talk class through exercise.)	
VI. Introduce (*demi-*) *pliés*. (These are preparation for all *pliés* that follow, also for jumps, hops, leaps.) A. First position (3-IX). B. Second position (3-XII). C. Add *relevé* (1-III-D, E).	Keep shoulders over hips, knees over toes when knees bend, heels on floor. Go only as low as you can and still control your torso and waist. Maintain back alignment and feeling of every part lifting up, but easily.	

OBJECTIVES, MATERIAL TO BE TAUGHT	TEACHING POINTERS AND SAFETY FACTORS	FORMATION, ACCOMPANIMENT
VII. Basic locomotion. (Preparation for all locomotion that follows. Preparation for being on beat [3-XIII].)		Large circle. Drum.
A. Even: walk; run; leap; hop; jump.	Step as beat sounds. You are the beat. (Keep this very short.)	Even beat.
B. Uneven: slide; gallop; skip.		Uneven beat.
VIII. Locomotion across floor (3-XIII).	Keep changing leaders across floor.	From corner in threes. Drum. Even beat.
A. Light forward run.	Very light, pick heels up behind you.	
B. Sideward run: grapevine.	Alternate side, front, back, very light and fast; keep hips front.	
C. Step-hop.	Step is unimportant; important part is going up into the air. Feel the air supporting you.	Uneven beat.
If time:		
D. Step-leap		
IX. Creative study (preparation for improvisation).		Square, sides numbered 1, 2, 3, 4.
A. Sides 1 and 3, four skips forward and back.	Talk class through action.	
B. Sides 2 and 4 repeat.		
C. A jump and turn around—each side in turn.	Any kind of jump, turn, or spin you want to do. You do not need to be like your neighbors.	
D. Mosquito on your head.	What would you do?	
E. Repeat C.		
F. Girl in calico.	Girls show new calico dress. Boys admire it.	
G. Repeat C.		
H. Sides 1 and 3 change places.	Use any step that fits music.	
I. Sides 2 and 4 change places.		
J. All break square formation; go any place on floor.	Really travel; use all the space you can find. Try some turns. Can you change level—go lower and higher? Music is getting faster—stay with it.	
X. Brief resumé.	Compliment class on specific activity.	Sit, facing teacher.

Lesson 3

Obj. To increase understanding of and facility in control of center and alignment.
To introduce relaxation.
To add to dance vocabulary.
To provide practice in basic controls and in creative exploration.

OBJECTIVES, MATERIAL TO BE TAUGHT	TEACHING POINTERS AND SAFETY FACTORS	FORMATION, ACCOMPANIMENT
I. Introduce concept of efficiency in movement (preparation for all that follows.)	Energy used only in moving part and only in amount needed for the activity, expended in direction needed. Demonstrate some examples.	Sit, facing teacher.
II. Review alignment from Lesson 1 (1-III-D).		Scattered.
III. Stretch and relax.	Really stretch; let go completely.	Lying on back.
IV. Hip thrust (4-III).	Lift hips as high as possible.	Lying on back, knees bent.

V. Chest arch (4-III; 5-I-B, C).
  A. Just the arch.
  B. Repeat arch but continue arch to a sit, bending forward; roll back down to floor.
	Lift chest until top of head is on floor. Being sure top of head is on floor, keep chest leading with head back until you are sitting; head goes toward knees. Keep back rounded as you roll down to floor. Keep it flowing, continuous, sequential.	Lying on back.

VI. Preparation for stretches (preparation for all following sitting stretches) (4-II-C).
 	
  A. From relaxation, starting with head.
 	
  B. Return to sit.
 	
  C. Repeat in stride sit.
 	
  D. Repeat with legs in front.
	Keep voice very quiet. Start by dropping head forward. The head is very heavy. Let it pull you forward.
	Go only as far as the weight of the head can pull you. Hang there a while to see if your muscles can relax more to let you go further.
	Start movement at base of spine; let movement progress up back. Head is last to come to place.
	Legs only as far apart as you can sit comfortably with back straight. Try to get tail off floor.
	Have knees straight, back straight and well lifted.
		Sitting, bottoms of feet together.
		
		Stride sit.
		
		Legs together, straight front.

VII. Transition to stand; stretch legs behind, one at a time.	Keep hips low, stretch one leg way back and bounce a little; repeat with other leg; stand.	Face floor.
VIII. Introduce concept of energy going in opposite directions (preparation for most of following lessons).		Stand scattered, facing teacher.

IX. Review (demi-) pliés (3-XII) first and second positions. (Add deep [grand] pliés [only as deep as students can control alignments] if class seems ready.)
  A. In first position: 2 small, 1 deep plié, relevé. Repeat.
  B. In second position, repeat sequence.
	Feel gravity pulling down as knees bend; at same time, pull up in torso, with an equal energy going through top of the head. Keep shoulders over hips, knees over toes. Keep knees straight coming down from relevé.
	
	In second position, heels stay on floor in deep plié.
		Music with even $\frac{4}{4}$ beat.

OBJECTIVES, MATERIAL TO BE TAUGHT	TEACHING POINTERS AND SAFETY FACTORS	FORMATION, ACCOMPANIMENT

X. Introduce brushes (*petits battements*) (4-V) (preparation for all brushes that follow and for leaps), first position, brushes to side.
  A. Do 4 slow brushes on floor; then 4 slightly faster ones (3-XIII-D).
  B. *Plié* and change to parallel position. Repeat the above sequence, foot goes forward.
	Keep both knees straight. Have enough pressure on floor so you have to work to extend the leg. When leg comes in, try to bring inside of upper thighs together. Think of pointing toe as an ankle extension.
	
	Movement in hip joint must be free. Keep knee straight, but hip joint and ankle must move freely. Be efficient. Do not let the tension of keeping knee straight carry into tightening hip and ankle joints.
		Drum.
		Scattered, facing teacher.

XI. Introduce prances.
  A. Preparation: Exploration of foot and ankle movement.
  B. Perform 8 prances. Start and end with one leg lifted.
	Feel all sections of foot and ankle in sequential movement.
	
	The push with toes lifts the knee, not thigh.
		Drum.

XII. Jumps. Perform 8 jumps (each) in parallel and in first and second positions (all *pliés*).	Use the push of the toes and ankle extension as in the prance. Be sure to *plié* on landing. Land quietly, trying for no sound.	

XIII. Locomotion across floor (4-VII).
  A. Review step-hop.
  B. Introduce step-leap.
  C. Take two steps and a hop.
  D. Two steps and a leap.
		From two centers, alternate sides; 2 students from a corner at a time. Drum.

XIV. Creative exercise (1-III-B; 2-II).
  A. Slow movement with eyes closed. Be touching someone in your group. Interweave with others in your group, changing contacts.
  B. After students get into this, add suggestions for movement: try some turning; try flexion and extension of torso; change level.
  C. Tell them to find another group without opening eyes to see where they are going.
  D. After trying to find another group (some will, some will not), have them open eyes.
	Concentrate. No giggling or talking. No peeking. This is for a new experience in feeling movement; it will be lost if you peek. It is not fair to yourself or others if you talk or giggle.
	
	If necessary, keep reminding them to move slowly and not to peek or talk.
		Groups of 4 or 5, scattered. Close together within group. Try this in silence. However, students are so accustomed to noise, they may do better with very soft, slow background music.

OBJECTIVES, MATERIAL TO BE TAUGHT	TEACHING POINTERS AND SAFETY FACTORS	FORMATION, ACCOMPANIMENT
XV. End class quietly. Try indicating by gestures rather than words that they should leave.		

Lesson 4

Obj: To add to dance vocabulary.
To provide practice in basic controls for more facility and coordination.
To increase ability to combine movements.
To provide further experience in creative exploration.

I. Introduce dance positions (1-III-D).	Work for complete efficiency; no tension where not needed. You should feel that your instrument (yourself) is differently organized in each of the positions.	Scattered, standing.

II. Floor exercises.
  A. Hip thrust (5-I-B).
  B. Chest arch (5-I-C).
  C. Sitting stretches, 8 each; soles of feet together, stride sit, legs straight ahead. Also, side bends in stride sit. (If students cannot sit with backs straight, do not include this.)
  D. Knee lifts (5-I-G; 5-II-D).
 	
  E. Back leg stretch to stand.
	Talk class through movement.
	
	Start with back well pulled up, straight, and in good alignment. Bend comes from hips, not from waist. Keep both buttocks on floor for side bend.
	
	Keep back lifted. This is a leg extension, not a knee bounce; no slap.
	Keep hips low.
		Lie on backs.
		
		Sit, soles of feet together. Drum or just count.

III. Standing exercises. *Pliés.* Alternate small and deep in each position, each with *relevé.* First, second, and fifth positions on both sides. Do 2 sets of each position. To change position, add *relevé* and brush to side—then into new position (for all jumps, hops, leaps).	Remember feeling of energy going equally in opposite directions. Be aware of the difference in feeling (dynamics) between the small and deep *pliés.*	Stand facing teacher. Music with even $\frac{4}{4}$ beat.

IV. Brushes (5-II-B).
  A. Review brushes from first position.
  B. Fifth position. Do 4 each: front; side (closing to first); back; side. *Plié,* point back foot to side and close in fifth in front. Repeat on other side.
  C. Repeat B, bringing foot slightly off floor.
	Remember, keep knees straight, press slightly against floor as foot brushes out. When closing, pull upper thighs together. Point toe by extending ankle.
	
	Toes are last to leave floor going out and first to touch coming down.
		Scattered, standing and facing teacher. Drum or music with moderately fast $\frac{2}{4}$ or $\frac{4}{4}$ beat.

OBJECTIVES, MATERIAL TO BE TAUGHT	TEACHING POINTERS AND SAFETY FACTORS	FORMATION, ACCOMPANIMENT
V. Review prancing. 8 to 16 sets of 3 prances with a hold on fourth count (3-X-A; 5-III-A).	Remember, keep back well lifted and aligned; push with toes. When foot is in the air, toes are pointed down and foot is under knee.	Drum.
VI. Locomotion (2-VII). A. Review step-step-leap. B. Introduce schottische with variations in position of free leg, and in direction of traveling (preparation for combining movements). If time: C. Introduce polka. Also try with turn if they are performing step easily (5-III-A).	Keep changing leaders. Try for feeling of holding in the air; ride on the air under you.	In lines of 4 or 5, depending on width of studio. Go length of room. Drum or music. Any good polka music.
VII. Creative exercise (all preceding creative exercise is preparation for this). A. Explore localized leads (6-I). B. From a sitting position (choose own way of sitting), start with one arm leading torso in movement and turning on floor. Let lead go to other arm; gradually let arm lead to a standing position; then into locomotion; change leads, other than arms. The leads can include flexion, extension, and rotation of various joint areas; let some part lead back to floor. C. Free movement to music.	Find the feeling for one part leading and the rest following; sense of sequential action and the relationship of one part to another. Try to find feeling of suspension as leads change and as directions change. Be prepared to suggest movements if needed.	Scattered, standing. Slow, quiet music. Sit. Lively music, possibly syncopated.

From here on, for the warmup exercises and exercises previously introduced, try to go from one exercise to the next without stopping between exercises. Name the next exercise as they are finishing the one before.

Lesson 5

Obj: To increase dance vocabulary.
To practice and increase coordination in combining movements.
To increase awareness of self and belief in self.
To introduce turns.

OBJECTIVES, MATERIAL TO BE TAUGHT	TEACHING POINTERS AND SAFETY FACTORS	FORMATION, ACCOMPANIMENT
I. Floor exercises.		
A. Relaxed roll. On back, leg leads; on face, arm leads (3-VI).	Completely relaxed everywhere except for leading part. Remember the use of the center when coming down from hip thrust.	Scattered, lying on backs.
B. Introduce contraction on back (7-I-B).		
C. Chest arch.	Top of head, not back of head on floor.	
D. Introduce flex and point on each leg (G below).	Keep thigh in place as knee and ankle flex and extend.	Drum or record.
E. Sitting stretches in all positions; 4 each position.	Lift in center before starting bend from hip joint.	
F. Side bends in sit-stride position.	Keep both buttocks on floor.	
G. Sitting knee lifts (for brushes and jumps.	Keep back well-lifted when knees bend. As knees extend, add an extra stretch and lift in torso between hip bone and lowest rib. This stretch will help you understand relationship of torso and hips when performing standing brushes and extensions.	
H. Introduce sitting torso rotation (2-IV).	Talk class through movement. Feel as though hip is pushing to start torso on the turn and then is leading back by pushing toward floor. (Do not worry if you cannot get both buttocks on floor.) As you return, lift in torso, similar to the torso lift on knee lifts, all energy going in two directions.	
I. Back leg extension to stand.	Keep hips low.	
II. Standing exercises.		
A. *Pliés*. Perform 2 in each position: first, second, fifth (both sides); all deep (within individual control); *relevé* after each. Hold one count going down just before heels have to lift. Coming up, get heels to floor as soon as possible and hold one count before straightening knees.	Feel that the *relevé* is a continuation of the rise on the *plié*. Be sure knees are completely straight before starting *relevé*. Coming down, be sure heels are on floor before starting next *plié*.	Scattered. Stand with back to teacher. Vary music used. (If you have been using classical music, use jazz this time.)
B. Brushes. 4 on each of 3 levels: on floor; medium high; and high. Complete both sides in 3 positions: parallel, brush forward; first, brush side; fifth, brush front, back with other foot. (Repeat fifth on other side.)	Remember: extend ankle completely when foot is out; knee is straight; back well-lifted but shoulders down; free movement in hip and ankle joints.	Drum.
C. Achilles stretch at wall.	Keep back and hips aligned. No break or bend at hips.	Find place at wall.

OBJECTIVES, MATERIAL TO BE TAUGHT	TEACHING POINTERS AND SAFETY FACTORS	FORMATION, ACCOMPANIMENT
D. Ankle push to lift knees (similar to prance but freer and faster) (4-II-D).	Be sure ankles are warmed up.	Scattered, facing teacher.
E. Alternate a jump on both feet and a hop on one foot, alternating foot for hop.	Try to go as high on the hop as on the jump.	
F. Introduce 3-step turn (*tour*); gradually increase tempo (6-V; 6-VI-B).	Keep steps small. Perform almost in place. Aim yourself. Know where front is and make yourself get there. Spot or focus eyes on one place in front. Try not to see anything else as you go around.	
III. Locomotion (preparation for combining movements).		
A. Polka sideward with a partner, taking half-turn on hop.	Alternate face-to-face and back-to-back.	In two's, use diagonal path from one corner. Good polka music.
If time:		
B. Ask class for requests for locomotor exercises.		
C. Slow back walk with long reach of leg backwards.	Bend supporting knee to permit longer reach.	Drum.
IV. Creative exercise. Free movement to music.	Be ready to give suggestions if needed.	Scattered—free use of space. Use several short pieces of varied moods, tempos, rhythms.
V. Have each student bow to mirror as though each is a star and bowing to applause of the audience after an exciting performance.	Use mirror as though it were an audience. Be believable.	

Lesson 6

Obj: To continue development of coordinations for turns.
To continue development of coordination and ability to combine movements.
To expand creative exploration.
To provide for experience in performing for an audience.

No floor exercises.

I. Warm up; cat exercises. Flex; extend; rotate all joint areas (5-I-A, B; 7-I-B).	Remember there are joints in the face area. Let movement flow from one part to another as when a cat stretches its back or when movement flows along a squirrel's back and tail.	Scattered. No accompaniment.

OBJECTIVES, MATERIAL TO BE TAUGHT	TEACHING POINTERS AND SAFETY FACTORS	FORMATION, ACCOMPANIMENT
II. Combine *pliés* and brushes. In fifth position, 2 each direction: small *plié* and forward brush; small *plié* and brush side; small *plié* and brush back; small *plié*, *relevé*; lift back so toe touches knee (*passé*); bring foot to fifth in front, still on half-toe; hold for a second; *plié*. Repeat on other side.	Both knees bend and extend at same time. Feel as though the straightening from the *plié* sends the foot out for the brush. On the coda, as the back foot comes to the front after the *relevé*, hold the half-toe position of the front leg with back and thigh well pulled up. The back foot going to the floor in front should be like a rapier going to the floor. Energy equally in two directions: up on standing leg to equal down thrust of back leg passing standing leg and coming down in front.	Drum or music.
III. Review swing and circle exercise from Lesson 2 (2-V).		Drum.
IV. Review twist and turn from Lesson 2 (2-IV).		
V. Review 3-step turn.		
VI. Locomotor exercises. A. Introduce triplets.	Down, up, up. Small *plié* on down. Very high on the ups; feel as though you are leaving the floor but don't. Even in tempo and distance of each step.	Drum.
B. Combine triplet and 3-step turn. Do two triplets and two 3-step turns, one to each side.	Remember to know where front is—the direction you are traveling.	Drum.
VII. Creative exercise (practice in improvisation). Develop a short movement study using a piece of furniture. Do not use it for its intended purpose. Give choice: to work alone or with a partner. Tell class how many minutes they have to complete the study. Allow time for one-half of class to perform for other half (8-IV).	Use your imagination to see how many ways you can use the object you selected, or how many interesting movements you can work out around or with the object.	Scattered, alone or with partner.

Lesson 7

Obj. To increase dancer vocabulary and range of movement.
To increase ability to think for themselves.
To increase ability to combine movements.
To increase ability in making own decisions in creative exploration.

OBJECTIVES, MATERIAL TO BE TAUGHT	TEACHING POINTERS AND SAFETY FACTORS	FORMATION, ACCOMPANIMENT
I. Floor exercises.		
A. Relaxed roll (5-I-A).	Leg lead when on back, arm lead when on face.	Scattered, lying on back. Quiet background music.
B. Cat stretches—lying on face and on side (6-I).	These positions limit movement possibilities and will feel very different than when sitting or standing.	
C. Flex and point. One leg at a time, perform 4 slow flex and point, then 8 double time.	Keep trying to get leg as far forward or over face as possible and still hold thigh in place and straighten knee.	Drum.
D. Sitting stretches; 2 each position.	Move smoothly from one exercise to the next with no waits between.	Sitting. Quiet background music.
E. Knee lift—4 to 8 times (whole series).		
F. Sitting torso rotation. Perform 2 preparations, then 2 going to floor. Stretch legs to side and swing around to other side.		
G. Introduce sitting front leg extensions. (4-II-C, D).	Keep thigh in place as knee straightens. Keep legs turned out and knee of working leg as high as possible. The height of the foot on the extension will depend on how high the knee is at the start.	
1. Experiment; find what height to hold knee, what is possible for each student for extension. Hold thigh with arm for first experiments with the extension.		
2. Complete 4 front extensions on each side.		
H. Each find own way to stretch and stand.		
II. Standing exercises.		
A. *Plié* and brushes; each perform own combinations of *pliés* and brushes (1-III-E).		
B. Jump preparatory exercise.		Drum.
C. Jump and hop in first position. Take 2 jumps and 2 hops; repeat with hops on other side. At end, jump from both feet into a side lunge; land on one foot with the other foot off floor. Repeat with lunge on other side.	Keep knees turned out. Jump, jump, hop, hop; jump, jump, hop, hop; jump, jump, hop, hop; jump, jump, side lunge. Keep torso well-lifted, shoulders down; use small *plié* on all landings. Keep all very light.	
D. Review 3-step turn. Add a hop after each turn (5-II-F).	Step, step, step, hop.	

OBJECTIVES, MATERIAL TO BE TAUGHT	TEACHING POINTERS AND SAFETY FACTORS	FORMATION, ACCOMPANIMENT
E. Introduce jump turn. 4 quarter-turns, each side; 4 half-turns, each side; 4 full turns, each side.	Hold straight alignment with sense of pivot around own center. Be efficient. Find how easily you can turn.	Drum.
III. Locomotion.		
A. Polka sideways (5-III-A). Perform a half-turn on the hop (4-VI-C).	Do not work technically on this. First, see how easily they can pick it up.	
B. Combine triplet, 3-step turn, and side hop. Perform 2 triplets forward; step and 2 hops; repeat on other side; two 3-step turns (one set to each side) (6-VI-B).	Be very clear on directions: Straight forward on triplet and really sideways on 3-step turn and hops.	
IV. Creative exercise.		
A. Explore balance going directly to a perch on half-toe (piqué); forward, sideways, backward (1-III-E).	Efficiency is important. Find the exact amount of energy needed to get you there. Keep well pulled up in torso and thighs. Keep equal energy in both legs.	Slow music.
B. Explore balance on whole foot, bending and turning torso in as many ways as possible. Also, vary the direction and position of free leg and arms.		
C. Free movement to music.		Let class choose music.

Lesson 8

Obj: To increase awareness of previously introduced exercise through review and addition of other elements.
To increase students' ability to think for themselves.
To increase dance vocabulary through slightly more complex movements and combinations.

I. Floor exercises.		
A. Sitting stretches. Start from standpoint of relaxation with head pulling forward. When over as far as possible, start a small stretch; increase it to a real pull with hands on ankles. Include all leg positions and side bend with legs spread (3-VI-A,B,C; 4-II-C; 7-I-D).	Start with back and middle well pulled up. Be sure bend is from hip joint and not from waist.	Scattered, sitting.

OBJECTIVES, MATERIAL TO BE TAUGHT	TEACHING POINTERS AND SAFETY FACTORS	FORMATION, ACCOMPANIMENT
B. On hands and knees, bring knee toward chest, then extend leg back and up. Do several on each side.	Keep center strong. Be sure not to drop into a swayback when leg lifts in back.	Drum: Use triplets with swinging rhythm.
C. Sitting front leg extensions, with ankle flexion and extensions. Perform 4 on each side (4-II-C; 7-I-G).	Be sure to keep thigh in place as knee extends.	Scattered, sitting. Drum.
D. Perform stretches and torso rotations; work up to standing.	Be ready to correct any movements that may be harmful.	
E. *Pliés* and brushes. Perform 2 brushes in parallel position, small *plié*; brush out just off floor; flex ankle then extend to touch toe to floor; repeat 4 times; close; *plié*. Repeat on other side. Repeat all in first position with brush to side.	Moderately slow with ankle stretch.	Scattered, facing back of room.
F. One moderately deep *plié*, 4 fast brushes with accent out. Just off floor, hold last half a count; 4 brushes with accent in. Repeat on other side. Complete above in first position, brushing side. Repeat all in fifth position, brushing forward with front foot, backward with back foot. Repeat with other leg.	Medium fast. Remember all alignments. Bring foot in hard. Be aware of difference in feeling and dynamics as accents change.	Face side of room.
G. Jumps. Start very fast and small (barely leave floor); gradually slow tempo, jumping higher until jumping as high as possible. Reverse, gradually getting faster and smaller.	Each decide on own arm movements (*port de bras*).	Drum.
H. Review jump turn from Lesson 7 (7-II-E).	Work for complete efficiency. Try to discover how easy it is to make the full turn.	
II. Creative study. Each student work out a short combination of movement using at least 2 different locomotor steps and some kind of turn. Each step may be repeated as many times as student wishes. Have students practice combination so they can remember it and repeat it. Quarter of class show studies at a time.	Tell class how long they have to finish working out the study. Give a 1-minute warning.	

OBJECTIVES, MATERIAL TO BE TAUGHT	TEACHING POINTERS AND SAFETY FACTORS	FORMATION, ACCOMPANIMENT

Lesson 9

Obj: To experience new orientation through change of direction of facing for familiar exercises.

To increase awareness of purpose of warmup exercises and awareness in thinking for themselves.

To increase ability to extend movement exploration.

No floor exercises.

I. Warmup: Cat stretches (6-I).

Think in terms of flexing, extending, and rotating in all joint areas.

See if class can do this in complete silence.

II. Standing exercises.
  A. Each student perform own series of *pliés* and brushes.

  Each choose own way of facing, but no one faces front (or usual place of facing).

  B. Foot and ankle exercises.
    1. Try to lift metatarsal arch, one foot at a time.

    Try to isolate this area. Do not get action by curling toes under or by lifting longitudinal arch.

    2. Explore flexion and extension of foot and ankle in flowing, sequential movement.

    Work for flowing, sequential action.

  C. Jumps.
    1. Repeat jumps from 8-I-G.

    Land with no sound.

    2. Combination: 8 jumps in parallel position; 4 alternating parallel and first positions; 8 in second position; 4 in fifth position with one foot in front; 4 with other foot in front; end in second position *plié*.

    3. Introduce jump in fifth position, changing feet (front foot goes to back, back foot to front, etc.) (*changement*) (3-XII; 1-III-D).

    Think of heels changing places. Be sure there is no change in torso. When students are secure in this, possibly add a further complication. Make a smooth arm circle while jumping: one arm circle for 4 jumps. Arms start down (*en bas*) in front, lift forward, up over head (*en haut*), out to sides (*à la seconde*), down to starting position. Keep it smooth with no jerks. This takes real control in center of torso.

  D. Achilles stretch at wall.

OBJECTIVES, MATERIAL TO BE TAUGHT	TEACHING POINTERS AND SAFETY FACTORS	FORMATION, ACCOMPANIMENT

III. Locomotion. 2 steps with side hop.
  A. Step across in front to start.
  B. Repeat, starting with foot in line of direction. Lift free leg up to side.
  C. Repeat using 3 steps. This will alternate feet for hop.
	Step, step, hop.
	
	Emphasize hop, go high in air. Steps are fast, unimportant.
	
	Try to travel while in air for hop.
		In lines moving length of room.
		
		Drum, uneven beat.

IV. Creative study. Explore swinging movements that carry into a suspension; carry suspension into a loss of balance that returns to swinging movement. After experimentation in place, try to carry it into some traveling in space. Select 2 or 3 of most interesting for whole class to try.		

Lesson 10

Obj: To increase ability to move completely, involving all parts of the body.
To increase dance vocabulary through more complex movement combinations.
To introduce falls and recoveries.
To introduce compositional form.
To provide practice in performing for an audience.

I. Warmup. Each student complete own warmup. Each select exercises that work best for self.	Flexing and stretching; remember to involve all parts of body. Make suggestions if needed.	Scattered. Quiet, background music.
II. Two arm swings and circle. Arm circle carry into a jump to the side. This will alternate sides (2-V).	Swing, swing, circle. Make the arm circle strong enough to lift you into air and to travel to side.	Drum.
III. Leg swing (*battement en clôche*) (11-II-C). Swing leg across in front, then out to side as high as possible; then step out to side as leg lowers. Keep alternating legs.	Find arm movements that will help with the leg swing.	Drum, use triplet beat.
IV. *Plié* and side brush (*petite battement à la seconde*) traveling. Start in fifth, *plié*, brush back foot to side, close in front, *plié*; other foot brushes side, close in front. Perform 8 moving forward, then 8 moving backward.	The brush to the side starts while straightening from *plié*. The *plié* starts as foot closes from brush. It is all connected. Each select own arm positions or movements.	Drum, even beat.

OBJECTIVES, MATERIAL TO BE TAUGHT	TEACHING POINTERS AND SAFETY FACTORS	FORMATION, ACCOMPANIMENT
V. Jumps and hops (7-II-C, E). Take 2 jumps and hops; on repetition alternate feet on hop; 2 jump and side lunge, alternating sides; 2 jumps in place with a half-turn in air on second jump; hold. Repeat.	Be sure to hold alignment in torso. Make lunges big. Jump, jump, hop, hop; jump, jump, hop, hop; jump, lunge; jump, lunge; jump, turn, hold.	Drum, uneven beat.
VI. Locomotion. Leaps in circle. Combination, 4 of each: 2 steps and leap; 3 steps and leap; 4 steps and leap. End with 8 straight leaps.	If a person in front of you isn't covering as much space as you want to, pass them on the outside of the circle.	Large circle, drum.
VII. Introduce front falls and recoveries. Allow time to practice. Slide feet out to get as close to floor as possible.	Talk class through exercise. Keep back straight with strong control of center. Minimize impact by sequential bending of arm joints (an elbow *plié*). The landing should be silent, with no sound on impact with floor.	No accompaniment.
VIII. Creative study. Work out a study with 3 parts. Have the first part a short combination using slow, sustained movements with some change of level. Have the second part go into a faster combination using locomotor movements, but end so you can repeat your first slow combination. If time, have each show study individually. If not, a few at a time.	A-B-A form. Brief explanation of A-B-A form.	No accompaniment.

Lesson 11

Obj: To review various areas introduced through course.

I. Warmup, cat stretches standing; some on one leg.		Scattered. Quiet background music.
II. Standing exercises. A. *Plié* and side brush (10-IV) traveling 8 forward and 8 backward.	Keep torso well pulled up. Connect *pliés* and brushes.	
B. Brushes: parallel forward; first position sideways; fifth position forward and back with repeat with other foot in front. For each, do 3 sets: 4 on floor (*petit*), 4 middle level, 4 high (*grand*). *Plié* between positions.	Maintain all alignments. Maintain tempo on high brushes.	Drum.

OBJECTIVES, MATERIAL TO BE TAUGHT	TEACHING POINTERS AND SAFETY FACTORS	FORMATION, ACCOMPANIMENT
C. Leg swing sideways (10-III). Swing leg across in front; out to side; across in front; out to side with a high lift; suspend and land in lunge with *plié*; pull feet together and repeat with other leg. Try various arm positions.	Really swing leg. Let final swing lift you to half-toe for the suspension. See how long you can suspend before gravity pulls you into lunge. Watch knee alignment on landing.	Music or drum.
D. Jump in fifth position changing feet (9-II-C).	Try with arm circle.	Music or drum.
III. Locomotion. Combination: Do 2 triplets traveling forward; face side with a half-toe perch, stepping on other foot with small *plié*; step to back with half-toe perch, stepping in small *plié*; step to other side on half-toe perch, stepping in small *plié* (this is a turn in place).	Theme and variation on a rhythmic pattern; 1,2,3; 1,2,3; 1,2; 1,2; 1,2 (two three's, three two's). The triplets are the two three's; the turn stepping into perch on half-toe are the three two's. Cover ground on the triplets. Make step into perch as big as you can control.	Drum.
First variation: Swivel slightly to step across in front; 2 steps in place. Repeat on other side.	The two three's.	
Turn in place by stepping up on half-toe behind other foot, pivoting; step down on other foot. Perform 3 of these for one complete turn.	The three two's.	
Second variation: 2 triplets forward.	The two three's.	
Take a big step across in front with a *plié*, letting hips turn; take a small step on half-toe turning back to face front. Complete 3 of these.	This is a twisting step.	In lines moving across floor.
Practice each of these separately, then perform whole combination with one following the other. This can be performed in groups with each succeeding group starting after preceding group finishes first theme. Each group will be performing a different version (like a round).	The three two's.	
IV. Free movement to music.		If time, several short pieces with variation in mood and rhythm.

Lesson 12

Obj: To have fun and enjoy selves while reviewing some areas of course and stressing creative aspects.

OBJECTIVES, MATERIAL TO BE TAUGHT	TEACHING POINTERS AND SAFETY FACTORS	FORMATION, ACCOMPANIMENT
I. Warmup. Have each do own, or ask for requests, or for several volunteers, each to lead one exercise.		Scattered. Background music.
II. Introduce floor patterns. Draw on chalkboard. All walk through pattern. Move straight forward; diagonally back; straight to side; curving path diagonally front and up to back to starting location.		
III. Creative study. Each work out a movement pattern using this floor pattern.	Students have many choices. Any steps or movements they wish. They can face any direction while following the floor pattern. The amount of space used can be big or small. The floor pattern can be inverted. It can all be performed down on the floor. Two can work together like a mirror image. Any rhythmic pattern or several can be used. Make it as interesting and different as possible.	Scattered.
IV. Group composition. Divide class into groups of 3, 4, or 5. Each group decide who will be first, second, etc. Each group performs for class. If time permits, each group could work out a group statement for opening and closing with the solos in the middle. Again, if time permits, the group statement could be performed between each solo (*rondo*).		
V. Very brief statement to class about course: enjoy class; pick up handout sheets when they leave.		Sit, facing teacher.
VI. Free movement to music. Have them continue dancing to dressing room (stand by door and say ''good-bye'').		Students' favorite music.

Some teachers may feel it necessary to have a class discussion of the course and a summing up of what has been covered. However, it is generally better to give mimeographed handout sheets with an outline of course work and to end with dancing rather than with talk.

If you must give a test during this period, use Lesson 11 for a review and Lesson 12 for the test. In this case, you need to change lessons 6 through 10 to incorporate into them some of the material used in lessons 11 and 12.

Final Comment

The lesson plans just completed are not intended to be complete; they are not formulas to be lifted out and used as is. Like the rest of the book, these plans are offered as guidelines, as a takeoff point from which students and beginning teachers can begin to think for themselves. Success with their use depends on what you put into them. And no matter how well you plan the lesson, its success still depends your enthusiasm, energy, and ability to instill in your students the feeling of magic and excitement that comes from moving completely: the feeling of really dancing.

There are holes in these plans (not indicated) for you to find and fill in for yourself. Good luck.

Appendix A

Labanotation *

Labanotation is a system for recording human and animal movement and behavior. Rudolph von Laban published this system in 1928.

Historians believe that the Egyptians and Romans attempted to record their dances with some method of notation, but there is no evidence of this. The earliest known recordings of written dance, which are preserved in the Municipal Archives of Cervera in Spain, date from the last half of the 15th century. Since then many systems have been tried—some are still used, but most have disappeared. Modern music notation, first used in the 11th century, was not unified until the 18th century. Of course, dance movement exists in space and time and is thus more complex than music. As with music, however, dance notation has followed dance innovations; therefore, it is continually being revised.

Ann Hutchinson[1] states that because Laban was interested in movement in every phase of life it was inevitable that he should devise a system based not only on personal style but on the universal laws of kinetics. He studied all aspects of the theater. When he was 25, he founded his school in Munich, where he developed theories of movement he called "eukinetics." Laban became director for movement at the Berlin State Opera in the 1930s and at other state theaters. In England, Laban worked with F. C. Lawrence in examining movements of industrial workers, and they coauthored the book *Effort*. This study in 1947 led to the effort-shape analysis of movement, which is used for business, medical, and psychiatric purposes. Effort-shape analysis describes how movement occurs in human beings, its rhythms and patterns. The presence or absence of effort variables and the combinations and sequences in which they occur in a person's movement reflect important aspects of adaptation, function, and expression in human activity.

It was in the midst of all these activities that Laban devised his notation system, Kinetography Laban. Since publication of his text, the system has developed even further, not only in dance but in other fields of movement.

Hutchinson calls notation the "language of movement," and as all language is taught or learned, training should begin at an early age. According to Albrecht

* The author expresses her appreciation to Toni Intravaia for preparing this information as well as all the Labanotation that appears in this book.

[1] *Labanotation: The System of Analyzing and Recording Movement* (New York: Theatre Arts Books, 1977).

Knust[2], Labanotation answers the questions of what movement happened, when it happened, how long it lasted, and what part of the body caused it.

Hutchinson notes that Labanotation is a means of international communication:

> It is a triple-edged tool because it provides a means of recording movement on paper for future reference, a sound, fundamental analysis of movement and a carefully selected terminology which is universally applicable. . . . Labanotation serves the art of dance much as music notation serves the art of music. . . .Work in each comparable area—studying, teaching, rehearsing, and composing—is expedited through the use of notation. . . . The use for movement notation, which is immediately obvious, is the preservation of choreography for future re-creation. . . . Labanotation is a complement to film as a tool for movement analysis and choreographic preservation; neither can replace the other. A comparison with music makes the point for notation clear. Recorded music has not made the printed sheet unnecessary. . . . The Laban system has proved a valuable tool for movement education ranging from work with four- to five-year-old children to postgraduate and doctoral studies. . . . Labanotation has provided a similar visual method for the dance and for physical education as an additional channel through which knowledge can be imparted at every age and level of study. . . . By Motif writing the first broad statement (Motif writing gives a general statement about a theme or the most important part of a movement. By adding more details it can come to a point of full structured description. Motif writing gives the idea of the movement.) of the action can gradually be defined in greater detail with structural Labanotation producing an increasingly specific description until finally a very precise form has been achieved in which the exact use of the body, time, direction, and energy have been stated. . . . The handing down of detailed knowledge in any field requires a system of notation for recording facts so that comparisons can be made, differences evaluated, new ground broken.[3]

And with notation comes the new profession of notator and new sections in the library to further the art of movement.

For purpose of illustration, Labanotation can be compared with music notation. The music staff, a five-line horizontal staff, reads from bottom to top, with the center line dividing the left side of the body (left of the center line) from the right side of the body (right of the center line). In music, the staff is divided to indicate measures to groups of sounds; in Labanotation, the staff is divided to indicate measures or groups of movement. The basic music symbol is egg-shaped. The basic movement symbol is a rectangle. To show duration, the music symbol is shaded or has a stem and ''flags'' attached. The movement symbol is lengthened or shortened to show duration. To show pitch, the music note is placed appropriately on the staff. By its shading, the movement notation symbol shows level; by the addition of pointers, the symbol shows direction; and by its placement on the staff, the symbol shows the part of the body that moves.

It is important to use notation. This visual aid helps not only the student but the teacher, not only the performer but the composer.

As you begin to analyze movement, write only what is needed. Add details as learning and need progress. The complexity of the human body and its behavior need a notation to record as much or as little as necessary to fit a given situation. Add word notes to the notation; musicians do.

[2] *Dictionary of Kinetography Laban* (London: Macdonald & Evans, 1982).
[3] *Labanotation*, pp. 6–9.

Notation should be used in technique class to illustrate the craft of movement. In composition class, it should be used to give examples from scores to show form, content, theme, and the theme's development, phrasing, etc., or to write down the assignments: that is, it should be used as a tool to teach the craft of composition.

The Dance Notation Bureau, Inc., acts as a clearinghouse for furthering the understanding, documentation, and preservation of movement primarily based on Labanotation. The Bureau was founded in 1940 and incorporated as a nonprofit service-educational organization in 1952. The Dance Notation Bureau includes: the DNB Press, publisher of notation texts, scores, and reading materials; the DNB library, the world's most extensive collection of dance and movement notation materials; the DNB School; and a licensing agency that arranges performing rights for a number of notated choreographic works for dance companies throughout the world. For further information about Labanotation contact the Dance Notation Bureau, Inc., 33 West 21st Street, New York, New York 10010.

Appendix B

Glossary

Abstract Main essence, nonliteral, nonrealistic.
Accelerando (accel.), Stringendo (string.) Getting faster and faster.
Accent Added intensity or stress.
Accumulative A bringing together.
Adagio Slowly; sustained, smooth. In ballet, used to indicate a portion of the duet between a man and a woman featuring lifts, pirouettes, and other movements performed by the ballerina to exhibit her grace and skill.
Ad libitum At will freely.
Agitato Agitated.
Aire Air.
Allegro Lively, bright.
Alongé Stretched, extended.
Andante At a walking tempo.
Animato Animated.
Arabesque A position in which weight is supported on one leg with the other leg raised behind with knee straight.
Arrière To the back.
Assemblé A movement in which one foot is brushed out to the side; as this leg lifts there is a hop on the supporting leg, and both feet land at the same time in fifth position.
Asymmetrical Opposite of symmetrical; an unbalanced grouping in a design.
Attitude A position in which weight is supported on one leg with the other leg lifted either in front or behind with knee bent and turned out.
Augment Add, enlarge, increase.
Avant Forward, in front.
Axial Around an axis. In dance, usually refers to non-locomotor movements.

Balancé A movement involving three changes of weight: step down on whole foot, up on half-toe, down on whole foot.
Barre A horizontal, wooden (sometimes metal) rod used for practicing some dance techniques. May be portable or attached to wall.

Bas Low.
Battement A movement in which a leg moves out from a centered position and returns. The foot brushes the floor when moving out or in.
Bras Arms.
Brush *See* Battement.

Cabriole A jumping movement in which one leg is brought up to touch the other leg while in the air.
Calando Gradually dying away and getting slower at the same time.
Canon Two or more voices exactly duplicating each other, with each voice starting at a different point (also called a "round").
Cantable, Cantilena Singing style.
Chaînes Small, very fast half-turns in first position.
Changé Changed or to change.
Changement A jump in place in fifth position with feet changing places while in the air.
Chassé A sliding step in which the legs are brought together while in the air.
Choreographer A person who composes a dance.
Choreography A dance composition.
Cinq Five.
Cinquième Fifth.
Coda "Tail" or ending.
Contraction A tightening of a muscle or group of muscles to cause flexion of a joint area or several body parts.
Couru Running.
Crescendo (cresco) A progressive increase in volume, tempo, or intensity.
Croisé Crossed.

Da Capo (D.C.) Go back to the beginning and repeat the first part of the piece, and end at the word *FINE* (Italian, meaning finish or end).
Deciso With decisive feeling for the beat.
Dedans Inward.
Dégagé Disengage (usually from the floor).

208

Dehors Outward.
Demi Half.
Derrière Behind, in back.
Devant Forward, in front.
Dimension Size of a movement or the space used.
Dimuendo (dim.), Decrescendo (decresc.) Getting gradually softer in volume.
Dolce Sweetly.
Dolente, Lamentoso Sorrowful, sad.
Dotted notes A dot after a musical note adds one-half the value of the note.
Downbeat An accent on first note of a measure.
Downstage Toward the audience.
Dramatico Dramatic.
Dynamics The amount of intensity or energy used in a movement.

Écarté Separated.
Éffacé Shaded.
Elevation A rising up, lifted.
Elevé A jump.
Energico Energetic.
Entrechat Crossings.
Enveloppé A movement in which a straight leg is raised, then the knee is bent to return to place.
Épaulé Shouldered.
Espressivo In an expressive manner.
Extension Lengthening, elongating, reaching.

Fermé Closed.
Feroce Fiercely.
Flexion Bending in a joint area of the body.
Floor pattern The path covered during a movement sequence.
Focus Center of attention.
Form Compositional shape or design.
Forte (f) Loud. **Fortissimo (ff)** very loud.
Fouetté Whipped.
Frappé Struck.
Fugue A compositional form in which a theme is introduced by one voice, then developed contrapuntally by others voices.

Giocoso Happily.
Giusto Exact.
Glissade Glide.
Grand (grande) Big.
Grazioso Gracefully.

Half-toe On ball of foot with heel off floor.
Harmony Two or more musical sounds played or sung at the same time that are pleasing or satisfying to the ear.
Haut High, raised.
Hop A rising into the air, with the takeoff and the landing on the same foot.

Intensity Degree or amount of energy or strength used.

Jambe Leg.
Jazz A particular style of music or dance characterized by syncopation, accented rhythms, dissonance, and individualized tonal effects.

Jeté Leap.
Jump A rising into the air and landing on both feet at the same time, though the takeoff may be from one or both feet.

Kinesthetic Awareness of, perception of, or sensitivity to variations in movement, tension, or position of the body.

Largo Stately.
Leap Going into the air, taking off from one foot and landing on the other.
Legato Smoothly.
Leggiero Lightly.
Lento Slowly.

Mazurka A folk dance of Polish origin in 3/8 or 3/4 time (slide, cut, hop).
Measure A partitioning of pulses or beats into units. These units are marked by vertical lines on the music staff, usually with a designated number of counts per unit or measure.
Meter Number of beats in a measure.
Moderato At a moderate tempo or speed.
Motif *Music:* central theme or idea. *Notation:* an abbreviated or partial notating of the movement.

Note value The duration or time value of a musical note.

Ouverte Open.

Pas Step.
Pas de Basque A movement of three steps in which one foot steps (or leaps) to the side, the other foot steps forward, and the first foot closes to the other foot. This may be reversed to travel backward.
Pas de bourrée A movement in three steps in which one foot takes the weight behind the other foot, the free foot steps to the side on half-toe, and the first foot takes the weight in front on the whole foot.
Pas de chat Literally, "step of the cat." A springing, elevated step.
Pas de cheval Literally, "step of the horse." A pawing, brushing movement of the foot, resembling a horse's foot movement.
Passé Passed.
Perch A step onto half-toe, with knee straight. (*See Piqué*).
Percussive Sharp, stopped action or sound.
Petit Little.
Phrase A musical thought or theme sometimes ending in a cadence.
Piano (p) soft. **Pianissimo (pp)** very soft.
Pied Foot.
Piqué A position in which weight is on one leg and the other foot is lifted so the foot is halfway between the knee and the ankle, with toe well-pointed and knee turned out. The heel is against the leg, with toes showing on the outside of the standing leg. A movement in which weight is taken on half-toe with leg straight, and the free foot often assuming the above piqué position.

Pirouette A turn in place on one foot.

Plié A knee bend with careful alignment of the knee and torso.

Poco Little.

Polka A social dance of Polish origin; developed in the early 19th century with a lively rhythm (hop, step, close, step).

Polyharmonies Two or more chords occurring simultaneously that are not key related.

Polyrhythms More than one rhythm occurring simultaneously, such as two against three.

Polytonality Two or more music keys played simultaneously.

Pomposo Pompous.

Port de bras Carriage of the arms.

Posé Poised, position.

Poser To position the foot on the floor, in place.

Precipité Hurried.

Première First.

Presto Rapid.

Promenade Walk, travel.

Quality Essential character.

Quasi Almost, as if.

Quatrième Fourth.

Rallantando (rall.), Ritardando (rit.), Allargando (allarg.) Getting gradually slower.

Range Size of a movement, area, or space.

Relaxation A state of being free of tension.

Release Change from a state of tension to a letting go or a release of the tension.

Relevé A rise to half-toe (or to full pointe).

Rests In music, resting places.

Rhythm An organization of music or movement in respect to time. Organization of repetition in a visual design.

Rond Around.

Rondo Compositional form of three or more themes with a return to the principal theme between the other themes.

Round *See* Canon.

Rubato "Robbed time," that is, to alter time at player's discretion.

Sauté Hop.

Schottische A social dance of Scotch origin popularized in Germany (three steps and a hop).

Seconde Second.

Sforzando (sf, sfz) Forced, strongly accented.

Sissonne A springing into air from both feet at the same time, then landing on one foot with the other foot closing neatly to the first foot in fifth position.

Soutenu Smoothly.

Spotting Keeping eyes focused on one spot during turns. Or, standing ready to assist another who is learning difficult movements such as lifts or gymnastic-type movements.

Staccato Sharp, accented.

Style, Stylization A manner of moving; nonliteral representation.

Sur le cou-de-pied At the neck of the foot (ankle).

Sustained Smooth, continuous.

Swinging Pendulum-like movement.

Symmetry, Symmetrical Even proportion in arrangement of parts (dance groups, visual design).

Syncopation A shifting of the accent from the beginning of a measure to other beats or notes.

Tempo Speed; how fast or slow.

Temps Time.

Tendu Stretched.

Teneramente Tenderly.

Terre Ground or floor.

Tombé (tombée) Lowered, accented.

Tour, Tournant Turn.

Tranquillo Quietly.

Triplet A movement pattern of three steps. In music, three notes played in the same amount of time as one note in the time signature.

Troisième Third.

Turnout The outward rotation of the feet and legs from the hip joint.

Underlying beat The basic pulse on which a rhythmic pattern is developed.

Upbeat Beat that occurs on the last note of a measure.

Valse *See* Waltz.

Vibration, vibratory Very fast, staccato, repetitive movement.

Vivace Lively, fast.

Vivo Brisk, fast.

Waltz A social dance step consisting of three steps in an even triple time.

Bibliography

History and General Background

Anderson, Jack, *Ballet and Modern Dance: A Concise History.* Princeton: Princeton Book Company, 1986.

Balanchine, George, and Francis Mason, *Complete Stories of the Great Ballets.* NY: Doubleday, 1977.

Banes, Sally, *Terpsichore in Sneakers* (2nd ed). Middletown, CT: Wesleyan University Press, 1988.

Brown, Jean Morrison (ed), *Vision of Modern Dance.* Princeton: Princeton Book Company, 1979.

Cohen, Selma Jeanne (ed), *The Modern Dance: Seven Statements of Belief.* Middletown, CT: Wesleyan University Press, 1966.

———, *Dance as a Theatre Art.* NY: Harper & Row, 1974.

Emery, Lynne Fauley, *Black Dance: From 1619 to Today* (2nd ed). Princeton: Dance Horizons, 1987.

Foster, Susan Leigh, *Reading Dancing: Bodies and Subjects in Contemporary American Dance.* Berkeley: University of California Press, 1986.

Ghiselin, Brewster, *The Creative Process.* NY: Mentor, 1958.

Grant, Gail, *Technical Manual and Dictionary of Classical Ballet.* NY: Dover, 1967.

Gruen, John, *People Who Dance: 22 Dancers Tell Their Own Stories.* Princeton: Dance Horizons, 1988.

Jacob, Ellen, *Dancing: A Guide for the Dancer You Can Be.* NY: Danceways, 1981.

Jowitt, Deborah, *Time and the Dancing Image.* NY: Morrow, 1988.

Kirstein, Lincoln, *Dance: A Short History of Classic Theatrical Dancing.* Princeton: Dance Horizons, 1987.

Kraus, Richard, and Sara Chapman, *The History of Dance in Art and Education* (2nd ed). Englewood Cliffs, NJ: Prentice-Hall, 1969.

Kreemer, Connie, *Further Steps: 15 Choreographers on Modern Dance.* NY: Harper & Row, 1987.

Lloyd, Margaret, *The Borzoi Book of Modern Dance.* Princeton: Dance Horizons, 1987.

Mara, Thalia, *The Language of Ballet: A Dictionary.* Princeton: Dance Horizons, 1987.

Martin, John, *The Dance in Theory.* Princeton: Dance Horizons, 1990.

———, *The Modern Dance.* Princeton: Dance Horizons, 1965.

Mazo, Joseph H. *Prime Movers: The Makers of Modern Dance in America.* Princeton: Princeton Book Company, 1984.

McDonagh, Don, *The Complete Guide to Modern Dance.* NY: Doubleday, 1976.

———, *The Rise & Fall & Rise of Modern Dance.* Pennington, NJ: A Cappella Books, 1990.

Nagrin, Daniel, *How to Dance Forever: Surviving Against the Odds.* NY: Morrow, 1988.

Nahmuck, Nadia Chilkovsky, *Dance Curriculum Resource Guide.* NY: American Dance Guild, 1980.

Ryan, Allan J., and Robert E. Stephens (eds), *The Healthy Dancer.* Princeton: Dance Horizons, 1989.

Sorell, Walter, *The Dance in Its Time.* NY: Columbia University Press, 1987.

Steinberg, Stephen Cobbett (ed), *The Dance Anthology.* NY: New American Library, 1980.

Stodelle, Ernestine, *Deep Song: The Dance Story of Martha Graham.* NY: Schirmer Books, 1984.

Vincent, L.M., *The Dancer's Book of Health.* Princeton: Dance Horizons, 1988.

Warren, Larry, *Lester Horton.* NY: Marcel Dekker, 1977.

Technique, Composition, and Notation

Arnheim, Daniel, *Dance Injuries* (3rd ed). Princeton: Dance Horizons, 1990.

Blom, Lynne and L. Tarin Chaplin, *The Intimate Act of Choreography*. Pittsburgh: University of Pittsburgh Press, 1982.

_____, *The Moment of Movement*. Pittsburgh: University of Pittsburgh Press, 1989.

Brown, Ann Kipling, and Monica Parker, *Dance Notation for Beginners*. London: Dance Books Limited, 1984.

Cheney, Gay, *Basic Concepts in Modern Dance* (3rd ed). Princeton: Dance Horizons, 1989.

Chmelar, Robin, and Sally Fitt, *Dancing At Your Peak: Diet*. Princeton: Dance Horizons, 1990.

Cunningham, Merce, *Changes: Notes on Choreography*. West Glover, NY: Something Else Press, 1969.

Duncan, Isadora, *The Art of the Dance*. NY: Theatre Arts Books, 1969.

Ellfeldt, Lois, *A Primer for Choreographers*. Palo Alto, CA: Mayfield, 1971.

Fitt, Sally Sevey, *Dance Kinesiology*. NY: Schirmer Books, 1988.

H'Doubler, Margaret, *Dance: A Creative Art Experience*. Madison: University of Wisconsin Press, 1957.

Hackney, Peggy, et al., *Study Guide for Elementary Labanotation*. NY: Dance Notation Bureau Press, 1977.

Hammond, Sandra, *Ballet Basics*. Palo Alto, CA: Mayfield, 1974.

_____, *Ballet: Beyond the Basics*. Palo Alto, CA: Mayfield, 1975.

Harrison, Mary Kent, *How to Dress Dancers*. Princeton: Dance Horizons, 1988.

Hawkins, Alma, *Creating Through Dance* (Revised ed). Princeton: Dance Horizons, 1988.

Hayes, Elizabeth R., *Dance Composition and Production*. Princeton: Dance Horizons, 1981.

Horst, Louis, *Pre-classic Dance Forms*. Princeton: Dance Horizons, 1987.

_____, and Carroll Russell, *Modern Dance Forms*. Princeton: Dance Horizons, 1987.

Hutchinson, Ann, *Labanotation: The System of Analyzing and Recording Movement*. NY: Theatre Arts Books, 1977.

Knust, Albrecht, *Dictionary of Kinetography Laban*. London: Macdonald and Evans, 1982.

Kraines, Minda Goodman, and Esther Kahn, *Jump into Jazz: A Primer for the Beginning Jazz Dance Student*. Palo Alto, CA: Mayfield, 1983.

Laban, Rudolf, *The Mastery of Movement* (5th ed). Plymouth, UK: Northcote House, 1989.

_____, *Modern Educational Dance*. Plymouth, UK: Northcote House, 1989.

Lawson, Joan, *Ballet Class*. NY: Theatre Arts Books, 1988.

Lockhart, Aileene, and Esther Pease, *Modern Dance, Building and Teaching Lessons* (6th ed). Dubuque, IA: William C. Brown, 1990.

Marriet, Jane, and Muriel Topaz, *Study Guide for Intermediate Labanotation*. NY: Dance Notation Bureau Press, 1987.

Morgenroth, Joyce, *Dance Improvisation*. Pittsburgh: University of Pittsburgh Press, 1987.

Paskevska, Anna, *Ballet: From the First Plié to Mastery*. Princeton: Dance Horizons, 1990.

Penrod, James, and Janice Gudde Plastino, *The Dancer Prepares: Modern Dance for Beginners* (3rd ed). Palo Alto, CA: Mayfield, 1990.

Schlaich, Joan, and Betty DuPont, *Dance: The Art of Production* (2nd ed). Princeton: Dance Horizons, 1988.

Shawn, Ted, *Every Little Movement: A Book About Delsarte*. Princeton: Dance Horizons, 1968.

Smith, Jacqueline, *Dance Composition: A Practical Guide*. London: A & C Black, 1976.

Sparger, Celia, *Anatomy and Ballet*. NY: Theatre Arts Books, 1960.

Stodelle, Ernestine, *The Dance Technique of Doris Humphrey* (2nd ed). Princeton: Dance Horizons, 1990.

Stuart, Muriel, Lincoln Kirstein, Carlus Dyer, and George Balanchine. *The Classic Ballet*. NY: Knopf, 1952.

Todd, Mabel, *The Thinking Body*. Princeton: Dance Horizons, 1986.

Turner, Margery, *New Dance: Approaches to Nonliteral Choreography*. Pittsburgh: University of Pittsburgh Press, 1971.

van Praagh, Peggy, and Peter Brinson, *The Choreographic Art*. NY: Knopf, 1963.

Watkins, Andrea, and Priscilla Clarkson, *Dancing Longer, Dancing Stronger*. Princeton: Dance Horizons, 1990.

Wigman, Mary, *The Language of Dance*. Middletown, CT: Wesleyan University Press, 1966.